PERFORMING ARTS
RESEARCH

PERFORMING ARTS INFORMATION GUIDE SERIES

Series Editor: Louis A. Rachow, Librarian, The Walter Hampden
Memorial Library, New York, New York

Also in the Performing Arts Series:

THE AMERICAN STAGE FROM 1900 TO THE 1970s—*Edited by Don B. Wilmeth***

THE AMERICAN STAGE TO 1900—*Edited by Don B. Wilmeth***

BUSINESS OF THE THEATRE—*Edited by J. Kline Hobbs***

LAW OF THE THEATRE—*Edited by Daniel Jon Strehl***

STAGE SCENERY, MACHINERY, AND LIGHTING—*Edited by Richard Stoddard**

*in press
**in preparation

The above series is part of the
GALE INFORMATION GUIDE LIBRARY

The Library consists of a number of separate series of guides covering major
areas in the social sciences, humanities, and current affairs.

General Editor: Paul Wasserman, Professor and former Dean, School of
Library and Information Services, University of Maryland

PERFORMING ARTS RESEARCH

A GUIDE TO INFORMATION SOURCES

Volume 1 in the Performing Arts Information Guide Series

Marion K. Whalon

Collection Development Librarian
for Humanities and Fine Arts
University Library, University of California, Davis

Gale Research Company
Book Tower, Detroit, Michigan 48226

Library of Congress Cataloging in Publication Data

Whalon, Marion K
    Performing arts research.

    (Performing arts information guide series; v. 1) (Gale information
guide library)
    Includes index.
    1. Performing arts--Bibliography. I. Title.
Z6935.W5 [PN1584]   016.7902   75-13828
ISBN 0-8103-1364-2

VITA

Marion K. Whalon is Collection Development Librarian for Humanities and
Fine Arts in the Shields Library, University of California at Davis. She holds
a B.A. from Rutgers University, and an M.A. in English and M.L.S. from the
University of California at Berkeley. She has had eighteen years of experi-
ence in academic and public libraries, including service at a general reference desk, in special music and art departments, and as a humanities division
head.

Whalon is a member of the California Library Association, Theatre Library
Association, California Association of Theatre Specialists, and Phi Beta Kappa.

CONTENTS

Contents

Preface

PROBLEMS OF RESEARCH IN THEATER ARTS

People engaged in producing, directing, and acting rarely take time for writing until they sum up a life's experiences in a volume or two of memoirs. Few have a taste for either the bibliographer's or the historian's tasks. Hence vital data on individuals, companies, and productions may go unrecorded except in such ephemera as posters, programs, and ticket stubs. Even the promptbook of a production seems likelier found in an attic than in published form. Business records, ironically enough, may, especially if litigation has occurred, be preserved longer than evidence of the artistic elements that made the performances memorable. Fortunately, the plays themselves are often available to us now on record or tape, but the rehearsals and the arguments for one interpretation or another are lost to us until someone mulls them over years later.

Even when data exist, most theater groups have little money to use in publishing the history of their work. (A few notable exceptions such as Lincoln Center come to mind.) Occasionally a local historical society will take an interest, especially in theater buildings, and will publish their history. But the records of performances and personalities have been less well served. Particularly difficult of access is theater history in cities where no local newspapers have been retained in public collections. If such newsprint is still available or has been transferred to microcopy, there is still the problem of access, for local papers are never fully indexed, even by zealous local historians. There have been a few painstaking professional bibliographers in this field, and it is to their work one must turn for information buried in moldering newsprint.

Reviews, articles, and interviews in the metropolitan dailies and the major news weeklies are more readily accessible. However, the very short runs of some plays make for scanty reviews. Other plays which have achieved longer runs appeared in such out-of-the-way places that they may not have been reviewed in the usual media. Some companies have moved from cellar to loft and in reverse (with no thought for the historical consequences), leaving only a faint trail of articles. Some of these even appeared in the "little magazines." Some of these magazines have been indexed recently.

Until a performer attains either distinction or ill fame, one cannot be sure that biographical information will be printed or indexed anywhere. The most reliable of the indexes may omit all mention of a minor actor until his obituary appears. For such sad news the usual sources are BIOGRAPHY INDEX, the READERS' GUIDE TO PERIODICAL LITERATURE, and the indexes of the TIMES (London) and the NEW YORK TIMES. The latter has brought out a separate index to its obituaries from 1858 to 1968.

For immediate news of the living one may have to consult VARIETY or even BILLBOARD. Such trade journals are not fully indexed anywhere, although MUSIC INDEX does list some items from each. In the case of such specialized publications it would be wise to consult a librarian before assuming that no indexing exists.

Other difficulties abound in theater research. Foreign-language sources are hard to trace and evaluate, since they were ignored or given scant treatment in older reference works. Certain types of theater reference works are in short supply. There are one-volume "encyclopedias" of theater in English, but the major multivolume work, the ENCICLOPEDIA DELLO SPETTACOLO, has not been translated. A four-volume MCGRAW-HILL ENCYCLOPEDIA OF WORLD DRAMA has been issued recently, but this, while helpful, falls short of the scholar's need for a major encyclopedia of the theater in English.

Usually in any retrospective research, numerous reference works must be consulted even to pin down one fact, let alone to complete one's research. Fortunately, in recent years theater reference works have been proliferating rapidly, and the use of computers may lead to other helpful scholarly tools. However, the very rapidity of such publication makes individual evaluation desirable.

In such a wilderness, guides are needed. The neophyte should be aware of these difficulties. Likewise, the old hand at research should also be on the watch for new resources. Both would do well to consult one of the guides in Part I of this bibliography. None of these is perfect, comprehensive, or totally up to date. Some exhibit strange errors and incomprehensible omissions. (In a computerized world, will things be better?) However, the sources listed in Part I will lead to more specialized material. With their aid the resolution of many problems will take only the persistence, courage, and ingenuity for which theater people are famed.

As theater reference works, including bibliographies, have multiplied so exceedingly, it seemed imperative to cover both new reference works and the most usable from the past, but it was impossible to extend coverage to monographs. The closing date is roughly 1973, with a few notable 1974 titles included.

Since the reader, after examining the guides in Part I, will often need to use several reference books of the same kind (dictionaries, directories, etc.), the various parts of this guide are in classified arrangement. The many cross-references within each section should facilitate quick comparisons.

In describing all of these works, I have tried to bring out their theatrical aspects, sometimes ignoring their more general features, with the aim of helping especially graduate students and their instructors, as well as librarians and persons engaged in independent research.

Works cited were examined closely. Many likely sounding items were disappointing and had to be omitted. Unevenness of length in the notes may result from several factors, but it usually shows my opinion of the importance and/or intricacy of the work. Some very unwieldy tools seemed indispensable.

My sincere thanks go to friends and supervisors for encouragement and to the many typists who helped from time to time, especially Ellen Lange, Bohnda O'Donnell, and Dawn Nelson.

I am grateful, above all, to Dr. Robert K. Sarlos, Department of Dramatic Art, University of California at Davis, for fostering this work so kindly and helpfully.

Marion K. Whalon

Part I
GUIDES

A guide as here defined means a bibliographic reference work intended by its author to present a basic or comprehensive view of a field of knowledge. Such a guide may include both books and periodical articles. Most of the guides to theater arts and related studies listed here are single-volume works, in classified arrangement. Most are annotated in English, but if an English-language guide was not found, one in a foreign language was substituted.

Guides to "theater," broadly defined, often include motion pictures, radio, and television. Placed after the list of general theater guides are shorter lists for costume, dance, fine arts, literature, and rhetoric, concluding with general reference works and periodicals.

Less comprehensive bibliographies, many treating individual countries, periods, languages, or specialized subjects (e.g., theater architecture), appear in Part VI, "Bibliographies, Indexes, and Abstracts."

A. THEATER ARTS

Baker, Blanch M. THEATRE AND ALLIED ARTS. New York: H.W. Wilson, 1952. 536 p.

> Major classified bibliography with annotations for books and chapters in books published in English from 1885 to 1948. Omits television, radio, and motion picture material, but treats dance, music, and costume as related to theater. Baker's preface defines limitations on Shakespearean material. For medieval drama, see "Religious Drama and Festivals," pp. 190-93.
>
> Author and subject indexes follow main list.
>
> Note that Baker does not list texts of plays.

Blum, Eleanor. REFERENCE BOOKS IN THE MASS MEDIA; AN ANNOTATED SELECTED BOOKLIST COVERING BOOK PUBLISHING, BROADCASTING, FILMS, NEWSPAPERS, MAGAZINES, AND ADVERTISING. Urbana: University of Illinois Press, 1962. 103 p.

Leads to sources of biographical and bibliographical information as well as histories and treatises on the media.

See also Limbacher, James L., below.

_____. BASIC BOOKS IN THE MASS MEDIA; AN ANNOTATED SELECTED BOOKLIST COVERING BOOK PUBLISHING, BROADCASTING, FILMS, NEWS-PAPERS, MAGAZINES, AND ADVERTISING. 2d ed. Urbana: University of Illinois Press, 1972. 252 p.

Revision of Blum's REFERENCE BOOKS IN THE MASS MEDIA (1962). Four hundred titles have been added and the scope has been broadened. Among subjects treated are broadcasting and films.

See also Limbacher, James L., below.

Brockett, Oscar, et al. BIBLIOGRAPHICAL GUIDE TO RESEARCH IN SPEECH AND DRAMATIC ART. Chicago: Scott, Foresman, 1963. 118 p.

Cites materials in English appearing through 1962 and annotates them briefly. Part I introduces drama students to general reference works, but pp. 73-83 and 100-12 should also be noted. No index.

See also Lowe, Claudia Jean, below.

Cheshire, David. THEATRE: HISTORY, CRITICISM AND REFERENCE. Readers Guide Series. Hamden, Conn.: Archon Books, Shoe String Press, 1967. 131 p.

Annotated bibliography of 500 items, covering general reference, history, criticism, biography, theory, and current periodicals, with emphasis on British books in print. No literary aspects of drama are considered.

CIRCUS AND ALLIED ARTS; A WORLD BIBLIOGRAPHY, 1500-1962. Compiled by Raymond Toole-Stott. 4 vols. Derby, Eng.: Harpur, 1958-71.

Annotated bibliography of books and other materials (such as play-bills) found in several notable collections, public and private. Index in Volume III lists names and some subjects, e.g., midgets, clowns. Volume II, section 5, "Drama," pp. 183-226, lists pan-tomimes, plays, operas, etc., with a circus background. Volume IV: 3,500 more items.

See also Delannoy, J.C., in Part VI-A2.

Crothers, J. Francis. THE PUPPETEER'S LIBRARY GUIDE; THE BIBLIOGRAPHIC INDEX TO THE LITERATURE OF THE WORLD PUPPET THEATRE. Vol. 1. Metuchen, N.J.: Scarecrow Press, 1971- .

Volume I covers the history of puppetry and related topics. Books and articles are annotated briefly, and library locations are given for some items. Author index and list of publishers.

Five more volumes will treat the educational and entertainment aspects of puppetry.

See also McPharlin, Paul, in Part VI-A2.

CUMULATED DRAMATIC INDEX, 1909-1949. 2 vols. Boston: G.K. Hall, 1965.

A cumulation of the forty-one volumes of Faxon's DRAMATIC IN-DEX. Lists, without annotation, articles and illustrations in American and British periodicals over a period of fifty years. There are items on theater, musical theater, and motion pictures.

Entry is by subject, which includes names of persons (authors, actors), dramatic characters, titles of plays, and other topics (e.g., "Dramas in Foreign Languages").

A typical entry for an actor may yield the following: portraits, interviews, obituaries, articles by or about him, and books about him. Citations of book reviews follow notice of a book's publication. Play reviews are shown under title of play.

Note separate entries for HAMLET, a ballet; Hamlet, a character; and various dramas of that title. Costume plates listed under both characters' and actors' names.

Under "Dramas" or "Dramas--Author's Name" are noted play texts or published collections, contents of which are listed. Many entries are, however, only cross-references to Volume II: "Appendices."

Volume II: "Appendices," pp. 619-935: (1) author list of 6,500 books on drama and theater; (2) title list of 24,000 play texts, in collections, in periodicals, or separately published; (3) author list of published plays. (Refer from title list to author list for full data.)

Gottesman, Ronald. GUIDEBOOK TO FILM; AN ELEVEN-IN-ONE REFERENCE. New York: Holt, Rinehart and Winston, 1972. 230 p.

Partially annotated, classified guide to books, periodicals, and dissertations on aspects of the motion picture art and industry. Separate list of museums, archives, organizations, agencies, awards, etc.

Hunter, Frederick James. DRAMA BIBLIOGRAPHY; A SHORT-TITLE GUIDE TO EXTENDED READING IN DRAMATIC ART FOR THE ENGLISH-SPEAKING AUDIENCE AND STUDENTS IN THEATRE. Boston: G.K. Hall, 1971. 239 p.

A classified list, without annotations, covering books published through 1970. Excludes motion pictures.

Limbacher, James L. A REFERENCE GUIDE TO AUDIO-VISUAL INFORMATION. New York: R.R. Bowker, 1972. 197 p.

> Briefly annotates 400 reference books and one hundred periodicals. Added are a subject index, list of publishers, glossary of terms, and a selection of in-print supplementary reading.
>
> See also AUDIO VISUAL MARKET PLACE, in Part III, and Blum, Eleanor, above.

Lowe, Claudia Jean. A GUIDE TO REFERENCE AND BIBLIOGRAPHY FOR THEATRE RESEARCH. Columbus: Office of Educational Services, Ohio State University Libraries, 1971. 137 p.

> Classified, annotated guide. Can serve to introduce theater students to general library materials and major reference works on theater. Contains little on motion pictures. There is a general index.
>
> See also Brockett, Oscar, et al., above.

Santaniello, A.E. THEATRE BOOKS IN PRINT. 2d ed. New York: Drama Book Shop, 1966. 509 p.

> Classified, annotated guide to books in print, mainly in English. Covers theater, drama, radio, television, and motion pictures. Play texts and collections not included, except for major scholarly editions.
>
> First edition (1963) is also useful.
>
> Continued in revised form by Schoolcraft, Ralph Newman, PERFORMING ARTS BOOKS IN PRINT. See below.

Schoolcraft, Ralph Newman. PERFORMING ARTS BOOKS IN PRINT; AN ANNOTATED BIBLIOGRAPHY. New York: Drama Books Specialists, 1973. 761 p.

> Updates and continues Santaniello, A.E., above. Includes 10,000 items, well annotated. Author and title index.
>
> Updated quarterly by the ANNOTATED BIBLIOGRAPHY OF NEW PUBLICATIONS IN THE PERFORMING ARTS. See Part VI-A1.

Stratman, Carl J. DRAMATIC PLAY LISTS, 1591-1963. New York: New York Public Library, 1966. 44 p.

> Evaluative bibliography of play lists, mainly in English, arranged chronologically. It excludes lists of skits, monologs, and works by individual playwrights.

THEATRE BOOKS IN PRINT.

    See Santaniello, A.E., above.

Toole-Stott, Raymond.

    See CIRCUS AND ALLIED ARTS, above.

B. DANCE

Magriel, Paul David, comp. A BIBLIOGRAPHY OF DANCING; A LIST OF BOOKS AND ARTICLES ON THE DANCE AND RELATED SUBJECTS. 1936. Reprint. New York: Benjamin Blom, 1966. 229 p.

    Five thousand classified annotated entries for books and periodical articles on ballet, folk and social dancing, and the masque. Shows libraries owning copies.

    There are author and subject indexes.

_____. A BIBLIOGRAPHY OF DANCING; 4TH CUMULATED SUPPLEMENT, 1936-40. New York: H.W. Wilson, 1941. 104 p.

    Locates library copies of works on dance.

See also Beaumont, Cyril William; and Leslie, Serge, in Part VI-A1. The reader should also consult Part VII for illustrations of dance.

C. COSTUME

Hiler, Hilaire, and Hiler, Meyer, comps. BIBLIOGRAPHY OF COSTUME; A DICTIONARY CATALOG OF ABOUT EIGHT THOUSAND BOOKS AND PERIODICALS. New York: H.W. Wilson, 1939. 911 p.

    Most extensive multilingual guide to the subject. See note, "Theater and Cinema," p. xxxiv, and "Theatrical Costume," pp. 838-43, as well as references under Shakespeare, Moliere, etc.

For later books on costume, see Baker, Blanch M.; Santaniello, A.E.; and Schoolcraft, Ralph Newman, under "Theater Arts," above. See also Part VI, "Bibliographies, Indexes, and Abstracts" and Part VII, "Illustrative and Audiovisual Sources."

D. VISUAL ARTS, MUSIC, AND ESTHETICS

Carrick, Neville. HOW TO FIND OUT ABOUT THE ARTS. New York:

Pergamon Press, 1965. 164 p.

> Brief guide. Useful to update Chamberlin, Mary W., below, and to emphasize major reference sources. Concentrates on visual arts but treats broadcasting, cinema, dance, theater, pp. 155-60, and costume, pp. 130-34. Note the specimen pages of reference works with explanation of their use.

Chamberlin, Mary W. GUIDE TO ART REFERENCE BOOKS. Chicago: American Library Association, 1959. 418 p.

> Principal international guide for research in the visual arts. Chapters on periodicals, monographs in series, documents, and art libraries. Notes are evaluative.
>
> Theater per se is not treated, nor are individual artists.
>
> See also Lucas, Edna Louise, below.

Davies, J.H. MUSICALIA: SOURCES OF INFORMATION IN MUSIC. 2d ed. London: Pergamon, 1969. 184 p. plus unnumbered specimen pages.

> Selective, well annotated guide. Includes a chapter on "The Theatre Conductor and Researcher," pp. 13-24. Appendices list music publishers and sources for performing rights, pp. 127-55.

Duckles, Vincent. MUSIC REFERENCE AND RESEARCH MATERIALS; AN ANNOTATED BIBLIOGRAPHY. 3d ed. New York: The Free Press, 1974. xi, 526 p.

> Well balanced scholarly guide to reference books, histories, bibliographies, musical discographies, yearbooks, and the printed catalogs of music libraries.

Grout, Donald Jay. A SHORT HISTORY OF OPERA. 2d ed. 2 vols. New York: Columbia University Press, 1965.

> From the lyric theater of the Greeks to 1960. A comprehensive bibliography in Volume II, pp. 585-768, lists both books and articles on opera in U.S. and European periodicals. See pp. 769-86 for modern editions of pre-1800 operas.

Hammond, William A. A BIBLIOGRAPHY OF AESTHETICS AND OF THE PHILOSOPHY OF THE FINE ARTS FROM 1900 to 1932. Rev. ed. 1934 Reprint. New York: Russell and Russell, 1967. 205 p.

> Sparsely annotated list of books and periodical articles on esthetics. Selections relevant to drama deal with topics such as the history of esthetic theories, literature of drama and the theater, style, symbolism, empathy, laughter, caricature.
>
> See also ENCYCLOPEDIA OF PHILOSOPHY, in Part II-E.

Lucas, Edna Louise. ART BOOKS; A BASIC BIBLIOGRAPHY ON THE FINE ARTS. Greenwich, Conn.: New York Graphic Society, 1968. 245 p.

> Selective, unannotated list of books on visual arts classified by subject. Separate section on individual artists. Index.

> Useful to update and supplement Chamberlin, Mary W., above.

E. LITERATURE

1. Methods of Literary Research

Altick, Richard D. THE ART OF LITERARY RESEARCH. New York: Norton, 1963. 240 p.

> Chapter V, "Finding Materials," offers sound advice on developing bibliography. Chapter VI, "Libraries," surveys major research collections.

Bowers, Fredson. PRINCIPLES OF BIBLIOGRAPHICAL DESCRIPTION. Princeton, N.J.: Princeton University Press, 1949. 505 p.

> Detailed advanced treatise. Chapters 3, 8, and 10 deal with practices in the printing and publishing of English literature from the sixteenth to the twentieth century.

Esdaile, Arundell James Kennedy. ESDAILE'S MANUAL OF BIBLIOGRAPHY. 4th rev. ed., edited by Roy Stokes. Library Association Series of Library Manuals, 1. London: Allen & Unwin, 1968. 336 p. Illustrated.

> Supersedes Esdaile, Arundell James Kennedy. A STUDENT'S MAN-UAL OF BIBLIOGRAPHY, which first appeared in 1931 and reap-peared in a revised third edition (London: Allen & Unwin, 1963).

> Many generations of students are indebted to Esdaile's examination of books as physical objects, with emphasis on the identification and description of editions. A brief history of printing and publish-ing is also included.

McKerrow, Ronald B. AN INTRODUCTION TO BIBLIOGRAPHY FOR LITERARY STUDENTS. Oxford: Clarendon Press, 1928. 358 p.

> Aids in establishing texts, describing editions, and other techniques of scholarship. Pages 135-38 discuss the Stationers' Register, Term Catalogues, and other documents of English publishing history. Appendix 8 is a note on Elizabethan handwriting.

> McKerrow may be supplemented by Bowers, Fredson. See above.

Sanders, Chauncey. AN INTRODUCTION TO RESEARCH IN ENGLISH LITER-ARY HISTORY. New York: Macmillan, 1952. 423 p.

Advice on methods and problems of research. Note especially "Suggestions for Thesis-Writing," pp. 277-315. Good list of scholarly abbreviations and instructions for use, pp. 304-9.

Thorpe, James, ed. THE AIMS AND METHODS OF SCHOLARSHIP IN MODERN LANGUAGES AND LITERATURES. 2d ed. New York: Modern Language Association of America, 1970. 84 p.

Not a guide for quick reference, but a survey composed of essays by eminent scholars on aspects of criticism and scholarship.

2. English and American Literature

Altick, Richard D., and Wright, Andrew. SELECTIVE BIBLIOGRAPHY FOR THE STUDY OF ENGLISH AND AMERICAN LITERATURE. 3d ed. New York: Macmillan, 1967. 152 p.

Excellent guide, although few annotations are given. Includes cultural background. Note pp. 1-10, "On the Use of Scholarly Tools."

Bateson, Frederick W. A GUIDE TO ENGLISH LITERATURE. 2d ed. London: Longmans, 1967. 260 p.

Concise, lively, and scholarly. Discusses major editions and critical works in English to 1963-64. Shows special methods of period research. Treats individual authors chronologically by birthdate. See pp. 216-17 for a brief list of books on dramatic criticism and p. 7 for a short list of major histories of drama.

_____,ed.

See CAMBRIDGE BIBLIOGRAPHY OF ENGLISH LITERATURE, below.

Bond, Donald F. A REFERENCE GUIDE TO ENGLISH STUDIES. 2d ed. Chicago: University of Chicago Press, 1971. 198 p.

Standard work, with some treatment of auxiliary subjects such as art and philosophy. Chapter X lists periodicals carrying reviews and bibliographies. Note pp. 86-89, on drama, and pp. 45-48, on dissertations.

CAMBRIDGE BIBLIOGRAPHY OF ENGLISH LITERATURE. 5 vols. Edited by Frederick W. Bateson. New York: Macmillan, 1941-57.

Important guide to books and periodicals in English literature from 600 to 1900. Classified by period, thereunder by literary genre, and then by authors, whose works are listed in major editions, followed by contemporary and later criticism.

Preceding the literary section of each period are lists on "Social Background," "Intellectual Background," "Literary Relations with the Continent," etc.

Volume I, section 3, covers drama to 1660 (pp. 487–663); Volume II, section 3, drama to 1800 (pp. 392–485); Volume III, section 4, drama to 1900 (pp. 580–625). Note that the 1900 closing date means authors were well established by then. (Some works printed after that date are included.) Volume IV indexes the first three.

Volume V: SUPPLEMENT, contains additional material on all periods, ending with 1900. Has no index. See drama under periods: Medieval, pp. 156–58; Elizabethan, Jacobean, and Caroline, pp. 241–309; Restoration and Eighteenth Century, pp. 433–45; Nineteenth Century, pp. 651–53.

Anglo-Irish literature, including dramatists of the Irish Revival, will be found in Volume III, section 7, "The Literatures of the Dominions," pp. 1045–63 of the basic set, and also pp. 698–706 in the SUPPLEMENT.

A revised edition of the entire bibliography is nearly completed. See NEW CAMBRIDGE BIBLIOGRAPHY OF ENGLISH LITERATURE, below.

CONCISE CAMBRIDGE BIBLIOGRAPHY OF ENGLISH LITERATURE, 600–1950.

See Watson, George, below.

Gohdes, Clarence. BIBLIOGRAPHICAL GUIDE TO THE STUDY OF THE LITERA-TURE OF THE U.S.A. 3d ed., rev. Durham, N.C.: Duke University Press, 1970. 134 p.

Selective, classified, and annotated bibliography. Section 23 deals with American theater and drama, and section 25 with fashions in literary criticism down to the 1960s.

Subject and author indexes.

Jones, Howard Mumford, and Ludwig, Richard M. GUIDE TO AMERICAN LITERATURE AND ITS BACKGROUNDS SINCE 1890. 3d ed., rev. Cambridge, Mass.: Harvard University Press, 1964. 240 p.

Classifies, under broad topics, "Intellectual History," "Popular Arts," etc. Material on drama is scattered under various headings. Chapter VI is an annotated list of journals, old and new.

Kennedy, Arthur G., and Sands, Donald B. A CONCISE BIBLIOGRAPHY FOR STUDENTS OF ENGLISH. 4th ed. Stanford, Calif.: Stanford University Press, 1960. 467 p.

Unannotated list of books for English literature and its background. Note pp. 21–23, "Shakespeare," and pp. 110–41, "Stage and Drama."

LITERARY HISTORY OF THE UNITED STATES. 3d ed., rev. 2 vols. Edited by Robert E. Spiller et al. New York: Macmillan, 1966 c. 1963.

First supplement by Richard M. Ludwig.

BIBLIOGRAPHY SUPPLEMENT II. Compiled by Richard M. Ludwig. New York: Macmillan, 1972. 366 p.

> The major bibliography for American literature, its background, and its critics.

> Volume I: HISTORY. Progresses through the 1950s, including a survey of that decade's drama, pp. 1435–41. See index for drama of other periods. A revised, updated bibliography for the general reader is on pp. 1446–81.

> Volume II: BIBLIOGRAPHY. Consists of materials which appeared in Volume III of first (1948) edition and those in the 1959 SUPPLE-MENT. These have been left in separate lists. There is a combined index.

> In this bibliography a general historical section is followed by bibliography for individual authors. Gives dates of first editions, collections, and periodical publications as well as the many biographical and critical works on each writer.

> The fourth revised edition, which will appear in two volumes, is now in preparation by Robert E. Spiller and others.

NEW CAMBRIDGE BIBLIOGRAPHY OF ENGLISH LITERATURE. 5 vols. Edited by George Watson. Cambridge, Eng.: At the University Press, 1969––. Vol. III: 1890–1900 (1969), 1,006 p.; Vol. II: 1660–1800 (1971), 2,092 p.; Vol. IV: 1900–1950 (1972), 1,414 p.; Vol. I: 600–1600 (1974), 2,491 p. Vol. V (Index) in prep.

> Volumes I–III are a revision and updating of the CAMBRIDGE BIBLIOGRAPHY OF ENGLISH LITERATURE (1940) and its 1957 SUPPLEMENT (see above). Antiquated titles have been dropped and some nonliterary sections have been modified, but the scope and the arrangement, by period and genre, are essentially preserved. Volume IV is totally new and was edited by I.R. Willison and others.

> Each volume of the NEW CBEL is the work of numerous scholarly contributors.

Spiller, Robert E., et al., eds.

> See LITERARY HISTORY OF THE UNITED STATES, above.

Stokes, Roy

> See Esdaile, Arundell James Kennedy. ESDAILE'S MANUAL OF

BIBLIOGRAPHY, above.

Temple, Ruth Z. TWENTIETH CENTURY BRITISH LITERATURE: A REFERENCE GUIDE AND BIBLIOGRAPHY. New York: Ungar, 1968. 261 p.

> Part I is a classified list of reference books, works on literary history, critical monographs, and essay collections. Note pp. 13-14, a list of journals publishing annual bibliographies.
>
> Part II is a bibliography of first editions by 400 English authors of this century. Each entry is supplemented by a short list of biographical and critical studies.

U.S. Library of Congress. General Reference and Bibliography Division. A GUIDE TO THE STUDY OF THE UNITED STATES OF AMERICA. Washington, D.C.: Library of Congress, 1960. 1,193 p.

> Lists books only and gives more than 6,500 full annotations, up to 1955 (1958 in some parts). Theater is included in a weak chapter, "Entertainment," pp. 672-84. Note treatment of intellectual history, periodicals, journalism, etc.

Watson, George, ed. THE CONCISE CAMBRIDGE BIBLIOGRAPHY OF ENGLISH LITERATURE, 600-1950. 2d ed. Cambridge, Eng.: At the University Press, 1965. 270 p.

> Based on the CAMBRIDGE BIBLIOGRAPHY OF ENGLISH LITERATURE and its SUPPLEMENT but with coverage extended to the 1950s. General material on each period is followed by individual authors. For each author, bibliographies, if any, are listed first, followed by author's works, then principal biographies and/or critical studies.

Watson, George, ed.

> See also NEW CAMBRIDGE BIBLIOGRAPHY OF ENGLISH LITERATURE, above.

3. Shakespeare

Berman, Ronald. A READER'S GUIDE TO SHAKESPEARE'S PLAYS; A DISCURSIVE BIBLIOGRAPHY. Chicago: Scott, Foresman, 1965. 151 p.

> Selective critical list of books and articles. Grouped by play titles are references to important critiques and a separate list on the stage history of each play.

Ebisch, Walther, and Schuecking, Levin L. A SHAKESPEARE BIBLIOGRAPHY. Oxford: Clarendon Press, 1931. 294 p.

Classified bibliography of works in English and European languages concerned with the full range of Shakespeare studies. Includes books, some dissertations, and articles in periodicals and annuals through 1929. Analyzes contents of sets and Festschriften. Has a few evaluative notes.

Continued by SUPPLEMENT FOR THE YEARS 1930-1935 TO A SHAKESPEARE BIBLIOGRAPHY, below.

_____. SUPPLEMENT FOR THE YEARS 1930-1935 TO A SHAKESPEARE BIBLI-OGRAPHY BY WALTHER EBISCH AND LEVIN L. SCHUECKING. Oxford: Clarendon Press, 1937. 104 p.

Gives a few additions to the basic bibliography as well as new publications from 1930-36.

Continued by Smith, Gordon Ross. See below.

Howard-Hill, Trevor Howard, ed. SHAKESPEAREAN BIBLIOGRAPHY AND TEXTUAL CRITICISM: A BIBLIOGRAPHY. Index to British Literary Bibliography, vol. 2. London: Oxford University Press, 1971. 322 p.

Classified entries for British, Commonwealth, and U.S. books and periodical articles, 1890-1969. Indexed.

See also Smith, Gordon Ross, below.

Jaggard, William. SHAKESPEARE BIBLIOGRAPHY. Stratford on Avon: The Shakespeare Press, 1911. Reprint. New York: Ungar, 1959. 729 p.

Lists writings by and about Shakespeare, with annotations. Locates items in some large libraries, primarily in England and the United States.

Schuecking, Levin L.

See Ebisch, Walther, above.

Smith, Gordon Ross. A CLASSIFIED SHAKESPEARE BIBLIOGRAPHY, 1936-1958. University Park: Pennsylvania State University Press, 1963. 784 p.

Uses the same general classification as Ebisch, Walther, and Schuecking, Levin L., above. Smith continues the record chrono-logically. Not claiming comprehensiveness, Smith's work, is, however, a master bibliography of items in the major annual bibli-ographies. Also adds some dissertations not found in Ebisch and Schuecking. Notes are sparse.

See also Howard-Hill, Trevor Howard, above.

4. World Literature

Baldensperger, Fernand, and Friederich, Werner P. BIBLIOGRAPHY OF COM-
PARATIVE LITERATURE. Studies in Comparative Literature. Chapel Hill:
University of North Carolina Press, 1950. 701 p.

> Lists books, articles, and some serial publications such as proceed-
> ings of societies. Topics treated: influence of one author on
> another; influence of one nation's literature on another; the classi-
> cal tradition; literary genres; literature and politics.

> See also Osburn, Charles B., below.

> The Baldensperger and Friederich work is supplemented by an annu-
> al bibliography appearing in the YEARBOOK OF COMPARATIVE
> AND GENERAL LITERATURE.

Fomin, Aleksandr Grigor' evich. PUTEVODITEL' PO BIBLIOGRAFII, BIOBIBLI-
OGRAFII, ISTORIOGRAFII, KHRONOLOGII I ENTSIKLOPEDI I LITERATURY
V 1736-1932 GG. Leningrad: Goslitizdat, 1934. Reprint. New York:
Johnson Reprint Corp., 1966. 334 p.

> Classified and annotated list of reference books, periodical articles,
> and bibliographies on Russian literature.

Koerner, Josef. BIBLIOGRAPHISCHES HANDBUCH DES DEUTSCHEN SCHRIFT-
TUMS. 3d ed. Berne, Switzerland: Francke, 1949. 644 p.

> German literature from the Middle Ages to World War II is treated
> in one well indexed volume. Shows standard and newer editions
> of German authors, followed by annotated lists of critical works.

> For more detail and newer material, consult especially Arnold,
> Robert F., in Part VI-B.

McGuire, Martin R.P. INTRODUCTION TO CLASSICAL SCHOLARSHIP; A
SYLLABUS AND BIBLIOGRAPHICAL GUIDE. Rev. ed. Washington, D.C.:
Catholic University Press of America, 1961. 257 p.

> Guide for graduate students in Greek and Latin studies. There is
> a selective bibliography of Greek literature, philosophy, and sci-
> ence on pp. 201-8, and a similar section on Latin literature, pp.
> 223-27.

> See also Osburn, Charles B., below.

Osburn, Charles B. RESEARCH AND REFERENCE GUIDE TO FRENCH STUDIES.
Metuchen, N.J.: Scarecrow Press, 1968. 517 p.

SUPPLEMENT. 1972. 377 p.

> Classified unannotated guide for French language and literature and
> related subjects, including Latin and comparative literature. De-

scribes reference works and analyzes some sets.

Theater items in each historical period; individual authors treated separately.

The author index actually lists critics; the subject index includes literary authors as subjects.

See also Baldensperger, Fernand, and Friederich, Werner P.; and McGuire, Martin R.P., above, and Palfrey, Thomas Rossman et al., below.

Palfrey, Thomas Rossman, et al., comps. A BIBLIOGRAPHICAL GUIDE TO THE ROMANCE LANGUAGES AND LITERATURES. 8th ed. Evanston, Ill.: Chandler's, 1971. 122 1.

Entries for titles of books and periodicals (no articles) are arranged under French, Italian, Brazilian, Portuguese, Spanish, and Spanish-American sections, subdivided by period. There are few annotations. Useful as a general reference but not as a substitute for more specialized bibliographies. The latest edition includes many items published since 1966. No index.

See also Osburn, Charles B., above, and Simon Diaz, Jose, below.

Simon Diaz, Jose. MANUAL DE BIBLIOGRAFIA DE LA LITERATURA ESPANOLA. 2d ed., ampliada.... ADICIONES 1962-64; ADICIONES, 1965-70. Barcelona: Gili, 1971. 603 p.; 100 p.; 198 p.

One-volume classified guide to books, periodical articles, and chapters in books on Spanish and Spanish-American literature from Middle Ages to twentieth century. Few annotations. Under period, general material followed by individual authors.

See also Palfrey, Thomas Rossman, et al., above.

F. RHETORIC

Cleary, James W., and Haberman, Frederick W. RHETORIC AND PUBLIC ADDRESS: A BIBLIOGRAPHY, 1947-1961. Madison: University of Wisconsin Press, 1964. 487 p.

International annotated bibliography of speech and rhetoric. Touches little on theater. See names of playwrights (e.g., Shakespeare, Shaw) for their use of rhetorical devices.

See also Bailey, Richard W., in Part VI-B, and Mulgrave, Dorothy Irene, below.

Haberman, Frederick W.

See Cleary, James W., above.

Mulgrave, Dorothy Irene. BIBLIOGRAPHY OF SPEECH AND ALLIED AREAS, 1950-1960. Philadelphia: Chilton, 1962. 184 p.

> Theater is treated on pp. 153-84 in a classified but unannotated list of books and dissertations.

> See also Cleary, James W., and Haberman, Frederick W., above.

Thonssen, Lester, et al. BIBLIOGRAPHY OF SPEECH EDUCATION. New York: H.W. Wilson, 1939. 800 p.

> Limited to English-language materials on speech. Separate lists of books, pamphlets, and periodical articles, with some annotations. See section on "Dramatics," pp. 287-428.

_____. SUPPLEMENT: 1939-1948. New York: H.W. Wilson, 1950. 393 p.

> Classified, annotated list of books, theses, chapters in books, and some periodical articles. The section "Dramatics," pp. 121-212, is broader than title suggests, although emphasis both here and in basic volume, above, is on educational factors.

G. GENERAL REFERENCE WORKS

Malcles, Louise Noelle. LES SOURCES DU TRAVAIL BIBLIOGRAPHIQUE. 3 vols. in 4. Geneva: E. Droz, 1950-52.

> The major French-language guide to reference works. Volume I: GENERAL BIBLIOGRAPHIES. Volume II (Parts 1 and 2): SPECIAL BIBLIOGRAPHIES (Humanities). Volume III: SPECIAL BIBLIOGRA-PHIES (Science and Technology).

> A theater section under French literature emphasizes French reference works. See Volume II, Part 1, pp. 285-91.

Sheehy, Eugene P.

> See Winchell, Constance M., SECOND SUPPLEMENT, below.

Stevens, Roland E. REFERENCE BOOKS IN THE SOCIAL SCIENCES AND HUMANITIES. 3d ed. Champaign, Ill.: distributed by Illini Union Bookstore, 1971. 188 p.

> Very selective manual, well balanced and annotated.

Walford, Albert John. GUIDE TO REFERENCE MATERIALS. 2d ed. London: Library Association, 1963-   .

> Similar to Winchell, Constance M., below. International, but with British emphasis.

Winchell, Constance M. GUIDE TO REFERENCE BOOKS. 8th ed. Chicago: American Library Association, 1967. 741 p.

> Important general guide, classified and annotated. International in coverage.
>
> Note section BG, "Theater Arts, Dance and Motion Pictures," pp. 324-29; section BH, "Music," pp. 329-41; section BD, "Drama," pp. 245-47. But note also special subsections on drama and on a few individual authors under various national literatures in section BD, "Literature."

_____. FIRST SUPPLEMENT, 1965-66. Chicago: American Library Association, 1968. 122 p.

_____. SECOND SUPPLEMENT, 1967-68. Compiled by Eugene P. Sheehy. Chicago: American Library Association, 1970. 165 p.

_____. THIRD SUPPLEMENT, 1969-70. Chicago: American Library Association, 1972. 190 p.

H. PERIODICALS

This subsection contains general guides to currently published periodicals. Also included are a few specialized guides to periodicals in the fields of literature, drama, theater, and motion pictures. Stratman's lists are retrospective and will both identify a periodical and locate a library which owns it.

Identification of a periodical (with its entire publishing history, title changes, lapses, etc.) and location of copies in libraries are the chief functions of a major research tool, the UNION LIST OF SERIALS, which, with its continuation, NEW SERIAL TITLES, shows the holdings of large libraries in the United States and Canada. The BRITISH UNION-CATALOGUE OF PERIODICALS serves the same purpose for Great Britain. For a fuller description of these important catalogs, the reader is refered to Constance M. Winchell's GUIDE TO REFERENCE BOOKS in the previous section.

A new union catalog has begun to appear for periodicals in the libraries of Paris and the university libraries of France, including publications from the beginning of the seventeenth century to 1939 - Bibliotheque Nationale. Departement des periodiques. CATALOGUE COLLECTIF DES PERIODIQUES DU DEBUT DU XVII SIECLE A 1939 CONSERVES DANS LES BIBLIOTHEQUES DE PARIS ET DANS LES BIBLIOTHEQUES UNIVERSITAIRES DES DEPARTEMENTS. Paris: Bibliotheque Nationale, 1967- . To date Volumes IV (R-Z), 1967; III (J-Q), 1969; and II (C-I), 1973, have appeared.

DIRECTORY OF LITTLE MAGAZINES. Edited by Leonard V. Fulton. El Cerrito, Calif.: Dust Magazine, 1964- . Annual.

Gives publisher's name and address, subscription price, and brief
description for each magazine. The publications are usually literary and avant garde. A few print short plays (e.g., FIRST STAGE),
and some discuss films regularly. Others may carry interviews,
reviews, and articles of interest to students of theater. The IN-
DEX TO LITTLE MAGAZINES indexes contents of a few of these
publications.

Gerstenberger, Donna Lorine. DIRECTORY OF PERIODICALS PUBLISHING
ARTICLES ON ENGLISH AND AMERICAN LITERATURE AND LANGUAGE.
3d ed. Chicago: A. Swallow, 1970. 199 p.

Annotated, alphabetically arranged list of current periodicals. In
addition to literary material, some publish articles on speech,
theater, classical, and Renaissance studies. See subject index.

Notes on requirements for manuscripts and terms of payment for
publication.

See also LITERARY MARKET PLACE, below.

INTERNATIONAL DIRECTORY OF LITTLE MAGAZINES AND SMALL PRESSES.
Paradise, Calif.: Dustbooks, 1973-74-   . Annual.

Continues DIRECTORY OF LITTLE MAGAZINES, above.

See also INDEX TO COMMONWEALTH LITTLE MAGAZINES, in
Part V.

IRREGULAR SERIALS AND ANNUALS: AN INTERNATIONAL DIRECTORY.
Edited by Emery Koltay. 2d ed. New York: R.R. Bowker, 1972. 850 p.

Classified list showing price, frequency, sponsor, and editor, and
indicating availability of indexing.

Supplements ULRICH'S INTERNATIONAL PERIODICALS DIRECTORY,
below.

Katz, William Armstrong, ed. MAGAZINES FOR LIBRARIES. 2d ed. New
York: R.R. Bowker, 1972. 822 p.

Classified selective guide to periodicals, including "little magazines," and to abstracts and indexes. Critical notes to aid libraries in selection. Details on circulation, price, indexing, etc.
U.S. publications are emphasized, but some Canadian, British,
and foreign-language titles are entered.

Koltay, Emery, ed.

See: IRREGULAR SERIALS AND ANNUALS, above.

LITERARY MARKET PLACE, THE DIRECTORY OF AMERICAN BOOK PUBLISH-
ING. New York: R.R. Bowker, 1940-   . Annual.

Contains separate directories of book and magazine publishers with some comment. Also lists literary contests, editorial services, translators, etc.

See also WRITER'S MARKET, below.

STANDARD PERIODICAL DIRECTORY. New York: Oxbridge Publishing Co., 1964-65- . Annual.

Classified list of periodicals with brief, nonevaluative notes on typical contents. Gives addresses and subscription rates.

See also ULRICH'S, below.

Stratman, Carl J. AMERICAN THEATRICAL PERIODICALS, 1789-1967; A BIBLIOGRAPHICAL GUIDE. Durham, N.C.: Duke University Press, 1970. 133 p.

Preliminary list of serials owned by 137 libraries. (Complete runs of some serials could not be found in any library.) The 685 items include journals, newspapers, annuals, and directories.

Stratman excludes literary journals, even those with drama columns, and also omits film material in general, but journals of musical theater or the dance are included. The main list is organized chronologically. A separate table shows comparative duration of publications.

There is an index of titles, editors, and places of publication with some subject entries, e.g., "Circus."

_____. BRITAIN'S THEATRICAL PERIODICALS, 1720-1967: A BIBLIOGRA-PHY. 2d ed. New York: New York Public Library, 1972. 160 p.

This revision of the 1962 work, BIBLIOGRAPHY OF BRITISH DRA-MATIC PERIODICALS, has nearly doubled the number of entries and has updated the material and broadened its scope to include dance, magic, and vaudeville. The list is chronological, gives publishing information, and locates copies in U.S. and British libraries.

ULRICH'S INTERNATIONAL PERIODICALS DIRECTORY. 14th ed. 2 vols. New York: R.R. Bowker, 1971-72.

"A classified guide to current periodicals, foreign and domestic." This often-revised directory arranges periodicals under broad subjects. The title entries show publisher, address, frequency, and price as well as availability of standard indexing or abstracting services. The main directory is preceded by a list of abstracting and index-ing services and followed by a list of new periodicals (published since 1969).

United Nations Educational, Scientific, and Cultural Organization. Belgian

National Commission. REPERTOIRE MONDIAL DES PERIODIQUES CINEMA-
TOGRAPHIQUES. WORLD LIST OF FILM PERIODICALS. 2d ed. Brussels,
1960. Unpaged.

> Annotated list of 786 periodicals grouped by national origin. In-
> dexed by subject, title, geographical area, and sponsoring agency.
> Omits house organs and film society bulletins.

WRITER'S MARKET. Cincinnati: Writer's Digest, 1929-   . Annual.

> Fully annotated list of current periodicals, classified by subject
> matter. Each entry describes requirements for manuscripts, method
> of payment, etc. Also includes a note on marketing books in the
> United States and abroad.

> See also LITERARY MARKET PLACE, above.

Part II

DICTIONARIES, ENCYCLOPEDIAS, AND HANDBOOKS

Part II embraces motion pictures, stage, and television, with emphasis on the stage. Note separate sections for costume, dance, music, and musical theater, which follow the main "Theater" section. For the literary aspects of drama, consult both the "Theater" and "World Literature" sections.

Grouped under relevant headings are selected dictionaries, handbooks, glossaries, concordances, and plot digests, as well as more encyclopedic works. Biographical encyclopedias are included if they pertain especially to theater and related subjects. Most of the works described are retrospective. For sources of more current information on persons or institutions, see Part III, "Directories."

A. THEATER

Academy of Motion Picture Arts and Sciences. WHO WROTE THE MOVIE AND WHAT ELSE DID HE WRITE? AN INDEX OF SCREEN WRITERS AND THEIR FILM WORKS, 1936-1969. Los Angeles: Academy of Motion Picture Arts and Sciences, 1970. 491 p.

> The "Writers' Index" section lists screenwriters, with their works.
> The "Film Title Index" lists films by English-language title and
> original foreign title, and gives producer and release date, with
> cross-reference.

Adams, William Davenport. A DICTIONARY OF THE DRAMA. 1904. 2 vols. Reprint. New York: Franklin, 1965. 627 p. Reprint covers only volume I (A-G). Volume II, an unpublished manuscript, is available on microfilm only, in SOURCE MATERIALS IN THE FIELD OF THEATER. See Part VI-A1.

> The two volumes form a descriptive list of plays, dramatists, actors,
> characters, societies, and theaters (listed by city) in the United
> States and United Kingdom through the late nineteenth century.
> Notable productions are shown under play title.

American Film Institute. THE AMERICAN FILM INSTITUTE CATALOG OF MOTION PICTURES PRODUCED IN THE UNITED STATES. Edited by Kenneth W. Munden. New York: Bowker, 1971- .

Volumes I and II present feature films from 1921 through 1930 in an alphabetical title list, with distributor, release date, literary source, cast, characters, and a synopsis. Volume II has a cast and credit index as well as a subject index.

When completed, this major reference work will extend to 1970.

Anderson, Michael, et al. CROWELL'S HANDBOOK OF CONTEMPORARY DRAMA. New York: Crowell, 1971. 512 p.

Articles, by specialists, vary in length and are arranged alphabetically by topic. No index.

See also Matlaw, Myron; and Melchinger, Siegfried, below.

ATLANTISBUCH DES THEATERS.

See Huerlimann, Martin, below.

Baker, David Erskine. BIOGRAPHIA DRAMATICA OR A COMPANION TO THE PLAYHOUSE. 3 vols. in 2. London: Longman, Hurst, Rees, Orme, and Brown, 1812.

Volume I: Biographies of British and Irish dramatists. Note also Appendix, pp. 769–89.

Volumes II–III (in one volume): Alphabetical list of titles includes anonymous plays. Indicates when performed or printed; describes plot, style, and production.

Separate lists: Latin plays by English authors; oratorios. Addenda, pp. 471–78.

See also THESPIAN DICTIONARY OF DRAMATIC BIOGRAPHY OF THE PRESENT AGE, below.

Band-Kuzmany, Karin R.M. GLOSSARY OF THE THEATRE. IN ENGLISH, FRENCH, ITALIAN, AND GERMAN. Glossarium Interpretum, no. 15. Amsterdam and New York: Elsevier, 1969. 140 p.

Terms are in English, with foreign equivalents. There are indexes of the latter.

See also Giteau, Cecile; and Rae, Kenneth, and Southern, Richard, both below.

Bellour, Raymond, ed. DICTIONNAIRE DU CINEMA. Paris: Editions Universitaires, 1966. 771 p.

Mainly short biographies of selected directors from silent films onward. Includes a few essays on the history and recent state of the cinematic art.

See also Bessy, Maurice, and Chardans, Jean Louis; and Boussinot,

Roger, below.

Bessy, Maurice, and Chardans, Jean Louis. DICTIONNAIRE DU CINEMA ET DE LA TELEVISION. Paris: J.J. Pauvert, 1965-   . Illustrated.

Includes definitions and biographies, as well as essays on the history and art of motion pictures. Historical surveys are found under "Etats Unis d'Amerique" and "Evolution chronologique," etc.

See also Bellour, Raymond, above, and Boussinot, Roger, below.

THE BEST PLAYS [AND THE YEAR BOOK OF THE DRAMA IN AMERICA]. New York: Dodd Mead, 1899-   . Annual.

Title and coverage have varied. Sometimes referred to as the BURNS MANTLE YEARBOOK. Annual volumes include abridged versions of ten plays of the New York season and a discussion of trends in world theater. Lists of awards, obituaries, long runs, casts, and a discography; brief biographies of authors; annals of New York's season, with casts; list of plays found in earlier volumes of BEST PLAYS. Volumes from 1964 on carry a list of recently published plays.

For a cumulated index to BEST PLAYS, see DIRECTORY OF THE AMERICAN THEATER, 1894-1971, below.

BIOGRAPHIA DRAMATICA OR A COMPANION TO THE PLAYHOUSE.

See Baker, David Erskine, above.

BIOGRAPHICAL DICTIONARY OF ACTORS, ACTRESSES, MUSICIANS.

See Highfill, Philip H., Jr., et al., below.

Boussinot, Roger. ENCYCLOPEDIE DU CINEMA. Paris: Bordas, 1967. 1,550 p. Illustrated.

International encyclopedia of biographical and other entries, with brief bibliographies. Film titles appear in original language.

Volume II: L'ENCYCLOPEDIE DU CINEMA PAR L'IMAGE. 1970. 773 p. Illustrated. This volume is composed of 3,000 photographs, with text. Volume III, covering recent years, is in preparation.

See also Bellour, Raymond; and Bessy, Maurice, and Chardans, Jean Louis, above; Halliwell, Leslie; and WORLD ENCYCLOPEDIA OF FILM, below.

Bowman, Walter Parker, and Ball, Robert Hamilton, eds. THEATRE LANGUAGE: A DICTIONARY OF TERMS IN ENGLISH OF THE DRAMA AND STAGE FROM MEDIEVAL TO MODERN TIMES. New York: Theatre Arts, [1961]. 428 p.

Defines standard, technical, and slang terms used in American and British theater of the last 500 years.

Cf. Granville, Wilfred; Lounsbury, Warren C.; Rae, Kenneth, and Southern, Richard; and Taylor, John Russell, below.

THE BURNS MANTLE YEARBOOK.

See THE BEST PLAYS [AND THE YEAR BOOK OF THE DRAMA, IN AMERICA], above.

Cawkwell, Tim.

See WORLD ENCYCLOPEDIA OF FILM, below.

Centre Francais du Theatre. DICTIONNAIRE DES HOMMES DE THEATRE FRANCAIS CONTEMPORAINS. TOME I. DIRECTEURS, ANIMATEURS, HISTORIENS, CRITIQUES. Paris: Librairie Theatrale, 1967–

A "Who's Who" of the French theater.

See also ANNUAIRE DU SPECTACLE in Part III, "Directories."

Chardans, Jean Louis.

See Bessy, Maurice, above.

CONTEMPORARY DRAMATISTS OF THE ENGLISH LANGUAGE. Edited by James Vinson. Contemporary Writers of the English Language, vol. 3. London: St. James Press; New York: St. Martin's Press, [c.1973]. 926 p.

A bio-bibliography which adds critical comments and, sometimes, a statement by the author regarding his work. Three hundred living playwrights are discussed. In addition, the volume includes essays by various writers on radio, television, and motion picture writers, on librettists, on the theater of mixed means, and finally, "Theatre Collectives" by Theodore Shank. The preface is by Ruby Cohn.

CROWELL'S HANDBOOK OF CONTEMPORARY DRAMA.

See Anderson, Michael, et al., above.

DEUTSCHES THEATER-LEXIKON.

See Kosch, Wilhelm, below.

DICTIONARY OF FILM MAKERS and DICTIONARY OF FILMS.

See Sadoul, Georges, below.

DICTIONARY OF THE CINEMA.

See Graham, Peter, below.

A DICTIONARY OF THE DRAMA.

> See Adams, William Davenport, above.

DICTIONNAIRE DES HOMMES DE THEATRE FRANCAIS CONTEMPORAINS.

> See Centre Francais du Theatre, above.

DICTIONNAIRE DU CINEMA.

> See Bellour, Raymond, above.

DICTIONNAIRE DU CINEMA ET DE LA TELEVISION.

> See Bessy, Maurice, and Chardans, Jean Louis, above.

Dimmitt, Richard Bertrand. AN ACTOR GUIDE TO THE TALKIES, 1949-1964. 2 vols. Metuchen, N.J.: Scarecrow Press, 1967.

> Companion to Dimmitt's A TITLE GUIDE TO THE TALKIES, below. Volume I: eight thousand films listed by title. Volume II: name index.

> See also Weaver, John T., below.

_____. A TITLE GUIDE TO THE TALKIES: A COMPREHENSIVE LISTING OF 16,000 FEATURE-LENGTH FILMS FROM OCTOBER 1927 UNTIL DECEMBER 1963. 2 vols. Metuchen, N.J.: Scarecrow Press, 1965.

> Arranges films by title and shows literary sources, studio, and date of production. Author index. Bibliography.

> See also Dimmitt, Richard Bertrand, above.

DIRECTORY OF THE AMERICAN THEATER, 1894-1971. Compiled and edited by Otis L. Guernsey, Jr. New York: Dodd Mead, 1971. 343 p.

> Actually a cumulated index to BEST PLAYS (see above). Covers seventy-seven years, with references to authors, composers, and others as well as to play titles.

ENCICLOPEDIA DELLO SPETTACOLO. 9 vols. Rome: Casa Editrice le Maschere, 1954-   Illustrated.

> Authoritative articles in Italian treat the arts of entertainment in all aspects, artistic, social, legal, economic, etc. Approximately 30,000 items on persons, organizations, cities, and types of drama, with bibliographies and many illustrations. Play titles are given in Italian only.

> See also two appendices and index, "Indice repertorio," below.

> See also MCGRAW-HILL ENCYCLOPEDIA OF WORLD DRAMA, below.

ENCICLOPEDIA DELLO SPETTACOLO. AGGIORNAMENTO, 1955-1965.
Rome: Unione Editoriale, 1966. 1,291 p. Illustrated.

Appendix covering a decade's topics and personalities in dance,
theater, television, motion pictures, opera.

ENCICLOPEDIA DELLO SPETTACOLO. APPENDICE DI AGGIORNAMENTO:
CINEMA. Rome: Istituto per la Collaborazione Culturale, 1963. 178 p.
Illustrated.

Biographical sketches concern film celebrities only.

See also FILMLEXIKON DEGLI AUTORI E DELLE OPERE, below.

ENCICLOPEDIA DELLO SPETTACOLO. INDICE REPERTORIO. Rome: Unione
Editoriale, 1969. 1,024 p.

Index of all titles cited in the nine volumes and AGGIORNAMEN-
TO. Titles are in original language, followed by Italian translation. Author and date are given.

ENCYCLOPEDIE DU CINEMA.

See Boussinot, Roger, above.

ENCYCLOPEDIE DU THEATRE CONTEMPORAIN. 2 vols. Paris: Publications
de France, 1957-59. Illustrated.

Volume I: 1850-1914; Volume II: 1916-50. Well illustrated
articles. Indexes and historical tables.

Enser, A.G.S. FILMED BOOKS AND PLAYS FROM WHICH FILMS HAVE
BEEN MADE, 1928-1967. Rev ed., with a supplementary list for 1968 and
1969. London: Deutsch, 1971. 509 p.

Replaces earlier editions and supplements. Lists films by title and
author. Shows dates, producers, title changes, adaptations.

FILMGOER'S COMPANION.

See Halliwell, Leslie, below.

FILMLEXICON DEGLI AUTORI E DELLE OPERE. Rome: Ed. di Bianco e Nero,
1958-

Sponsored by the Centro Sperimentale di Cinematografia, this major
work will consist of two parts. The section yet to be published
will be devoted to individual motion pictures and to indexes.
The seven-volume author section was completed by 1968. "Author"
can mean scriptwriter, director, producer, actor, cameraman, composer, art director, or costume designer. The introduction is multi-
lingual; the biographies are in Italian. Titles are given in original language also.

See also Mitry, Jean; and Sadoul, Georges, entries, below, and
ENCICLOPEDIA DELLO SPETTACOLO entries, above.

FILMOGRAPHIE UNIVERSELLE.

See Mitry, Jean, below.

Frenzel, Herbert A.

See KUERSCHNERS BIOGRAPHISCHES THEATER-HANDBUCH, below.

Gassner, John, and Quinn, Edward G., eds. THE READER'S ENCYCLOPEDIA
OF WORLD DRAMA. New York: Crowell, 1969. 1,030 p.

Entries for literary terms, titles, persons; articles on criticism,
forms of drama, etc. Basic documents are appended.

See also MCGRAW-HILL ENCYCLOPEDIA OF WORLD DRAMA,
below.

Giteau, Cecile, comp. DICTIONNAIRE DES ARTS DU SPECTACLE. Paris:
Dunod, 1970. 429 p.

Terms in French, German, and English for circus, dance, films,
puppetry, radio, television, theater, and related topics.

See also Rae, Kenneth, and Southern, Richard, below, and Band-
Kuzmany, Karin R.M., above.

Graham, Peter. A DICTIONARY OF THE CINEMA. London: Tantivy Press;
New York: A.S. Barnes, 1964. 158 p.

Brief biographies of actors, directors, scriptwriters, and others.
Each entry has a list of films. Covers from earliest years to 1964.
Index of film titles, pp. 107-58.

See also Halliwell, Leslie, below.

Granville, Wilfred. THEATRE DICTIONARY: BRITISH AND AMERICAN TERMS
IN THE DRAMA, OPERA, AND BALLET. New York: Philosophical Library,
1952. 227 p.

Practical and traditional terms and phrases. British emphasis.
Some comparisons with U.S. terminology.

See also Bowman, Walter Parker, and Ball, Robert Hamilton, above,
and Lounsbury, Warren C.; Rae, Kenneth, and Southern, Richard;
and Taylor, John Russell, below.

Gregor, Joseph. DER SCHAUSPIELFUEHRER. Stuttgart: Hiersemann Verlag,
1953-   .

First six volumes form an international list of plays from Middle
Ages to twentieth century, arranged by period and then by author.

Summaries and brief histories of performances. Indexes by author, subject, and title in each volume with a special index of one-act plays and chronological table of first editions. Titles and text are in German.

Volume VI has supplementary material for various periods and nations and also a cumulated index for the six volumes (separate author and title lists), pp. 278-324.

Volume VII adds material but only on the twentieth-century drama to 1956. Main list is by author. Separate indexes are organized by title, country, and subject or type of play (e.g., "Absurdes Grotesktheater"). Separate list of one-act plays.

Volume VIII covers representative contemporary plays produced from 1956 to 1965. (No entries for the U.S.S.R.) Main list by author. Also separate indexes by country, title, and subject. Volume IX (1972) covers world drama from 1966 through 1970.

See also Hensel, George; Hoyo, Arturo del; Shank, Theodore J.; Shipley, Joseph T.; and Sprinchorn, Evert, below.

Guernsey, Otis L., Jr.

See DIRECTORY OF THE AMERICAN THEATER, 1894-1971, above.

Halliwell, Leslie. THE FILMGOER'S COMPANION. 3d ed., rev. New York: Hill and Wang, 1967. 847 p. (4th ed. in prep., 1974.)

Short entries for actors, writers, organizations, technical terms, and films, including title changes. Longer articles on such subjects as courtroom films, sex, Shakespeare. Emphasis throughout in on American and British motion pictures.

The older editions are still useful.

See also Graham, Peter, above.

Harsh, Philip Whaley. A HANDBOOK OF CLASSICAL DRAMA. Stanford, Calif.: Stanford University Press, 1944. 526 p.

Essays on Greek and Roman drama, followed by inventory of all extant plays. Comment on each major playwright and critical summaries of individual dramas, with discussion of sources and influences. Notes, bibliography, and index.

See also Hathorn, Richmond Y., below, and Feder, Lillian, in Part II-F.

Hartnoll, Phyllis.

See OXFORD COMPANION TO THE THEATRE.

Hathorn, Richmond Y. CROWELL'S HANDBOOK OF CLASSICAL DRAMA. New York: Crowell, 1967. 350 p.

Brief notes on characters, myths, persons, and places. Critical plot summaries. Some plays are listed under English title and some in original language.

See also Harsh, Philip W., above, and Feder, Lillian, in Part II-F.

Hensel, George. SPIELPLAN. SCHAUSPIELFUEHRER VON DER ANTIKE BIS ZUR GEGENWART. 2 vols. Berlin: Propylaenverlag, 1966.

This German work groups playwrights of all nations under headings such as "Poets," "Moralists," etc. For each author there are plot summaries, a brief discussion, and excerpts from criticisms. The critics are named, but sources are not identified. There are indexes of titles, dramatists, and others important in theater history, including critics. Bibliography.

See also Gregor, Joseph, above, and Hoyo, Arturo del, below.

Highfill, Philip H., Jr., et al. A BIOGRAPHICAL DICTIONARY OF ACTORS, ACTRESSES, MUSICIANS, DANCERS, MANAGERS, AND OTHER STAGE PERSONNEL IN LONDON, 1660-1800. By Philip H. Highfill, Jr., Kalman A. Burnim, and Edward A. Langhans. Carbondale: Southern Illinois University Press, 1973- . Illustrated.

To be completed in twelve volumes, with alphabetical entries for biographees, in all, more than 8,500 persons who performed occasionally or were regularly employed with theatrical companies in London and environs. Amateurs are excluded.

Includes patentees or servants of the patent theaters, opera houses, music rooms, fair booths, pleasure gardens, etc. In addition to categories named in the title, scene painters, machinists, prompters, and special entertainers, such as dwarfs and strong men, appear.

Among musicians named are some not found in GROVE'S DICTIONARY or other usual biographical sources.

Based on thorough research, entries provide all significant information, minimizing anecdote. Dates, places of residence, names of associates, and creative contributions are shown, and careers are traced both in England and abroad. Contemporary evaluations often are added.

Portraits of about 1,500 persons will be included. The work also includes maps of London and interior and exterior views of theaters.

Holzknecht, Karl J. OUTLINES OF TUDOR AND STUART PLAYS, 1497-1642. 1947. Reprint. New York: Barnes and Noble, 1963. 442 p.

Plot summaries and notes on characters. Locates plays in anthologies.

See also Shank, Theodore J.; and Shipley, Joseph T., below.

Hoyo, Arturo del, comp. TEATRO MUNDIAL. 2d ed. Madrid: Aguilar, 1961. 1,272 p.

Biographical and critical articles in Spanish on world drama, with plot summaries.

See also Gregor, Joseph; and Hensel, George, above.

Huerlimann, Martin, ed. DAS ATLANTISBUCH DES THEATERS. Zurich: Atlantis Verlag, 1966. 1,038 p. Illustrated.

One-volume encyclopedia in German, with universal coverage. Part I: "Art and technology of the theater"; Part II: "History of the theater"; Part III: "Dictionary of the theater." First two parts consist of long signed articles, well illustrated in color and in black and white, with some bibliographies. A table of chronology for the world's most important theater buildings from the sixteenth century on is on pp. 144-50. Part III defines terms and identifies places, persons, and theaters, etc., with cross-references to items and pictures in the main text.

See also ENCICLOPEDIA DELLO SPETTACOLO, above.

INTERNATIONAL ENCYCLOPEDIA OF FILM. Roger Manvell, general editor. London: Joseph, 1972. 574 p. Illustrated.

In dictionary arrangement and lavishly illustrated (partly in color), this work concerns the development of the art and industry of motion pictures worldwide. Definitions of terms, short biographies, and longer articles on subjects such as publicity, documentaries, and national cinematic history are interfiled. Bibliography, pp. 514-28. Indexes of films, of changed titles, and of names.

Jordan, Thurston C. GLOSSARY OF MOTION PICTURE TERMINOLOGY. Menlo Park, Calif.: Pacific Coast Publishers, 1968. 63 p.

Terms in English are listed alphabetically, with short explanations.

See also Townsend, Derek, below.

Kienzle, Siegfried. MODERN WORLD THEATER; A GUIDE TO PRODUCTIONS IN EUROPE AND THE UNITED STATES SINCE 1945. New York: Ungar, 1970. 509 p.

Modified and translated from the German work, MODERNES WELT-

THEATER. Entries for 578 plays arranged alphabetically under author, with plot summary, date, and place of first performance, as well as first edition, and known translations or adaptations. Plays are evaluated. Index of titles.

Kosch, Wilhelm. DEUTSCHES THEATER-LEXIKON. Edited by Wilhelm Kosch. Klagenfurt: F.V. Kleinmayr, 1951-60; Bern: Francke, 1965-   .

Limited to German theater. Brief articles on persons living or dead, on theatrical characters and subjects. Often the work includes, under the name of a city, a brief history of its musical and theatrical life, with bibliography.

See also KUERSCHNERS BIOGRAPHISCHES THEATER-HANDBUCH, below.

KUERSCHNERS BIOGRAPHISCHES THEATER-HANDBUCH. Edited by Herbert A. Frenzel and Hans Joachim Moser. Berlin: de Gruyter, 1956. 840 p.

Short biographies of persons in drama, motion pictures, opera, and radio in Austria, Germany, and Switzerland.

Supplements Kosch's DEUTSCHES THEATER-LEXIKON, above, which omits films and radio.

Lounsbury, Warren C. THEATER BACKSTAGE FROM A TO Z. Rev. ed. Seattle: University of Washington Press, 1972. 191 p. Illustrated.

Glossary of technical terms. List of manufacturers.

See also Bowman, Walter Parker, and Ball, Robert Hamilton; and Granville, Wilfred, above.

Lovell, John. DIGESTS OF GREAT AMERICAN PLAYS; COMPLETE SUMMARIES OF MORE THAN 100 PLAYS FROM THE BEGINNING TO THE PRESENT. New York: Crowell, [1961]. 452 p.

Chronological list from 1766 to 1959, with plot summaries. Supplementary lists of songs, actors, composers, lyricists, authors, awards, titles. List of historical eras covered in the plays, p. 443; list of themes treated, p. 445; historical personages, p. 447; types of drama, pp. 440-41.

See also Sprinchorn, Evert, below.

Lyonnet, Henry. DICTIONNAIRE DES COMEDIENS FRANCAIS (CEUX D'HIER): BIOGRAPHIE, BIBLIOGRAPHIE, ICONOGRAPHIE. 2 vols. Geneva: Bibliotheque de la Revue Universelle International Illustree, [1910-12?].

Biographical sketches, with sources for further reading and for portraits and costumed pictures of the French actors of past years.

MCGRAW-HILL ENCYCLOPEDIA OF WORLD DRAMA. 4 vols. New York: McGraw-Hill, 1972. Illustrated.

Articles on major and lesser authors and, in the same alphabet, essays on such topics as the "Baroque Age," "Comedy," and "Musical Comedy," as well as shorter entries for dramatic terms (e.g., "confidant"). The major author entries include biography and a full play list with date and place of production or publication. (Titles given in original language and in English.) English-language editions, single or collected, are shown and a list of criticism is added. Well illustrated.

See also ENCICLOPEDIA DELLO SPETTACOLO.

Mantle, Robert Burns, ed.

See THE BEST PLAYS.

Manvell, Roger.

See INTERNATIONAL ENCYCLOPEDIA OF FILM, above.

Matlaw, Myron. MODERN WORLD DRAMA: AN ENCYCLOPEDIA. New York: E.P. Dutton, 1972. 960 p.

A source for brief factual entries and suggestions for further reading. Indexes.

See also Anderson, Michael, above.

Melchinger, Siegfried. CONCISE ENCYCLOPEDIA OF MODERN DRAMA. New York: Horizon, 1962. 288 p.

A catchall of essays, biographies, chronology of performances, glossary of terms, list of new playwrights, and brief bibliography including drama reviews published in collections. Extends from Ibsen to Beckett.

See also Anderson, Michael, above.

Mitry, Jean. FILMOGRAPHIE UNIVERSELLE. Cours et Publications de l'IDHEC. Ser: Histoire et Sociologie. Paris: Institut des Hautes Etudes Cinematographiques, 1963-   .

Volume I: a chronology of film making from 1895 to 1962. Appended are lists of titles, prizes, etc. Volumes II through X: noted directors (Volume II: France, 1895-1915; Volumes III and IV: U.S., 1895-1915; Volume V: Europe, 1910-25; Volumes VI-X; U.S., 1910-25).

See also FILMLEXICON DEGLI AUTORI, above, and Sadoul, Georges; and WORLD ENCYCLOPEDIA OF FILM, below.

MODERN WORLD DRAMA: AN ENCYCLOPEDIA.

    See Matlaw, Myron, above.

Moser, Hans Joachim.

    See KUERSCHNERS BIOGRAPHISCHES THEATER-HANDBUCH, above.

Munden, Kenneth W.

    See AMERICAN FILM INSTITUTE CATALOG, above.

Nungezer, Edwin. A DICTIONARY OF ACTORS AND OTHER PERSONS
ASSOCIATED WITH THE PUBLIC REPRESENTATION OF PLAYS IN ENGLAND
BEFORE 1642. New Haven: Yale University Press, 1929. 438 p.

    Details concerning roles acted, memberships in acting companies,
    etc.

THE OXFORD COMPANION TO THE THEATRE. Edited by Phyllis Hartnoll.
3d ed. London: Oxford University Press, 1967. 1,088 p. Illustrated.

    Brief descriptions of persons, organizations, theaters, plays, world-
    wide, past and present.

    Bibliographies pp. 1029-74.

    See also Taylor, John Russell, below.

Parish, James Robert. ACTORS' TELEVISION CREDITS, 1950-72. Ed. associates: Paige Lucas, Florence Solomon, and T. Allan Taylor. Metuchen, N.J.:
Scarecrow Press, 1973. 869 p.

    Alphabetical index of actors, with references to television programs
    or episodes, insofar as actors' appearances are identifiable from in-
    complete early records. Based mainly on the New York market
    edition of TV GUIDE.

PENGUIN DICTIONARY OF THE THEATRE.

    See Taylor, John Russell, below.

Philpott, A.R. DICTIONARY OF PUPPETRY. Boston: Plays, Inc., 1969.
286 p.

    Definitions and brief articles.

Rae, Kenneth, and Southern, Richard, eds. AN INTERNATIONAL VOCABU-
LARY OF TECHNICAL THEATRE TERMS IN EIGHT LANGUAGES. Edited for
the International Theatre Institute. [London]: M. Reinhardt, [1959]. 139 p.

    Parallel columns of terms in Italian, French, Spanish, English,

Dutch, German, and Swedish.

See also Band-Kuzmany, Karin R.M.; and Giteau, Cecile, above.

READER'S ENCYCLOPEDIA OF WORLD DRAMA.

See Gassner, John, and Quinn, Edward G., above.

Rigdon, Walter, ed. THE BIOGRAPHICAL ENCYCLOPEDIA AND WHO'S WHO OF THE AMERICAN THEATRE. New York: James H. Heinman, 1966. 1,101 p.

A dictionary of living persons in the American theater, including motion pictures, is followed by the necrology, which gives dates of birth and death for persons in world theater from ancient times to 1964.

Also included are a bibliography of 600 biographical sources; list of awards; chronology of American playwrights' works first performed abroad; titles of 10,000 plays seen in New York from 1900 to 1964; list of playbills for New York and for American repertory groups; a history of more than fifty such groups; and a "genealogy" of theater buildings in New York, some of which have been demolished.

A few flaws have been noted: A section, "Stage Periodicals," seems misplaced in the midst of theater group biographies, p. 951. Missing dates can often be found in such sources as DICTIONARY OF AMERICAN BIOGRAPHY.

Sadoul, Georges. DICTIONARY OF FILM MAKERS. Translated, edited, and updated by Peter Morris. Berkeley: University of California Press, 1972. 288 p.

Peter Morris's translation, revision, and updating of Sadoul's DICTIONNAIRE DES CINEASTES, 1965, below. The evaluative entries, each with filmography, represent notable film makers in sixty countries. Included are directors, scriptwriters, cinematographers, art directors, composers, producers, and inventors. Actors are included only as principal authors of a film. Omitted are editors and sound engineers.

Morris has added some cameramen, composers, and writers omitted by Sadoul, along with directors newly prominent in the 1960s. The Morris entries are headed by an asterisk. Asterisks following film titles indicate a fuller discussion is available in Sadoul's DICTIONARY OF FILMS. Both of these works lack the illustrations of the French edition.

See also FILMLEXICON DEGLI AUTORI above, and WORLD ENCYCLOPEDIA OF FILM, below.

_____. DICTIONARY OF FILMS. Translated, edited, and updated by Peter Morris. Berkeley: University of California Press, 1972. 432 p.

Peter Morris's translation, revision, and updating of Sadoul's DICTIONNAIRE DES FILMS, 1965, and companion volume to DICTIONARY OF FILM MAKERS. (See Sadoul, above.) Adds 100 new entries to the 1,000 and more in the original French work. Revisions include longer plot summaries and other additions and corrections. Films are cited by original titles, with cross-references from various English titles. Following French practice, Morris has alphabetized under full title, including initial article (e.g., UN CHIEN ANDALOU, under the U's).

The year given for a film is that in which production was completed, not the release date. Running times are shown. No illustrations.

See also WORLD ENCYCLOPEDIA OF FILM, below.

_____. DICTIONNAIRE DES CINEASTES. Paris: Editions du Seuil, 1965. 245 p. Illustrated.

Companion to Sadoul's DICTIONNAIRE DES FILMS, below. International biographical dictionary of designers, directors, photographers, film producers, and others. Actors are excluded.

For an English-language revision of the work see Sadoul, Georges. DICTIONARY OF FILMS and DICTIONARY OF FILM MAKERS, both above. See also WORLD ENCYCLOPEDIA OF FILM, below.

_____. DICTIONNAIRE DES FILMS. Paris: Editions du Seuil, 1965. 288 p. Illustrated.

For 1,168 films listed by title (usually in French), there are plot summaries, with criticisms. An index of directors leads both to the title entries and also to illustrations in a companion volume, DICTIONNAIRE DES CINEASTES. For an English-language revision of this work see Sadoul, Georges. DICTIONARY OF FILM MAKERS and DICTIONARY OF FILMS, both above. See also WORLD ENCYCLOPEDIA OF FILM, below.

Sarris, Andrew. THE AMERICAN CINEMA; DIRECTORS AND DIRECTIONS, 1929-1968. New York: E.P. Dutton, 1968. 383 p.

Biographical and critical sketches of directors. Chronology of films, 1915-67, pp. 269-300. Index of film titles, 1929-67, pp. 301-83.

See also Mitry, Jean, Volumes III and IV, above.

DER SCHAUSPIELFUEHRER.

See Gregor, Joseph, above.

Shank, Theodore, J., ed. A DIGEST OF FIVE HUNDRED PLAYS. New York: Collier Books, 1963. 475 p.

> Summaries of plays from ancient times to the twentieth century. Description of sets, costumes, characters; publication and royalty data given. Index of titles, English and foreign.

> See also Shipley, Joseph T.; and Sprinchorn, Evert, below, and Gregor, Joseph, above.

Sharp, Harold S., comp. INDEX TO CHARACTERS IN THE PERFORMING ARTS. 4 parts in 6 vols. Compiled by Harold S. Sharp and Marjorie Z. Sharp. New York: Scarecrow Press, 1966-73.

> Part I: NON-MUSICAL PLAYS. 2 vols. 1966. 30,000 characters in world drama from fifth century B.C. to 1965 are named with play in which character appeared, playwright's name, and date of first production. Includes plays written in or translated into English.

> Part II: OPERAS AND MUSICAL PRODUCTIONS. 2 vols. 1969.

> Part III: BALLETS, A-Z AND SYMBOLS. 1972. 324 p.

> Part IV: RADIO AND TELEVISION. 1973. 697 p.

Sharp, Marjorie Z.

> See Sharp, Harold S., above.

Shipley, Joseph T. GUIDE TO GREAT PLAYS. Washington D.C.: Public Affairs Press, 1956. 867 p.

> Author list, showing works in chronological order.

> Concise plot summaries of 700 plays, with critical analyses and some notes on productions.

> List of reviewers cited, pp. vi-vii, and glossary, pp. viii-xi. Title index, pp. 861-67, includes foreign and variant English titles.

> See also Gregor, Joseph; and Shank, Theodore J., above.

Smith, John M.

> See WORLD ENCYCLOPEDIA OF FILM, below.

Sobel, Bernard. THE NEW THEATRE HANDBOOK AND DIGEST OF PLAYS. 8th ed. New York: Crown, 1959. 749 p.

> People, trends, theaters, listed with brief comment. Includes some unusual items.

> Bibliography, pp. 727-49, by George Freedley.

Sprinchorn, Evert, ed. TWENTIETH-CENTURY PLAYS IN SYNOPSIS. New York: Crowell, 1965. 493 p.

> Summarizes 133 plays from Strindberg to Albee, some not yet translated into English. Biographical notes on playwrights, pp. 467-90.

> See also Gregor, Joseph; Lovell, John; Shank, Theodore; and Shipley, Joseph T., all above.

Taylor, John Russell. PENGUIN DICTIONARY OF THE THEATRE. Harmondsworth: Penguin, 1966. 296 p.

> In one alphabet: brief definitions of theatrical terms; biographical notes; histories of individual theaters and companies. Includes some film and television celebrities as well as stage performers of all periods. Title entry for a play refers to fuller notes under author.

> See also OXFORD COMPANION TO THE THEATRE, above.

TEATRAL'NAIA ENTSIKLOPEDIA. Moscow: the Publisher of the Soviet Encyclopedia, 1961-   . Illustrated.

> Russian-language encyclopedia of the theater. Some articles include bibliographies. For each play included there is a chronology of productions.

> A supplement indexes the first five volumes.

THE THESPIAN DICTIONARY OF DRAMATIC BIOGRAPHY OF THE PRESENT AGE. 2d ed. London: J. Cundee, 1805. [390 p.]

> Biographies of eighteenth-century composers, critics, dramatists, managers, and major actors of the United Kingdom.

> See also Baker, David Erskine, above.

Townsend, Derek. PHOTOGRAPHY AND CINEMATOGRAPHY; A FOUR LANGUAGE ILLUSTRATED DICTIONARY AND GLOSSARY OF TERMS. London: A. Redman, 1964. 178 p.

> Separate glossaries in English, French, German, and Italian, referring from foreign term to English definition.

> See also Jordon, Thurston C., above.

Vinson, James, ed.

> See CONTEMPORARY DRAMATISTS, above.

Vizcaino Casas, Fernando. DICCIONARIO DEL CINE ESPANOL, 1896-1966. 2d ed. Madrid: Editora Nacional, 1968. 323 p.

> Short biographies of actors, dancers, singers, directors, producers, writers, and others associated with Spanish films. Bibliography, pp. xiii-xiv.

Weaver, John T., comp. FORTY YEARS OF SCREEN CREDITS, 1929-1969.
2 vols. Metuchen, N.J.: Scarecrow Press, 1970.

> Credits listed for 4,000 screen actors. Index of film titles and
> list of awards also provided.
>
> See also Dimmitt, Richard Bertrand. AN ACTOR GUIDE..., above.

WHO'S WHO IN THE THEATRE. London: I. Pitman & Sons, 1912-   .
Issued irregularly.

> Notes on British theater celebrities. "Jubilee" edition (1967) in-
> cludes many American names.
>
> Lists as follows: playbills for London, Stratford-on-Avon and
> Stratford, Ont.; London revivals and notable productions of past
> years; long runs in London and New York; seasons of the Old Vic
> and its road companies; repertory theaters in Great Britain; main
> London theaters, with seating charts (omitted in 1967 edition);
> dates of opening of London theater buildings since 1806; the same
> for New York; nineteenth and twentieth-century honors; obituaries;
> theater research centers. See earlier editions for items currently
>
> See also THE STAGE YEAR BOOK in Part III.

WORLD ENCYCLOPEDIA OF FILM. Edited by Tim Cawkwell and John M.
Smith. London: Studio Vista, 1972. 444 p. Illustrated.

> Illustrated biographical sketches and an index of 22,000 film titles.
>
> See also Boussinot, Roger; Mitry, Jean; and all Sadoul, Georges,
> items, above.

THE YEAR BOOK OF THE DRAMA IN AMERICA.

> See THE BEST PLAYS [AND THE YEARBOOK OF THE DRAMA IN
> AMERICA], above.

B. MUSIC AND MUSICAL THEATER

Apel, Willi, and Daniel, Ralph T. HARVARD BRIEF DICTIONARY OF MUSIC.
Cambridge, Mass.: Harvard University Press, 1960. 341 p.

> Concise definitions and historical summaries relating to music and
> dance. Biographies excluded. Titles of compositions included.

Blom, Eric.

> See Grove, Sir George, below.

BLUE BOOK OF BROADWAY MUSICALS.

See Burton, Jack, below.

BLUE BOOK OF HOLLYWOOD MUSICALS.

See Burton, Jack, below.

Blume, Friedrich. DIE MUSIK IN GESCHICHTE AND GEGENWART; ALLGE-MEINE ENZYKLOPAEDIE DER MUSIK. 14 vols. Kassel: Baerenreiter, 1949-68. Illustrated.
SUPPLEMENT, A-D, 1973. Illustrated.

Detailed scholarly treatment of all aspects of music, including the biographical. Bibliographies. Excellent sources for illustrations.

See also Grove, Sir George, below

Burton, Jack. BLUE BOOK OF HOLLYWOOD MUSICALS; SONGS FROM THE SOUND TRACKS AND THE STARS WHO SANG THEM SINCE THE BIRTH OF THE TALKIES...Watkins Glen, N.Y.: Century House, 1953. 296 p.

Completes a three-volume set published by Century House which includes Burton's BLUE BOOK OF TIN PAN ALLEY (1951) and the BLUE BOOK OF BROADWAY MUSICALS (1952). Burton's INDEX OF AMERICAN POPULAR SONG (1957) indexes the three volumes. In 1969 the BLUE BOOK OF BROADWAY MUSICALS appeared in a new edition with additions by Larry Freeman. The BLUE BOOK OF TIN PAN ALLEY also appeared in an expanded edition (1962-65) of two volumes, with a 1950-65 supplement by Larry Freeman.

See also Freeman, Graydon La Verne; and Mattfeld, Julius, below.

Celletti, Rodolfo, ed. LE GRANDI VOCI. DIZIONARIO CRITICO-BIOGRAFI-CO DEI CANTANTI. Rome: Istituto per la Collaborazione Culturale, 1964. 1,044 p. Illustrated.

This biographical dictionary, in Italian, covers famous singers and serves to supplement the ENCICLOPEDIA DELLO SPETTACOLO. Includes operatic discography.

See also Kutsch, K.J., and Riemens, Leo, below.

Ewen, David. THE BOOK OF EUROPEAN LIGHT OPERA; A GUIDE TO 167 EUROPEAN COMIC OPERAS, OPERETTAS, LIGHT OPERAS, AND OPERA BUFFAS FROM THE "BEGGAR'S OPERA" (1728) and "LA SERVA PADRONA" (1733) TO IVOR NOVELLO'S "KING'S RHAPSODY" (1949) by 81 COMPOSERS, WITH PLOT, PRODUCTION HISTORY, MUSICAL HIGHLIGHTS, CRITICAL EVALUATIONS, AND OTHER RELEVANT INFORMATION. New York: Holt, Rinehart and Winston, 1962. 297 p. Illustrated.

Mainly plot summaries, with history of production and critical comment. The appendix is a chronology of European musical theater, which runs from THE BEGGAR'S OPERA (1728) to 1949.

_____. NEW COMPLETE BOOK OF THE AMERICAN MUSICAL THEATER.
New York: Holt, Rinehart and Winston, 1970. 800 p.

A history centered on American composers, in chronological order.

An earlier edition of this Ewen work was entitled COMPLETE
BOOK OF THE AMERICAN MUSICAL THEATER (New York: Holt,
1958).

_____. THE NEW ENCYCLOPEDIA OF THE OPERA. New York: Hill and
Wang, 1971. 759 p.

Based on Ewen's ENCYCLOPEDIA OF THE OPERA (New York:
Hill and Wang, 1963), this work has been rewritten and expanded
to include more than 5,000 items. There are entries for persons,
organizations, operatic roles, opera titles, and terms (e.g.,
Sprechstimme). Longer articles treat opera performance and other
topics.

Titles may be in English or in their original language. Some
librettists are listed by name, but many must be sought under the
opera title.

See also Rosenthal, Harold D., and Warrack, John, below.

Freeman, Graydon La Verne. THE MELODIES LINGER ON; FIFTY YEARS OF
POPULAR SONG. By Larry Freeman. Watkins Glen, N.Y.: Century House,
'951. 212 p. Illustrated.

Surveys popular song in the United States from 1900-50. Illustrations reproduced from sheet music covers exemplify popular entertainment in each decade. There is a chronology of hit-songs,
pp. 193-212, in which publishers and performing rights affiliations
are shown but not composers or recording companies.

See also Burton, Jack, above, and Mattfeld, Julius, below, and
Shapiro, Nat, in Part VII-F.

Freeman, Larry.

See Freeman, Graydon La Verne, above.

Grove, Sir George, ed. DICTIONARY OF MUSIC AND MUSICIANS. Edited
by Eric Blom. 5th ed. 9 vols. London: Macmillan, 1954.

SUPPLEMENT, 1961. 493 p.

The chief encyclopedia of music in English. Useful for background.
Drama students may also seek specific entries for playwrights who
wrote librettos (e.g., Beaumarchais) and for opera houses and
theaters, entered under city. Bibliographies accompany articles.

For most composers there are chronological charts of their compositions.

The sixth edition is in preparation.

See also Blume, Friedrich, above.

Harewood, Earl of.

See Kobbe, Gustav, below.

Kobbe, Gustav. COMPLETE OPERA BOOK. Edited and revised by the Earl
of Harewood. London and New York: Putnam, [1963]. 1262 p. (New edition
in preparation, 1972.)

Grouped by composer's nationality and period are plot summaries
of operas in the standard repertoire and a few others. Some details on premieres in world capitals are given.

See also VICTOR BOOK OF THE OPERA, below.

Kutsch, K.J., and Riemens, Leo. A CONCISE DICTIONARY OF SINGERS
FROM THE BEGINNING OF RECORDED SOUND TO THE PRESENT. Translated
and annotated by Harry Earl Jones. Philadelphia: Chilton Book Co., 1969.
487 p.

Translation of the second edition of UNVERGAENGLICHE STIMMEN
(1966), corrected and expanded both in details and in more than
sixty added biographies.

Biographical sketches appear in alphabetical order, outlining careers and indicating major recordings or recording companies. Preceding this main section are a glossary of terms, a list of principal
operas, operettas, and composers, and short lists of opera houses
and festivals of music.

See also Celletti, Rodolfo, above.

Lewine, Richard, and Simon, Alfred. SONGS OF THE AMERICAN THEATER:
A COMPREHENSIVE LISTING OF MORE THAN 12,000 SONGS, INCLUDING
SELECTED TITLES FROM FILM AND TELEVISION PRODUCTIONS. Introduction
by Stephen Sondheim. New York: Dodd, Mead, 1973. 820 p.

Revision of the same authors' ENCYCLOPEDIA OF THEATER MUSIC
(New York: Random House, 1961), which listed about 400 songs.
In the new edition the main list is alphabetized by song title and
gives names of composer and lyricist, with date of New York
premiere. A separate alphabetical list of productions shows date,
length of run, composer, lyricist, and song titles. Also added
are a chronology of productions and an index of composers and
lyricists.

Mattfeld, Julius. VARIETY MUSIC CAVALCADE, 1620-1961; A CHRONOLO-

GY OF VOCAL AND INSTRUMENTAL MUSIC POPULAR IN THE UNITED STATES. 3d ed. Englewood Cliffs, N.J.: Prentice-Hall, 1971. 766 p.

General historical introduction followed by annual lists of famous songs, with description of current events. Index of song titles only.

See also Burton, Jack; and Freeman, Graydon La Verne, above.

DIE MUSIK IN GESCHICHTE UND GEGENWART.

See Blume, Friedrich, above.

OXFORD COMPANION TO MUSIC.

See Scholes, Percy A., below.

Rosenthal, Harold D., and Warrack, John. CONCISE OXFORD DICTIONARY OF OPERA. London and New York: Oxford University Press, 1964. xiv, 446 p.

One of several opera reference books, listing, in one alphabet, terms, titles, roles, arias, composers, conductors, and performers as well as organizations and theaters. There are brief plot summaries and biographies.

See also VICTOR BOOK OF THE OPERA, below, and Ewen, David, NEW ENCYCLOPEDIA, above.

Scholes, Percy A., et al. OXFORD COMPANION TO MUSIC. Edited by John Owen Ward. 10th ed., rev. New York: Oxford University Press, 1970. 1,189 p. Illustrated.

A dictionary identifying and describing persons and subjects related to music and dance. Interesting articles under such subjects as "Folk Song," "Masque," "Patronage," and "Publishing of Music"; also under name of country.

Note the pronouncing glossary of difficult or foreign terms, pp. 1131-89.

Simon, Henry W.

See VICTOR BOOK OF THE OPERA, below.

VARIETY MUSIC CAVALCADE.

See Mattfeld, Julius, above.

VICTOR BOOK OF THE OPERA. Edited by Henry W. Simon. 13th ed. New York: Simon and Schuster, 1968. 465 p. Illustrated.

Plot summaries for 120 operas, with historical notes. A discography includes opera recordings from several companies.

See also Kobbe, Gustav; and Rosenthal, Harold D., and Warrack, John, above.

Ward, John Owen.

See Scholes, Percy A., et al, above.

C. DANCE

Chujoy, Anatole, ed. THE DANCE ENCYCLOPEDIA. Revised and edited by Anatole Chujoy and P.W. Manchester. New York: Simon and Schuster, 1967. 992 p. Illustrated.

Brief entries on ballet terms and works, choreographers, composers, dancers, companies, festivals, theater buildings. Longer articles by authorities on Oriental dance, etc. Covers all periods.

Crosland, Margaret. BALLET LOVERS' DICTIONARY. London: Arco Publications, 1962. 183 p.

Short entries for personal names, ballet terms, titles of works. Premieres, revivals, and notable performances indicated. Some notes on television and film productions.

See also Wilson, George B.L., below. See also Granville, Wilfred, in Part II-A.

DICTIONARY OF MODERN BALLET. Francis Gadan and Robert Maillard, general editors. New York: Tudor, 1959. 360 p. Illustrated.

Brief description of ballets, companies, and dancers. Well illustrated.

Raffe, Walter G. DICTIONARY OF THE DANCE. New York: A.S. Barnes, 1964. 583 p.

Alphabetical entries for names of dances and topics related to the dance. No biographies. Little on ballet. Mainly ethnological in approach, but includes modern social dances. Very entertaining comments.

Verwer, Hans. GUIDE TO THE BALLET. New York: Barnes and Noble, 1963. 201 p.

Includes many essays on ballet. Plot summaries, with date, place, and cast of first production. Index will, in some instances, lead to several choreographic interpretations of one ballet.

See also Wilson, George B.L., below.

Wilson, George B.L. A DICTIONARY OF BALLET. Rev. ed. New York:
Barnes and Noble, 1961. 313 p. (Third edition in preparation, 1973.)

>   Short entries for terms, persons, institutions, theaters, ballet
>   companies, titles (with dates of premieres).

>   See also Crosland, Margaret; and Verwer, Hans, above.

D. COSTUME

Boucher, Francois. A HISTORY OF COSTUME IN THE WEST. London:
Thames & Hudson, 1967. 441 p. Illustrated.

>   An encyclopedic history arranged by period and then by area.
>   Contains some material on the ancient East and Egypt but is mainly
>   European in focus, from prehistory to mid-twentieth century. Elab-
>   orately illustrated with works of art and costume photographs.
>   Each section has a bibliography. General bibliography, p. 423.
>   Glossary of fashion terms, pp. 425-36.

Cunnington, Cecil Willett, et al. A DICTIONARY OF ENGLISH COSTUME
[900-1900]. London: Adam and Charles Black, 1960. 281 p.

>   Main section, pp. 1-240, lists names of 30,000 items of costume,
>   headgear, and accessories with description and history. Glossary
>   of materials used in costumes, pp. 241-80. List of obsolete names
>   of colors, p. 281.

Davenport, Millia. THE BOOK OF COSTUME. 2 vols. in 1. New York:
Crown, 1948. 958 p. Illustrated.

>   From the ancient Orient through the nineteenth century, essays on
>   each period are followed by 3,000 annotated illustrations from
>   period sources, mainly paintings and engravings. Bibliography,
>   pp. 935-45. Index of names and subjects, pp. 946-58.

LeLoir, Maurice. DICTIONNAIRE DU COSTUME ET DES ACCESSOIRES, DES
ARMES ET DES ETOFFES DES ORIGINES A NOS JOURS. Paris: Librairie
Gruend, 1951. 390 p. Illustrated.

>   Definitions of costume terms illustrated with numerous detailed
>   drawings. Progresses from earliest times to the twentieth century.

Planche, James Robinson. A CYCLOPAEDIA OF COSTUME OR DICTIONARY
OF DRESS; INCLUDING NOTICES OF CONTEMPORANEOUS FASHIONS ON
THE CONTINENT; A GENERAL CHRONOLOGICAL HISTORY OF THE COS-
TUMES OF THE PRINCIPAL COUNTRIES OF EUROPE, FROM THE COMMENCE-
MENT OF THE CHRISTIAN ERA TO THE ACCESSION OF GEORGE THE THIRD.
2 vols. London: Chatto and Windus, 1876-79. Illustrated.

>   An old reference work, useful still, especially for medieval and

Renaissance periods.

Volume I: an illustrated dictionary of details of costume, describing origins and uses of garments, armor, headdress, and accessories.

Volume II: a history of costume in Europe from ancient Greece to the accession of George III.

Note pp. 383–433, "Theatrical, Allegorical, and Fanciful Costume."

General index, pp. 435–48.

Wilcox, Ruth Turner. FIVE CENTURIES OF AMERICAN COSTUME. New York: Charles Scribner's Sons, 1963. 207 p. Illustrated.

From the Viking voyages to American costume in the 1950s. Illustrated by drawings. Good material on military uniforms. Chapter on children's dress, sixteenth to twentieth centuries. Bibliography, pp. 203–7.

E. VISUAL ARTS AND ESTHETICS

Becker, Felix.

See Thieme, Ulrich, below.

Benezit, Emmanuel. DICTIONNAIRE CRITIQUE ET DOCUMENTAIRE DES PEINTRES, SCULPTEURS, DESSINATEURS, ET GRAVEURS DE TOUS LES TEMPS ET DE TOUS LES PAYS. Rev. ed. 8 vols. Paris: Librairie Gruend, [1948]–57. (New rev. ed. in prep., 1974.)

International biographical dictionary of artists. Monograms of anonymous artists shown at end of each alphabetical section. Note also sections headed "Ecole" (e.g., "Ecole italienne") and "Maitres anonymes."

Benezit shows location of many works of art and gives auction sale prices for some.

See also Thieme, Ulrich; and Vollmer, Hans, below.

ENCYCLOPEDIA OF PHILOSOPHY. 8 vols. New York: Macmillan, 1967.

Authoritative signed articles on philosophical topics and on philosophers. Bibliographies follow most articles.

Note especially essays on "Aesthetics, history of and problems of," "Aristotle," "Beauty," "Drama," "Greek Drama," "Humor," "Tragedy," "Ugliness," etc.

See also Hammond, William A., Part I-D, and ENCYCLOPEDIA OF WORLD ART, below.

ENCYCLOPEDIA OF THE ARTS. Sir Herbert Read, consulting editor. New

York: Meredith, 1966. 966 p. Illustrated.

Many short definitions and biographies relating to literature and the visual and performing arts. Cross-references to related entries. Numerous unusual illustrations; some are in color.

ENCYCLOPEDIA OF WORLD ART. 15 vols. New York: McGraw-Hill, 1959-68. Illustrated.

The major art encyclopedia in English. Table of contents in each volume. Volume 15 is the index.

Long authoritative articles have excellent bibliographies which sometimes occur after subdivisions. Illustrative plates are grouped at the end of each volume.

Note long articles on countries. Relatively few biographical entries, e.g., "Jones, Inigo." Articles on "Acoustics," "Costume," "Interior Design," "Scenography," and "Tragedy," and "The Sublime."

MCGRAW-HILL DICTIONARY OF ART. Edited by Bernard S. Myers. 5 vols. New York: McGraw-Hill, 1969. Illustrated.

Numerous short items for persons, places, movements, techniques, individual works, and types of art, e.g., masks. Many entries have bibliographies.

OXFORD COMPANION TO ART. Edited by Harold Osborne. Oxford: Clarendon Press, 1970. 1,277 p.

Brief entries for persons, art movements, styles, etc.

Thieme, Ulrich. ALLGEMEINES LEXIKON DER BILDENDEN KUENSTLER VON DER ANTIKE BIS ZUR GEGENWART. 37 vols. Edited by Ulrich Thieme and Felix Becker. Leipzig: E.A. Seemann, 1907-50. Reprint. 1951-60.

International biographical encyclopedia including 150,000 artists and artisans. Final volume has artists known only as "Meister" and, in a separate list, those known by monogram only. Bibliographies.

Continued by Vollmer, Hans, below.

See also Benezit, Emmanuel, above.

Vollmer, Hans. ALLGEMEINES LEXIKON DER BILDENDEN KUENSTLER DES XX JAHRHUNDERTS. 6 vols. Leipzig: E.A. Seemann, 1953-62.

Continues Ulrich Thieme's work, above. Covers twentieth-century artists. These two works overlap somewhat. Artists famous in this century appear in the earlier Thieme work if their careers began early; Vollmer gives added information. See Volumes V and VI for a supplement to the main alphabet.

See also Benezit, Emmanuel, above.

F. WORLD LITERATURE

Avery, Catherine B.

See THE NEW CENTURY CLASSICAL HANDBOOK, below.

Bompiani, Valentino.

See DIZIONARIO LETTERARIO BOMPIANI, below.

CASSELL'S ENCYCLOPEDIA OF WORLD LITERATURE. J[ohn] Buchanan-Brown, general ed. Rev. and enl. ed. 3 vols. London: Cassell, 1973.

First published in 1953 under the title CASSELL'S ENCYCLOPEDIA OF LITERATURE, edited by S.H. Steinberg.

The 1973 edition follows the pattern of its predecessor, Volumes I, II, and III being revisions of Parts I, II, and III of the original edition. Volume I, HISTORIES AND GENERAL ARTICLES, has been much revised, because of new developments in literature and publishing, for example, in regard to copyright and censorship. New literary areas are touched upon, such as the Pre-Colombian literature of Central America, and a much fuller treatment of the literatures of Africa and Asia is provided. In general, however, the European emphasis still prevails. Ninety new articles have been added in this volume, excluding mere definitions of rhetorical terms.

Volume II covers BIOGRAPHIES, A-K; Volume III, BIOGRAPHIES, L-Z. In these volumes the old arrangement of two chronological sections has been eliminated in favor of one alphabet covering all periods, with entries under authors' names. There are helpful updated bibliographies for most entries in all three volumes. These include both primary and secondary materials.

See also COLUMBIA DICTIONARY OF MODERN EUROPEAN LITERATURE; and Shipley, Joseph T., below.

Clapp, Jane. INTERNATIONAL DICTIONARY OF LITERARY AWARDS. New York: Scarecrow Press, 1963. 545 p.

Main list is of awards, alphabetically by title. Consult index for names of prize winners and of subjects (e.g., "Drama awards").

COLUMBIA DICTIONARY OF MODERN EUROPEAN LITERATURE. Horatio Smith, general ed. New York: Columbia University Press, 1947. 899 p.

Offers brief biographies of major and minor authors as well as

articles on national literatures, beginning about 1870. Useful
for discovering original titles of works and their English translations.

See also CASSELL'S ENCYCLOPAEDIA OF LITERATURE, above.

DICTIONNAIRE DES OEUVRES DE TOUS LES TEMPS ET DE TOUS LES PAYS:
LITTERATURE, PHILOSOPHIE, MUSIQUE, SCIENCES. Edited by Robert Raoul
Laffont and Valentino Bompiani. 4 vols. and Index. Paris: Societe d'Edition
de Dictionnaires et Encyclopedies (S.E.D.E.), 1958-59. Illustrated.

International illustrated dictionary of titles of works of literature,
philosophy, music, and science. Summaries and analyses of each
work are in French. For dramas, places and dates of performances
are given. Index volume has list of illustrations, author index,
and parallel chronological tables of literary works in various nations to the end of the nineteenth century.

See also DICTIONNAIRE DES PERSONNAGES, below.

DICTIONNAIRE DES PERSONNAGES LITTERAIRES ET DRAMATIQUES DE TOUS
LES TEMPS ET DE TOUS LES PAYS. Edited by Robert Raoul Laffont. Paris:
Societe d'Edition de Dictionnaires et Encyclopedies (S.E.D.E.), 1960. Illus-
trated.

Companion to DICTIONNAIRE DES OEUVRES..., above. A selective rather than comprehensive list. Identifies and describes characters in literary works and historical personages if used as characters.
There are cross-references to literary works cited in Laffont's
DICTIONNAIRE DES OEUVRES, above.

Both French works are derived from DIZIONARIO LETTERARIO
BOMPIANI, below.

DIZIONARIO LETTERARIO BOMPIANI DELLE OPERE E DEI PERSONAGGI DI
TUTTI I TEMPI E DI TUTTE LE LETTERATURE. 9 vols. and Appendix. Milan:
Valentino Bompiani Editor, [1947-66]. Illustrated.

The first seven volumes comprise an alphabetical list of literary,
philosophical, historical, musical, and scientific works described
in Italian. Volume VIII is an index of literary and mythological
characters. Volume IX is an index of authors and works, with
titles in original language. (Classical names appear in Italian
form.) There is a comparative chronological table of works. All
volumes are well illustrated. This encyclopedia is available in
French. See DICTIONNAIRE DES OEUVRES, and DICTIONNAIRE
DES PERSONNAGES, above. Only the Italian edition has a
useful two-volume appendix, which appeared in 1966.

ENCYCLOPEDIA OF POETRY AND POETICS. Edited by Alex Preminger.
Frank J. Warnke and O.B. Hardison, Jr., associate eds. Princeton, N.J.:
Princeton University Press, 1965. 906 p. (Rev. ed. in preparation, 1974.)

Articles on history, theory, technique, and criticism of poetry in all periods and places. Bibliographies. No biographies.

Note articles on "Classical Poetics," "Dramatic Poetry," "Greek Poetry," "Mystery and Miracle Plays," "Renaissance Poetry," and definitions of verse forms.

ENCYCLOPEDIA OF WORLD LITERATURE IN THE TWENTIETH CENTURY. Wolfgang Bernard Fleischmann, general editor. 4 vols. New York: Ungar, 1967-71.

Entries are biographical and critical, with bibliographies. Longer articles cover national literatures, literary genres: e.g., "Drama and Theater," "Cinema and Literature," and influences; e.g., "Christianity and Literature."

No definitions of terms.

Feder, Lillian. CROWELL'S HANDBOOK OF CLASSICAL LITERATURE. New York: Crowell, 1964. 448 p.

Summaries of literary works. Also biographical sketches, essays on myths, etc.

See also THE NEW CENTURY CLASSICAL HANDBOOK, below, and Harsh, Philip W.; and Hathorn, Richmond Y., in Part II-A.

Fleischmann, Wolfgang Bernard.

See ENCYCLOPEDIA OF WORLD LITERATURE IN THE TWENTIETH CENTURY, above.

Hammond, Nicholas G.L.

See OXFORD CLASSICAL DICTIONARY, below.

Holman, Clarence Hugh. A HANDBOOK TO LITERATURE. 3d ed. Indianapolis: Odyssey Press, 1972. 646 p.

Brief discussions of literary terms (e.g., blank verse), motifs (Holy Grail), and genres (the masque), as well as descriptions of literary groups, movements, and institutions.

Originally published by Thrall and Hibbard in 1960 (Odyssey), this important handbook has been much expanded, greatly revised, and addressed to a broader audience. There are now over 1360 entries. Six hundred articles have been added. Definitions of literary terms are still interfiled with longer articles.

Mayer, Alfred, comp. ANNALS OF EUROPEAN CIVILIZATION, 1501-1900. London: Cassell, 1949. 457 p.

Chronology of nonpolitical cultural history. Annual sections show parallel developments in learning, literature, and the arts. Useful lists of names and dates under headings of painting, drama, music, periodicals, etc.

THE NEW CENTURY CLASSICAL HANDBOOK. Edited by Catherine B. Avery. New York: Appleton-Century-Crofts, 1962. 1,162 p. Illustrated.

Brief entries on all facets of classical culture, including biography. Pronounciations shown.

See also OXFORD CLASSICAL DICTIONARY, below, and Feder, Lillian, above.

OXFORD CLASSICAL DICTIONARY. Edited by Nicholas G.L. Hammond. 2d ed. Oxford: Clarendon Press, 1970. 1,176 p.

Scholarly articles on all aspects of classical civilization. Biographical material included. Many theatrical and rhetorical terms defined. Bibliographies.

See also THE NEW CENTURY CLASSICAL HANDBOOK, above.

The OXFORD COMPANIONS include the following literary handbooks:

Hart, James D. THE OXFORD COMPANION TO AMERICAN LITERATURE. 4th ed., rev. New York: Oxford University Press, 1965.

Harvey, Sir Paul. THE OXFORD COMPANION TO CLASSICAL LITERATURE. Oxford: Clarendon Press, 1937.

_____. THE OXFORD COMPANION TO ENGLISH LITERATURE. 4th ed., rev. Oxford: Clarendon Press, 1967.

_____. THE OXFORD COMPANION TO FRENCH LITERATURE. Oxford: Clarendon Press, 1959.

All of these consist of numerous brief entries. Fringe areas of the particular literature are discussed and biographies are included.

THE OXFORD DICTIONARY OF QUOTATIONS. 2d ed. New York: Oxford University Press, 1953. 1,003 p.

Author and keyword indexes of familiar quotations in English and foreign languages, including the BIBLE, BOOK OF COMMON PRAYER, and anonymous references. No proverbs.

Pauly, August Friedrich von. PAULYS REALENCYCLOPAEDIE DER CLASSISCHEN ALTERTUMSWISSENSCHAFT (Neue Bearbeitung). Edited by Georg Wissowa et al. Stuttgart: Alfred Druckenmueller, 1893- .

Important multi-volume set dealing with all aspects of classical antiquity, including biography. Subject headings are in Latin or

Greek, and text is in German. Articles include bibliographies.

Basic set is complete, but supplements continue to appear as research develops. A general index and a picture volume are also planned.

There are two series, and because of the volumes of corrections and additions, the organization is complex. Volume 23, no. 2 has an index to these. (See p. 2520, and note abbreviations at head of page indicating volume and page references.) Volume 23 also includes items PS to PY of the basic entries and a section of corrections and additions (pp. 2283-519).

An abridged edition is DER KLEINE PAULY. Stuttgart: Alfred Druckenmueller, 1964-   .

Preminger, Alex, ed.

See ENCYCLOPEDIA OF POETRY AND POETICS, above.

Scott, Arthur Finley. CURRENT LITERARY TERMS. New York: St. Martin's Press, 1965. 324 p.

Defines or identifies words, phrases, and names of literary significance, from Abbey Theatre to "yellow press."

Shipley, Joseph T., ed. ENCYCLOPEDIA OF LITERATURE. 2 vols. New York: Philosophical Library, [1946].

Long articles on literature of the world's peoples, from Accadian to Zuni. Bibliographies after each article. Volume II also contains biographies, pp. 1055-1188.

Useful for general literary background. For example, for references to Goethe as related to the Sturm und Drang movement, see "German Literature."

See also CASSELL'S ENCYCLOPEDIA OF LITERATURE, above.

Smith, Horatio, general editor.

See COLUMBIA DICTIONARY OF MODERN EUROPEAN LITERATURE.

Sonnino, Lee Ann. A HANDBOOK TO SIXTEENTH CENTURY RHETORIC. London: Routledge; New York: Barnes and Noble, 1968. 278 p.

Defines terms.

Thrall, William Flint, and Hibbard, Addison. HANDBOOK TO LITERATURE.

See Holman, Clarence Hugh, above.

Tilley, Morris Palmer. A DICTIONARY OF THE PROVERBS IN ENGLAND IN THE SIXTEENTH AND SEVENTEENTH CENTURIES; A COLLECTION OF THE PROVERBS FOUND IN ENGLISH DICTIONARIES OF THE PERIOD. Ann Arbor: University of Michigan Press, 1950. 854 p.

> Important result of thirty years' scholarship. The dictionary covers the years 1500 to 1700. Quotes and gives date and place of use in works of Shakespeare and other English authors. Bibliography, pp. 769-802.

> Note the "Shakespeare Index," pp. 803-8.

Wissowa, Georg, ed.

> See Pauly, August Friedrich von, above.

G. SHAKESPEARE

Bartlett, John. A NEW AND COMPLETE CONCORDANCE OR VERBAL IN-DEX TO WORDS, PHRASES, AND PASSAGES IN THE DRAMATIC WORKS OF SHAKESPEARE, with a SUPPLEMENTARY CONCORDANCE TO THE POEMS. New York: Macmillan, 1896. 1,910 p. Reprint. New York: St. Martin's Press, 1966 as A COMPLETE CONCORDANCE OR VERBAL INDEX TO WORDS, PHRASES, AND PASSAGES IN THE DRAMATIC WORKS OF SHAKESPEARE, WITH A SUPPLEMENTARY CONCORDANCE TO THE POEMS, BY JOHN BARTLETT.

> Standard concordance to Shakespeare. List of key words and phrases, traced to passages in the plays. Separate concordance to the poems, pp. 1771-910.

> See also Spevack, Marvin; and Stevenson, Burton, below.

Campbell, Oscar James, ed. THE READER'S ENCYCLOPEDIA OF SHAKE-SPEARE. New York: Crowell, 1966. 1,014 p.

> For everyone interested in Shakespeare and his times. Lively read-ing although based on weighty scholarship. Short subject entries in alphabetical order.

> Select bibliography of books and articles, pp. 983-1014; includes secondary material as well as a list of major modern editions for each of Shakespeare's plays.

> Shakespearean chronology, pp. 967-76; documents, pp. 977-79; genealogical tables of houses of York and Lancaster, pp. 980-81.

> See also Halliday, Frank Ernest, below.

EVERYMAN'S DICTIONARY OF SHAKESPEARE QUOTATIONS. Compiled by D.C. Browning. London: J.M. Dent, 1953. 560 p.

> Selected quotations grouped under each play, with plot summaries.

Separate list of quotations from poems. Index of lines.

Added features are a list of historical events, selections from early biographies of Shakespeare, etc.

Halliday, Frank Ernest. A SHAKESPEARE COMPANION, 1564-1964. New York: Schocken Books, 1964. 569 p. Illustrations.

A dictionary of names and subjects related to Shakespeare, his associates, his times, and the stage history of his plays. Many entries for actors, adapters, critics, producers, composers, and scholars concerned with Shakespeare.

Bibliography, pp. 545-66, includes important editions of Shakespeare's plays in English from 1795 to 1958.

See also Campbell, Oscar James, ed., above.

Irvine, Theodora. A PRONOUNCING DICTIONARY OF SHAKESPEARE'S NAMES. 1944. Reprint. New York: Barnes and Noble, 1947. 387 p.

Alphabetical pronouncing list of people and places, with cross-references from variant forms.

Separate list of "Dramatis Personae" for each play, pp. 341-87.

See also Koekeritz, Helge, below.

Koekeritz, Helge. SHAKESPEARE'S NAMES: A PRONOUNCING DICTIONARY. New Haven: Yale University Press, 1959. 100 p.

Names pronounced by International Phonetic Association alphabet. Some of Koekeritz's opinions have been disputed.

See also Irvine, Theodora, above.

Onions, Charles Talbut. A SHAKESPEARE GLOSSARY. 2d ed., rev. Oxford: Clarendon Press, 1958. 264 p.

Based on the OXFORD ENGLISH DICTIONARY. Supplies definitions and illustrations of words now obsolete or provincial. Some explanation also of proper names of special interest or difficulty.

See also Schmidt, Alexander, below.

THE READER'S ENCYCLOPEDIA OF SHAKESPEARE.

See Campbell, Oscar James, ed., above.

Schmidt, Alexander. SHAKESPEARE LEXICON; A COMPLETE DICTIONARY OF ALL THE ENGLISH WORDS, PHRASES, AND CONSTRUCTIONS IN THE WORKS OF THE POET. Revised by Gregor Sarrazin. 3d ed. 2 vols. New York: Blom, 1968. 6th unchanged ed. 2 vols. New York and Berlin: Walter de Gruyter, 1971.

An old work still considered indispensable. The sixth edition is unchanged from the edition revised by Sarrazin in 1901 after the author's death.

See also Onions, Charles Talbut, above.

Spevack, Marvin, ed. COMPLETE AND SYSTEMATIC CONCORDANCE TO THE WORKS OF SHAKESPEARE. 6 vols. Hildesheim: Georg Olms, 1968-70.

This computer-produced work includes the following concordances: Volume I: folio comedies; Volume II, histories and nondramatic works; Volume III, tragedies; and Volumes IV-VI: the complete works, with full entry and statistical analysis for every word found.

Appendices in Volume VI: A, word frequency list; B, reverse-word index; C, hyphenated words; D, homographs; E, conversion table to through line numbering. Postscript and Corrigenda, pp. 4339-42.

Spevack's work is intended for use with THE RIVERSIDE SHAKE-SPEARE, edited by G. Blakemore Evans et al. (Boston: Houghton, Mifflin, 1974).

See also Bartlett, John, above, and Stevenson, Burton, below.

Stevenson, Burton, ed. THE HOME BOOK OF SHAKESPEARE QUOTATIONS. New York: Scribner's, 1937. 2,055 p.

Quotations grouped under subject. There is also an "Index and Concordance," listing passages by keyword.

See also Bartlett, John; and Spevack, Marvin, above.

Stokes, Francis Griffin. A DICTIONARY OF THE CHARACTERS AND PROPER NAMES IN THE WORKS OF SHAKESPEARE. 1924. Reprint. New York: Peter Smith, 1949. 360 p.

Entries for titles, characters, places. All are identified and described briefly.

Sugden, Edward H. A TOPOGRAPHICAL DICTIONARY TO THE WORKS OF SHAKESPEARE AND HIS FELLOW DRAMATISTS. Manchester: The University Press, 1925. 580 p.

Brief accounts of places and buildings mentioned in the plays of Shakespeare and other Elizabethan and Jacobean dramatists. For Shakespeare, references to plays are by abbreviated title. References to other dramatists are identified by author and full title of play.

Part III

DIRECTORIES

Most of the following entries provide details on organizations and institutions such as agencies, archives, foundations, libraries, museums, schools, and theaters. A few of the directories list living persons active in theater, motion pictures, radio, or television.

As some directories make only one appearance and others do not appear regularly, present addresses of individuals must sometimes be sought in general sources which are frequently or regularly updated, such as WHO'S WHO IN AMERICA and its British counterpart, WHO'S WHO, or in such ongoing compilations as CONTEMPORARY AUTHORS or CURRENT BIOGRAPHY. These are available in most libraries and are not further described in this guide.

Fuller descriptions of some persons and institutions may be found in works discussed in Part II, "Dictionaries, Encyclopedias, and Handbooks."

AMERICAN ART DIRECTORY. New York: R.R. Bowker, 1898- . (Title and frequency vary.)

> Describes art museums, schools, and other organizations in the United States and Canada, noting scope, activities, and personnel. There are few direct references to theater design, but some collections mentioned may interest designers. Lists a few art schools abroad.

American Council on Education. FELLOWSHIPS IN THE ARTS AND SCIENCES. Madison, Wis.: American Council on Education, 1957- . (Title varies.)

> List of pre-and post-doctoral aids given by agencies other than universities. Summer study is included.

> See also FOUNDATION DIRECTORY; and Wasserman, Paul, below.

American Educational Theatre Association. DIRECTORY OF AMERICAN COLLEGE THEATRE.

> See DIRECTORY OF AMERICAN COLLEGE THEATRE, below.

American Film Institute.

> See GUIDE TO COLLEGE COURSES IN FILM AND TELEVISION, below.

American Society of Composers, Authors, and Publishers. ASCAP BIOGRAPHI-CAL DICTIONARY OF COMPOSERS, AUTHORS, AND PUBLISHERS. Compiled and edited by the Lynn Farnol Group. 3d ed. New York, 1966. 845 p.

> Brief biographies. List of music publishers. Earlier editions also are useful.

> See also MUSICIAN'S GUIDE, below.

ANNUAIRE DU SPECTACLE: THEATRE, CINEMA, MUSIQUE, RADIO, TELE-VISION. Paris: A. Raoult, 1942- . Annual. (Title varies.)

> Directory of theaters, societies, schools, and persons active in Belgian, French, and Swiss theater. Provides a survey of the year's productions and histories of some theaters.

Ash, Lee, comp. SUBJECT COLLECTIONS. 3d ed., rev. New York: R.R. Bowker, 1967. 1,221 p.

> Briefly describes libraries and special collections of books and related materials in the United States. Classified by subjects, which include "Acting," "Actors," "Ballet," "Drama," and "Theater." See also such headings as "French language and literature."

> See also Kruzas, Anthony T.; Lewanski, Richard Casimir; and International Federation of Library Associations. PERFORMING ARTS LIBRARIES, below.

Associated Councils of the Arts. DIRECTORY OF NATIONAL ARTS ORGANIZA-TIONS. MEMBERSHIP ASSOCIATIONS SERVING THE ARTS. 2d. ed. New York: 1972. 60 p.

> The 1972 edition lists national, nongovernmental, nonprofit membership associations of the arts but does not include those concerned with single disciplines or a single religion, race, nationality, or sex. The list is alphabetical by names of organizations. For each there is mention of purpose, type of membership, activities (such as conferences), publications, and annual budget.

> See also NATIONAL DIRECTORY FOR THE PERFORMING ARTS AND CIVIC CENTERS, below.

AUDIO VISUAL MARKET PLACE: A MULTIMEDIA GUIDE. Edited by Olga S. Weber. New York: R.R. Bowker, 1970- . Biennial. (Frequency varies.)

> Directory of distributors, manufacturers, theatrical producers, rental services, radio and television stations, associations, conferences, festivals, and libraries.

See also BROADCASTING. YEARBOOK, below.

See also LITERARY MARKET PLACE and WRITER'S MARKET, in Part I-H.

See also Limbacher, James L., in Part I-A.

Bentham, Frederick. NEW THEATRES IN BRITAIN. London: A TABS Publication, Rank Strand Electric, Ltd., 1970. 141 p. Illustrated.

Describes seventy-eight theaters built in the past twenty years. Photographs, seating charts, plans, with technical data summarized from fuller articles in the journal TABS. Alphabetically arranged by name of place or theater.

See also Birks, Reginald; Holden, Michael; and THE STAGE YEAR BOOK, below.

BIOGRAPHICAL ENCYCLOPEDIA AND WHO'S WHO OF THE AMERICAN THEATRE.

See Rigdon, Walter, below.

Birks, Reginald. CIVIC THEATRES AND ENTERTAINMENTS DIRECTORY. Harlow, Essex: National Council for Civic Theatres, 1971. 149 p.

A revision of the council's 1966 THEATRE AND ENTERTAINMENTS FACILITIES DIRECTORY. Found alphabetically under city are civic theaters and halls in Great Britain. Added are lists of agents, managers, companies, associations, tours, and suppliers.

See also Bentham, Frederick, above, and Holden, Michael; and THE STAGE YEAR BOOK, below.

BROADCASTING. YEARBOOK. Washington, D.C.: Broadcasting Publications, 1935- . Annual. (Title varies.)

Mainly useful to advertisers, this directory has separate sections for television stations by state, radio stations, equipment suppliers, program services, and agencies. The "Agencies" section embraces schools and colleges, research services, government offices and officials, public relations bureaus, news and advertising agencies.

See also AUDIO VISUAL MARKET PLACE, above, and CELEBRITY SERVICE and INTERNATIONAL TELEVISION ALMANAC, below.

CELEBRITY SERVICE INTERNATIONAL CONTACT BOOK; TRADE DIRECTORY, ENTERTAINMENT INDUSTRY. New York: Celebrity Service, Inc., 1944- Appears at eighteen-month intervals.

Addresses of agents for motion pictures, radio, and television, in London, New York, Paris, Rome, and Hollywood.

See also BROADCASTING. YEARBOOK, above, and INTERNATION-

AL TELEVISION ALMANAC and THEATRICAL VARIETY GUIDE, below.

Cinematheque Royale de Belgique. WORLD DIRECTORY OF STOCKSHOT AND FILM PRODUCTION LIBRARIES; UN REPERTOIRE MONDIAL DE CINEMATHEQUES DE PRODUCTION. Edited by John Chittock. Oxford: Pergamon Press, 1969. 63 p.

> Describes 310 libraries in fifty-nine countries. "Stock material" means "filmed materials divorced from their original use and gathered...for possible inclusion in later complete productions." Terms of loan, exchange, or purchase are explained.

DANCE DIRECTORY. Washington, D.C.: American Association for Health, Education, and Recreation, 1954-55- . Biennial. (Title varies.)

> Describes programs of professional and general dance studies in U.S. colleges and universities.

Davis, Jed Horace, comp. A DIRECTORY OF CHILDREN'S THEATRES IN THE UNITED STATES. Washington, D.C.: American Educational Theatre Association, 1968. 205 p.

> Organized by state and city. Brief notes on each theater, its classes, programs, etc. A director or contact is named.

DEUTSCHES BUEHNENJAHRBUCH. Berlin: F.A. Guenther, 1890- . Annual. (Title varies.)

> Includes lists of the following: German, Swiss, and Austrian premieres; theatrical archives; institutes, foundations, and schools; networks; periodicals and publishers; film and television producers.

> Main section is a geographical arrangement of German theaters, with names of personnel and information on stage facilities. Austrian and Swiss theaters are grouped separately.

> For Swiss entries, see also ANNUAIRE DU SPECTACLE, above.

DIRECTORY OF AMERICAN COLLEGE THEATRE. East Lansing, Mich.: American Educational Theatre Association, 1967. 195 p.

> Drama departments and theater clubs at colleges and universities are noted, showing course requirements, facilities, grants, and scholarships. Criteria for junior college and college drama departments, pp. 192-93. Representative theses, dissertations, and projects from 1961 to 1965, pp. 177-85.

> See also such standard reference works as ANNUAL GUIDES TO GRADUATE STUDY and the COLLEGE BLUE BOOKS (not included in this guide).

DIRECTORY OF CHILDREN'S THEATRES IN THE UNITED STATES.

> See Davis, Jed Horace, comp., above.

DIRECTORY OF FILM LIBRARIES IN THE U.S.A. Edited by Joan Clark. New York: Film Library Information Council, 1971- . Biennial. (Not examined.)

> A list of libraries owning 16mm films or other audiovisual materials. Briefly describes collections and gives addresses.

> See also Mirwis, Allan, below.

DIRECTORY OF SCENERY AND PROPERTY SOURCES FOR FILMS, TV, AND THEATRE. New York: Gerard Designs, Inc. Annual.

> See SIMON'S DIRECTORY OF THEATRICAL MATERIALS, below.

DIRECTORY OF SPECIAL LIBRARIES AND INFORMATION CENTERS.

> See Kruzas, Anthony Thomas, comp., below.

DOCUMENTS OF AMERICAN THEATER HISTORY, Vols. I and II.

> See Young, William C. FAMOUS AMERICAN PLAYHOUSES, below.

THE FOUNDATION DIRECTORY. New York: Russell Sage Foundation, 1960- . Issued irregularly.

> Arranged by state. Describes activities and grants of foundations in the United States. Has indexes of persons; of foundations; and of subjects (e.g., "Arts, performing").

> See also American Council on Education. FELLOWSHIPS, above; and PRIVATE FOUNDATIONS ACTIVE IN THE ARTS; WASHINGTON INTERNATIONAL ARTS LETTER; and Wasserman, Paul, below.

Gard, Robert E. COMMUNITY THEATER: IDEA AND ACHIEVEMENT. New York: Duell, Sloan, and Pearce, 1959. 182 p.

> A survey, with interviews and bibliographies. Contains list of community theaters, arranged by state, pp. 150-82.

> See also NATIONAL DIRECTORY FOR THE PERFORMING ARTS AND CIVIC CENTERS, and SUMMER THEATRES, below.

GUIDE TO COLLEGE COURSES IN FILM AND TELEVISION. Washington, D.C.: American Film Institute, 1969- . Annual. (Title varies.)

> Published in 1969-72 as GUIDE TO COLLEGE FILM COURSES, listing schools in the United States with film majors or courses. Briefly describes programs and facilities.

Hamer, Philip May.

> See United States. National Historical Publications Commission.

Henderson, Mary C. THE CITY AND THE THEATRE; NEW YORK PLAYHOUSES FROM BOWLING GREEN TO TIMES SQUARE. Clifton, N.J.: J.T. White, 1973. xiv, 323 p. Illustrated.

> A history of New York's commercial and establishment theaters (excluding Off-Broadway), pp. 1-199, handsomely illustrated with photographs, reproductions of architects' drawings, etc. Chapters trace development of various theatrical districts. Each ends with a map and list of theaters.
>
> On pp. 201-86, theaters are listed alphabetically, whether extant or demolished. Every entry has an exterior view and a brief account of the building's history and present use.
>
> Notes, bibliography, and index.
>
> See also Young, William C. FAMOUS AMERICAN PLAYHOUSES, below.

Holden, Michael.

> See THE STAGE GUIDE, below.

Howard, Diana. LONDON THEATRES AND MUSIC HALLS, 1850-1950. London: Library Association, 1970. 291 p.

> Part I: Lists alphabetically and describes theaters, music halls, and pleasure gardens in London from 1850 to 1950. For each history, sources are given. Part II: An eight-page bibliography. Part III: Directory of theater collections in London.
>
> See also Mander, Raymond, entries, below.

Huenefeld, Irene Pennington. INTERNATIONAL DIRECTORY OF HISTORICAL CLOTHING. Metuchen, N.J.: Scarecrow Press, 1967. 175 p.

> Notes major costume and accessory collections in museums and historical societies of North America, pp. 24-32, and Europe, pp. 110-19. Separate lists for types of costume, etc.
>
> See also International Centre of Arts and Costumes, below.

International Centre of Arts and Costumes. INTERNATIONAL GUIDE TO MUSEUMS AND PUBLIC COLLECTIONS OF COSTUMES AND TEXTILES; GUIDA INTERNAZIONALE AL MUSEI E ALLE COLLEZIONI PUBBLICHE DE COSTUME E DI TESSUTI. Venice: Centro Internazionale delle Arti e del Costume, Palazzo Grassi, 1970. 594 p.

> Museums are entered in geographical arrangement, with names in the language of the country. The first section has descriptions in

Italian. This material is repeated in separate French and English sections.

See also Huenefeld, Irene Pennington, above.

International Federation of Library Associations. PERFORMING ARTS LIBRARIES AND MUSEUMS (BIBLIOTHEQUES ET MUSEES DES ARTS DU SPECTACLE DANS LE MONDE). Edited by Andre Veinstein and Rosemond Gilder. 2d ed., rev. Paris: Centre National de la Recherche Scientifique, 1967. 801 p.

Revision of the same organization's PERFORMING ARTS COLLECTIONS: AN INTERNATIONAL HANDBOOK (Paris: Centre national de la recherche scientifique, 1960).

Describes libraries and theater collections (including dance and musical theater).

See also Ash, Lee, above, and Young, William C. AMERICAN THEATRICAL ARTS, below.

INTERNATIONAL MOTION PICTURE ALMANAC. New York: Quigley Publishing Co., 1929-   . Annual. (Title varies--1929-36, THE MOTION PICTURE ALMANAC.)

Companion to INTERNATIONAL TELEVISION ALMANAC, below. Compendium of statistics, biographies, and lists of awards, agencies, producers, services, etc., in the United States. Some British and global materials are appended.

INTERNATIONAL TELEVISION ALMANAC. New York: Quigley Publishing Co., 1956-   . Annual.

Directory of agencies, awards, performers, stations, world meetings, etc.

See also BROADCASTING. YEARBOOK; CELEBRITY SERVICE INTERNATIONAL CONTACT BOOK; and INTERNATIONAL MOTION PICTURE ALMANAC, all above.

INTERNATIONAL THEATRE DIRECTORY.

See Pride, Leo Bryan, below.

Kruzas, Anthony Thomas, comp. DIRECTORY OF SPECIAL LIBRARIES AND INFORMATION CENTERS.

See Young, Margaret Labash; Young, Harold Chester; and Kruzas, Anthony T., below.

Lewanski, Richard Casimir. SUBJECT COLLECTIONS IN EUROPEAN LIBRARIES.

New York: R.R. Bowker, 1965. 789 p.

> Collections are classified by subject and include theater libraries. See pp. 516-21.

> See also Ash, Lee, above.

Litto, Fredric M. DIRECTORY OF USEFUL ADDRESSES. Washington, D.C.: American Educational Theatre Association, 1966. (Various pagings.)

> Intended as a desk-top aid. Lists selected organizations, publishers, agents, periodicals, library collections, suppliers for the theater, etc., with addresses, which may need updating.

McCallum, Heather. THEATRE RESOURCES IN CANADIAN COLLECTIONS. Research Collections in Canadian Libraries. II: Special Studies. Ottawa: National Library of Canada, 1973. 114 p.

> Describes materials for international theater research available in 114 Canadian institutions, public and private. Indexed.

Mander, Raymond, THE LOST THEATRES OF LONDON. London: Hart-Davis, 1968. 576 p.

> Brief histories of twenty-eight theaters in the central city which have vanished. Indexes of architects and theaters. Maps, plans, and illustrations.

> See also Howard, Diana, above, and Mander, Raymond, THE THEATRES OF LONDON, below.

Mander, Raymond, and Mitchenson, Joe. THE THEATRES OF LONDON. 2d ed., rev. London: Hart-Davis, 1963. 292 p.

> A directory and historical handbook of buildings, limited to those still in use as theaters. Includes an index of architects and a geographical grouping of theaters.

> See also Howard, Diana; and Mander, Raymond, THE LOST THEATRES OF LONDON, above.

Mirwis, Allan. A DIRECTORY OF 16mm. FILM COLLECTIONS IN COLLEGES AND UNIVERSITIES IN THE UNITED STATES. Rev. ed. Bloomington: Indiana University Audio Visual Center, [1972]. 74 p.

> Institutions are listed geographically, with information on their film holdings, terms of rental or exchange, and available catalogs. Addresses and telephone numbers are given.

> See also DIRECTORY OF FILM LIBRARIES IN THE U.S.A., above.

Mitchenson, Joe.

> See Mander, Raymond, above.

MOTION PICTURE ALMANAC.

See INTERNATIONAL MOTION PICTURE ALMANAC, above.

THE MUSICIAN'S GUIDE. New York: Music Information Service, 1954- .

Offers information on the following: organizations in the United States and Canada; conservatories and music colleges; competitions, grants, and awards; music books and periodicals; critics and editors; festivals; opera companies; symphony orchestras; agents; union locals.

See also American Society of Composers, Authors, and Publishers, above.

NATIONAL DIRECTORY FOR THE PERFORMING ARTS AND CIVIC CENTERS. Dallas, Tex.: Handel & Co., 1974- .

Will list geographically entries for organizations, centers, and other facilities for the performing arts in the United States.

See also Associated Councils of the Arts. DIRECTORY; and Gard, Robert E., above. SUMMER THEATRES; and Young, William C. FAMOUS AMERICAN PLAYHOUSES, below.

THE OPERA DIRECTORY.

See Ross, Anne, below.

PERFORMING ARTS LIBRARIES AND MUSEUMS.

See International Federation of Library Associations, above.

Price, Julia S. THE OFF-BROADWAY THEATER. New York: Scarecrow Press, 1962. 279 p.

Mainly a treatise, conservative in tone. Contains list of new productions and revivals, 1950-62, pp. 192-253.

Pride, Leo Bryan, ed. and comp. INTERNATIONAL THEATRE DIRECTORY; A WORLD DIRECTORY OF THE THEATRE AND PERFORMING ARTS. New York: Simon and Schuster, 1973. 577 p. Illustrated.

Arrangement is geographical, with prefatory remarks on the state of theater in each country. Listed, with address and brief description, are dance troupes, professional acting or opera companies, and theaters, including some in community centers or in universities.

PRIVATE FOUNDATIONS ACTIVE IN THE ARTS. The Arts Patronage Series, vol. 1. By the editors of the WASHINGTON INTERNATIONAL ARTS LETTER.

Washington, D.C.: Washington International Arts Letter, 1970. 138 p.

> Briefly describes foundations in the United States which have given $10,000 or more in initial grants.

> See also THE FOUNDATION DIRECTORY, above, and WASHINGTON INTERNATIONAL ARTS LETTER, below.

Rigdon, Walter, ed. THE BIOGRAPHICAL ENCYCLOPEDIA AND WHO'S WHO OF THE AMERICAN THEATER.

> See Part II-A.

Ross, Anne, ed. THE OPERA DIRECTORY. London: John Calder, 1961. 566 p.

> Information on festivals, theaters, opera and operetta organizations worldwide, as well as on composers, conductors, designers, librettists, producers, singers, and technicians.

> See also THE STAGE YEAR BOOK, below.

SIMON'S DIRECTORY OF THEATRICAL MATERIALS, SERVICES, AND INFORMATION. New York: B. Simon, 1955-   .

> A guide to buying or renting costumes, equipment, etc. Also lists new theaters, festivals, competitions, and awards.

> See also DIRECTORY OF SCENERY AND PROPERTY SOURCES, above.

THE STAGE GUIDE: TECHNICAL INFORMATION ON BRITISH THEATRES; PUBLISHED BY THE "STAGE" NEWSPAPER. New edition compiled by Michael Holden. Association of British Theatre Technicians, technical advisers. London: Carson and Comerford, Ltd., 1971. 408 p.

> First revision of this publication since 1952. Older editions are still useful for information on theaters no longer used. The new edition has more complete descriptions.

> Theaters are listed alphabetically under cities. Most entries show date of construction, architect, original and present use, with technical notes on stage, backstage, and public areas. Appendices.

> See also Bentham, Frederick; and Birks, Reginald, above.

THE STAGE YEAR BOOK. London: Carson and Comerford, 1908-   .

> A theatrical directory as well as a yearbook of British and Australian theater (opera, ballet, and television included). Details on casts, tours, festivals, clubs, repertory groups, theater managers, and film and musical recording companies. A directory of theaters is provided. Earlier editions still useful for their international data. (Title has varied--STAGE GUIDE, STAGE DIRECTORY.)

See also Bentham, Frederick; Birks, Reginald; and Ross, Anne, above, and WRITERS' AND ARTISTS' YEARBOOK, and WHO'S WHO IN THE THEATRE, below.

STUBS; THE THEATRE GUIDE, CONTAINING STAGE DIMENSIONS AND SEATING CAPACITIES OF NEW YORK THEATRES. ALSO SEATING PLANS OF STUDIO THEATRES AND MUSIC HALLS. New York: L. Tobin, 1942- . Annual.

Latest issues cover Off-Broadway, too.

SUBJECT COLLECTIONS.

See Ash, Lee; and Lewanski, Richard Casimir, above.

SUMMER THEATRES. (SUMMER THEATRE DIRECTORY). Edited by Claire Shull. New York: Leo Shull Publications. Annual.

Lists approximately 250 U.S. and Canadian theaters, with details on management, seasonal plans, openings for actors and apprentices, theaters for sale or rent, etc.

See also NATIONAL DIRECTORY FOR THE PERFORMING ARTS AND CIVIC CENTERS, and Gard, Robert E., above, and Young, William C. FAMOUS AMERICAN PLAYHOUSES, below.

TABS.

See Bentham, Frederick, above.

THEATRICAL VARIETY GUIDE. Los Angeles: Issued on Behalf of the American Guild of Variety Artists by Theatrical Variety Publications, 1966- .

Names and addresses of producers, agents, managers; officers of Actors' Equity, Screen Actors' Guild, and the American Federation of Television and Radio Artists; lecture bureaus, clipping services, recording companies, theaters, etc.

See also CELEBRITY SERVICE INTERNATIONAL CONTACT BOOK, above, and WEST COAST THEATRICAL DIRECTORY, below.

United Nations Educational, Scientific, and Cultural Organization. Department of Mass Communications. WORLD COMMUNICATIONS, PRESS, RADIO, TELEVISION, FILM. 4th ed., rev. New York: UNESCO, 1964. 380 p. 5th ed. in prep. Epping, Eng.: Gower Press, 1974.

Surveys activities in the communications media throughout the world. Names governmental, press, and other influential agencies. Statistics and bibliography are added.

U.S. National Historical Publications Commission. GUIDE TO ARCHIVES

AND MANUSCRIPTS IN THE UNITED STATES. Edited by Philip May Hamer. New Haven: Yale University Press, 1961. 775 p.

> Records manuscripts and other materials in 1,300 archives, libraries, and other collections. Index of subjects and of persons whose papers are preserved, e.g., Edwin Booth. Subjects treated: theater, theaters, theatrical posters, and individual theater collections, e.g., Hampden (Walter) Memorial Library.

> See also Modern Language Association, American Literature Group. AMERICAN LITERARY MANUSCRIPTS, in Part IV of this guide.

> See also International Federation of Library Associations. PERFORM-ING ARTS LIBRARIES AND MUSEUMS, above, and Young, William C. AMERICAN THEATRICAL ARTS, below.

Veinstein, Andre.

> See International Federation of Library Associations. PERFORMING ARTS LIBRARIES AND MUSEUMS, above.

WASHINGTON INTERNATIONAL ARTS LETTER. 1962- .

> Looseleaf bulletin with news of grants, lists of foundations, survey articles.

> See also THE FOUNDATION DIRECTORY and PRIVATE FOUNDA-TIONS ACTIVE IN THE ARTS, above.

Wasserman, Paul. AWARDS, HONORS, AND PRIZES: A DIRECTORY AND SOURCE BOOK. 2d ed. Detroit: Gale Research Co., 1972. 579 p.

> A directory for the United States and Canada, with entries under sponsors. Treats motion pictures, radio, television, and theater, among other fields. Contains about 3,000 entries. Indexes.

> See also American Council on Education. FELLOWSHIPS IN THE ARTS AND SCIENCES; and THE FOUNDATION DIRECTORY, above.

Weber, Olga S., ed.

> See AUDIO VISUAL MARKET PLACE: A MULTIMEDIA GUIDE, above.

WEST COAST THEATRICAL DIRECTORY. Los Angeles: Tarcher Gousha Guides, 1970- . Annual.

> The second edition, 1970, shows addresses for various agencies connected with motion pictures, radio, television, music, and legitimate theater. Has sections for Los Angeles, San Francisco, and Hawaii and some material on Chicago, Nashville, and New York.

See also THEATRICAL VARIETY GUIDE, above.

WHO'S WHERE. New York: Leo Shull Publications, 1941- . Annual. (Title varies.)

> Lists thousands of names, with address and telephone number, for people and companies in U.S. theater.

> See also THEATRICAL VARIETY GUIDE, above, and WHO'S WHO IN SHOW BUSINESS, below.

WHO'S WHO IN SHOW BUSINESS. THE NATIONAL DIRECTORY OF SHOW PEOPLE. Vol. 1. New York: Who's Who in Show Business, Inc., 1950- .

> Lists performing artists and entertainers under various categories.

> See also WHO'S WHERE, above.

WHO'S WHO IN THE THEATRE.

> See Part II-A.

WORLD DIRECTORY OF STOCKSHOT AND FILM PRODUCTION LIBRARIES.

> See Cinematheque royale de Belgique.

WRITERS' AND ARTISTS' YEARBOOK. London: A. & C. Black, 1907- . Annual.

> Describes societies, journals, publishers, and agents of interest to authors, artists, musicians, and theater people. Advises on British marketing of plays and scenarios, on censorship, copyright, etc. See earlier editions for items not currently treated.

> See also Ross, Anne, ed. THE OPERA DIRECTORY, and THE STAGE YEAR BOOK, above.

Young, Margaret Labash; Young, Harold Chester; Kruzas, Anthony T. DIRECTORY OF SPECIAL LIBRARIES AND INFORMATION CENTERS. 3d ed. 3 vols. Detroit: Gale Research Co., 1974.

> U.S. and Canadian listings only. See subject index for theater items.

> See also Ash, Lee, above.

Young, William C. AMERICAN THEATRICAL ARTS; A GUIDE TO MANUSCRIPTS AND SPECIAL COLLECTIONS IN THE UNITED STATES AND CANADA. Chicago: American Library Association, 1971. 166 p.

> Limited to materials on theater arts of the United States and Cana-

da found in 357 libraries and archives. An entry for each institution briefly outlines its holdings. There is an index of persons and subjects.

See also United States, National Historical Publications Commission, above.

_____. FAMOUS AMERICAN PLAYHOUSES, 1716-1899. Documents of American Theater History, vol. 1. Chicago: American Library Association, 1973. xxii, 327 p. Illustrated.

_____. FAMOUS AMERICAN PLAYHOUSES, 1900-1971. Documents of American Theater History, vol. 2. Chicago: American Library Association, 1973. xxii, 297 p. Illustrated.

Theaters from East to West Coast are described and illustrated. Under opening date of each theater, its history is summarized. More detail is given in quotations of contemporary news items or in an account by members of the theater's staff, e.g., the Vivian Beaumont Theater.

Each volume has a selective bibliography, the first for American theater generally and the second for the playhouses. Each volume has several indexes--geographical index, alphabetical index of theater names, and an index of persons, interfiled with entries for theatrical specialties, e.g., architects, builders, lighting and scene designers, directors, managers, and owners.

Each volume is subdivided into chapters for (1) New York playhouses; (2) regional; (3) college and university; (4) summer playhouses. Within each section there is chronological arrangement by opening dates.

See also Henderson, Mary C.; and NATIONAL DIRECTORY FOR THE PERFORMING ARTS AND CIVIC CENTERS, above.

Zwerdling, Shirley, ed. FILM AND TV FESTIVAL DIRECTORY. New York: Back Stage Publications, 1970. 174 p.

Festivals of the world in classified arrangement. Abbreviations for world organizations are identified.

Part IV
PLAY INDEXES AND FINDING LISTS

A. PLAYS IN ENGLISH, INCLUDING TRANSLATIONS

The following entries will provide access to play texts published in several media. Only plays in English originally or translated into English are considered here. (See Part IV-B for foreign-language plays.)

After using the card catalog, the reader sometimes feels that he confronts a blank wall. The play he needs does not <u>seem</u> to be available either as a single title or in the complete, collected, or selected works of the author.

If it is a matter of translation into English, the reader should realize that a play title can vary in several translations, sometimes unrecognizably. This difficulty can be resolved with the aid of a good bibliography of translations, e.g., LITERATURES OF THE WORLD IN ENGLISH TRANSLATION, which will relate the original to the various translated titles.

Even a work originally in English can be published under strikingly different titles in England and the United States. Often a book review or a bibliography on the author will clear this up.

But the ordinary bibliographic problem is access to an English-language play which has not changed title but which is apparently not in the library. Yet it is still very likely to be there, either in a collection of plays by various authors, or, more rarely, in a periodical. The same play may also exist in one of the large microcopy sets which the library owns. These are usually based on a published bibliography, which will identify the various editions of a single work included in the microcopy set. Often such contents are not noted in the card catalog, which may have only an entry for the microcopy set itself. Ideally the relationship of the set to the bibliography should be shown in the card catalog, but this is not always so. The reference librarian can supply the link.

Most plays, however, can be found readily in bound form by using one of the numerous indexes to plays in collections located in most reference departments. These works are frequently revised or supplemented so that current access to plays of all periods is possible. Yet, when a new author comes to the fore, there may be a lag during which his play is being performed in London or New York and, as a consequence, has not been published in any form. When the run of the play has ended, there may for a new author be a paperback edition only. Very much later the play may appear in a collection. Still later an index will pick it up.

Indexes to plays in collections exist for many kinds of drama, such as one-acts, monologs, plays for all-female casts, plays for young audiences, religious dramas, etc.

A few new bibliographies cover publication of plays in periodicals. This is the least likely form of publication at this time, but in the first half of the century many more plays did appear in periodicals.

A further resource is the published catalog of a large library or of a special theater library. A number of research libraries have published their card catalogs in book form, usually in multivolume sets. Other libraries have acquired these catalogs, which make it possible to identify editions and often to borrow them. In such catalogs there is sometimes, under the author entry for a play, a helpful parenthetical note showing that the play was published in a miscellaneous collection, which may be available locally. This should be checked out before attempting to borrow from another library.

Relatively few screenplays have been published, although recently several representative series have begun and will be found in many library book collections. Such catalogs as those of the New York Public Library (Theatre and Drama Collections) and of the Theater Arts Library at the University of California, Los Angeles, include many screenplays, both published and unpublished. See also Part VI-A of this guide: BIBLIOGRAPHIE INTERNATIONALE DU CINEMA ET DE LA TELEVISION; INTERNATIONALE FILMBIBLIOGRAPHIE; McCarty, Clifford; Rehrauer, George; and Vincent, Carl.

AMERICAN BIBLIOGRAPHY.

> See Evans, Charles, below.

American Library Association. Board on Library Service to Children and Young People. SUBJECT INDEX TO CHILDREN'S PLAYS. Chicago: ALA, 1940. 277 p.

> Compiled by a subcommittee of the ALA, with Elizabeth D. Briggs as chairman, the list shows plays printed in 202 collections suitable for children in grades one through eight.

> See also Kreider, Barbara, below.

AMERICAN PLAYS.

> See Hill, Frank Pierce, below.

ANNALS OF ENGLISH DRAMA.

> See Harbage, Alfred, below.

Belknap, Sara Yancey.

See GUIDE TO THE PERFORMING ARTS, below.

Bentley, Gerald Eades. THE JACOBEAN AND CAROLINE STAGE; DRA-
MATIC COMPANIES AND PLAYERS. 7 vols. Oxford: Clarendon Press,
1941-68.

Carries on from 1616, final date of Chambers's THE ELIZABETHAN
STAGE. (See below.) Ends with the closing of the theaters, 1642.
Volumes I and II name companies and players. Volumes III-V,
under author, group references to manuscripts, editions, and some
criticism. Volume VI describes theater buildings. Volume VII is
the index.

Bergquist, William, ed. THREE CENTURIES OF ENGLISH AND AMERICAN
PLAYS, A CHECKLIST: ENGLAND, 1500-1800; UNITED STATES, 1714-1830.
New York: Readex Microprint, 1963. 281 p.

Indexes the plays in Henry W. Wells's THREE CENTURIES OF
DRAMA, 1500-1830, [New York, Readex Microprint, 1952-56
(5471 cards in 24 boxes)]. Bergquist lists, by title and author,
approximately 5,350 British and 250 American plays. (Some plays
as found in manuscript, and others in the earliest edition published.)
Cross-references are shown for pseudonyms, anonymous titles, disputed authors, and foreign or classical authors whose works were
translated or adapted into English. Under author are found publisher and date of the earliest known edition, information needed
for use of the microprint series.

THE BIBLE IN ENGLISH DRAMA.

See Coleman, Edward D., below.

Birmingham Shakespeare Library. A SHAKESPEARE BIBLIOGRAPHY: THE CAT-
ALOGUE OF THE BIRMINGHAM SHAKESPEARE LIBRARY. 7 vols. London:
Mansell, 1971.

Catalog of 35,000 volumes by and about the playwright, in England's most famous Shakespeare library. Especially notable are
the eighteenth and nineteenth-century adaptations and translations.

See also Folger Shakespeare Library. CATALOG OF PRINTED
BOOKS, below.

Boston Public Library. Allen A. Brown Collection. A CATALOGUE OF THE
ALLEN A. BROWN COLLECTION OF BOOKS RELATING TO THE STAGE IN
THE PUBLIC LIBRARY OF THE CITY OF BOSTON. Boston: The Trustees of
the Boston Public Library, 1919. 952 p.

A collection of 3,500 volumes, mainly on stage history, listed by
author and subject. Contents of some sets are analyzed (e.g.,
BRITISH DRAMA) to show plays contained, but there are no cross-

references from names of authors.

List of periodicals, pp. 602-15.

British Drama League. THE PLAYER'S LIBRARY; THE CATALOGUE OF THE LIBRARY OF THE BRITISH DRAMA LEAGUE. London: Faber and Faber, 1950. 1,115 p.

SUPPLEMENTS. 1951, 1954, and 1956.

Catalog of the largest special collection of theater books in England. Includes books on theater and a separate play list, which shows date and publisher for first editions. Notes many rare items such as pantomimes and adaptations. Locates plays in anthologies.

The third supplement, 1956, also has an index of plays in French.

British Museum. Department of Printed Books. GENERAL CATALOGUE OF PRINTED BOOKS. PHOTOLITHOGRAPHIC EDITION TO 1955. 263 vols. London: The Trustees of the British Museum, 1959-66.

Complete record of books in the Library of the British Museum, from the fifteenth century to the end of 1955 in all languages except the Oriental. Mainly an author catalog. Some anonymous, keyword, and geographical entries are included.

A ten-year and a five-year SUPPLEMENT have been published to date.

Brown, Allen A.

See Boston Public Library. Allen A. Brown Collection, above.

California, University of. Los Angeles. Library. MOTION PICTURES: A CATALOG OF BOOKS, PERIODICALS, SCREEN PLAYS, AND PRODUCTION STILLS. 2 vols. Boston: G. K. Hall, 1973.

Records primary and secondary sources in a large research collection. The "screenplays" section of the catalog lists unpublished scripts of more than 3,000 American, British, and foreign films. The section on "Books and Periodicals" includes some personal papers.

CAMBRIDGE BIBLIOGRAPHY OF ENGLISH LITERATURE.

See Part I - E 2.

Chambers, Edmund K. THE ELIZABETHAN STAGE. 4 vols. Oxford: Oxford University Press, 1923.

Each volume of this major work has a bibliography. The fourth volume contains a list of printed plays, masques, etc., citing single editions and plays in anthologies. Chambers's work was followed by Gerald Eades Bentley's. (See above.)

See also Greg, Walter W.; Harbage, Alfred; and Stratman, Carl J.,
BIBLIOGRAPHY OF ENGLISH PRINTED TRAGEDY, below.

CHICOREL THEATER INDEX TO PLAYS IN ANTHOLOGIES, PERIODICALS,
DISCS AND TAPES. Vol. I. Edited by Marietta Chicorel and Veronica Hall.
New York: Chicorel Library Publishing Co., 1970-   .

> The first volume (1970) of a projected six-volume set lists plays in
> print in English. Volume II (1971) adds 9,000 recent and 500
> retrospective entries.

> Author and title entries are interfiled. There are indexes by
> author, title, editor, and broad subject.

> See also Firkins, Ina Ten Eyck; and the four Logasa, Hannah items
> below.

Clarence, Reginald.

> See Eldredge, H.J., below.

Coleman, Edward D. THE BIBLE IN ENGLISH DRAMA; AN ANNOTATED
LIST OF PLAYS, INCLUDING TRANSLATIONS FROM OTHER LANGUAGES.
1931. Reprint. New York: New York Public Library, 1968. 212 p.

> The 1968 edition is a reprint of the 1931 (also published by the
> New York Public Library), with an added survey of recent major
> plays.

> Following the historical introduction are these lists: collected
> plays and collections; miracle plays arranged by cycle; Old Testa-
> ment plays, grouped under books of the Bible; the Apocrypha;
> New Testament plays; Jewish festival plays, etc. There are in-
> dexes of authors, titles, special topics, and English translations.

> See also Farrar, Clarissa P., and Evans, Austin P.; Harbage,
> Alfred; and Stratman, Carl J. MEDIEVAL DRAMA, below.

Columbia University. Columbia College. A GUIDE TO ORIENTAL CLASSICS.
New York: Columbia University Press, 1964. 199 p.

> Evaluates editions, whether adapted, abridged, or complete. Lo-
> cates translations in journals and collections or singly published.
> Sections on drama: "The Little Clay Cart" of Shudraka, pp. 90-92;
> "Shakuntala" of Kalidasa, pp. 86-89; plays by Tagore, pp. 108-10;
> puppet and "Kabuki Plays," pp. 196-99; "Noh Plays," pp. 190-91.

> See also Davidson, Martha; and Nihon Pen Kurabu, below.

Cooper, Gayle. A CHECKLIST OF AMERICAN IMPRINTS FOR 1830-   .
Metuchen, N.J.: Scarecrow Press, 1972-   .

Continues the work of Richard H. Shoemaker. (See below.)

Courtney, Winifred.

See THE READER'S ADVISER.

CUMULATED DRAMATIC INDEX. 2 vols.

Lists play texts published in books and in periodicals from 1900 to 1949. See Part I-A for full annotation.

CUMULATIVE INDEX TO ENGLISH TRANSLATIONS, 1948-1968. 2 vols. Boston: G.K. Hall, 1973.

Based on the annual volumes of INDEX TRANSLATIONUM. (See below.) Translations indexed include those published in the United Kingdom, the United States, Canada, New Zealand, the Republic of Ireland, and the Union of South Africa. Entry is under author.

Davidson, Martha. A LIST OF PUBLISHED TRANSLATIONS FROM CHINESE INTO ENGLISH, FRENCH, AND GERMAN. Ann Arbor, Mich.: J.W. Edwards for the American Council of Learned Societies, [c.1957]. 462 p.

Only Part I concerns literary translations. Drama listings, pp. 135-76, are under author. Addenda, pp. 177-79. A guide to complete or excerpted translations whether published singly, in periodicals, or in collections. Also shows where reviews and synopses are found.

DRAMATIST'S GUIDE.

See Plummer, Gail, below.

Drury, Francis Keese Wynkoop. DRURY'S GUIDE TO BEST PLAYS. By James M. Salem. 2d ed. Metuchen, N.J.: Scarecrow Press, 1969. 512 p.

The guide recommends royalty plays for specific types of audiences and describes cast and setting. Plays are traced to published collections if not singly available from a major publisher.

EARLY AMERICAN IMPRINTS. First series.

See Evans, Charles, below.

EARLY AMERICAN IMPRINTS. Second series.

See Shaw, Ralph Robert, and Shoemaker, Richard H., below.

EARLY AMERICAN PLAYS.

See Wegelin, Oscar, below.

EARLY ENGLISH BOOKS, 1475-1640.

See ENGLISH BOOKS, 1475-1640, below.

EARLY ENGLISH BOOKS, 1641-1700.

See ENGLISH BOOKS, 1641-1700, below.

Eldredge, H.J., comp. [Clarence, Reginald, pseud.]. THE STAGE CYCLO-
PEDIA; A BIBLIOGRAPHY OF PLAYS. London: The Stage, 1909. 503 p.

> This work first appeared in THE STAGE. The compiler states that
> more than 50,000 plays (and a span of 500 years) are covered.
> Said to be comprehensive for English drama, selective for foreign
> plays. Gives date of first performance, of publication, etc.

ENGLISH AND AMERICAN DRAMA OF THE NINETEENTH CENTURY, 1801-1900.
Edited by George Freedley and Allardyce Nicoll. New York: Readex Microprint, 1966- .

> Play texts in microprint are being issued over a period of seven
> or eight years. The number will surpass 25,000. Plays are re-
> produced from the earliest available edition or from manuscript.
> Acting editions and promptbooks will also be included. So far,
> there is no cumulated index, but a checklist is being issued in
> parts.

ENGLISH BOOKS, 1475-1640. Ann Arbor, Mich.: University Microfilms,
1938- . The title changed, in thirty-second year, to EARLY ENGLISH
BOOKS, 1475-1640.

> This microfilm series is being issued over a number of years. It
> is accompanied by a catalog of the texts selected for microfilming
> from the list in Alfred William Pollard and G.R. Redgrave's
> SHORT TITLE CATALOGUE. (See below.) Lists items by SHORT
> TITLE CATALOGUE (STC) numbers. Under each number is a micro-
> film order number, which may be used to purchase copies. Oppo-
> site that is the reel number for the microfilm set. Entries are ar-
> ranged on reels by order number.

> For a convenient means of using this catalog and its companion,
> the microfilm set, see CONSOLIDATED CROSS INDEX, below.

ENGLISH BOOKS, 1475-1640. CONSOLIDATED CROSS INDEX BY STC
NUMBERS, years 1-19, and CROSS INDEX BY STC NUMBERS, years 20-25.
Ann Arbor, Mich.: University Microfilms, 1956 and 1964.

> This index to a microfilm series is being issued over a number of
> years. The user obtains the STC (SHORT TITLE CATALOGUE)
> numbers from the Pollard and Redgrave catalog. (See below.) He
> then finds this number in one of the cross indexes, where it tallies
> with a reel number. In the microfilm set, ENGLISH BOOKS,

1475-1640, he finds a table of contents at the start of each reel and can thus locate the desired text. Note, however, that the microfilming project is still continuing and has progressed beyond the indexes.

Continued by ENGLISH BOOKS, 1641-1700, below.

ENGLISH BOOKS, 1641-1700. Ann Arbor, Mich.: University Microfilms, 1961- . The title changed in sixth year, to EARLY ENGLISH BOOKS, 1641-1700.

> Catalog of literary and other texts selected from Wing's SHORT TITLE CATALOGUE. (See below.) The texts are being reproduced in a major microfilm series which includes pamphlets, contemporary criticism, etc. See introduction for scope of project and method of purchase for photocopy or microcopy. Reel numbers in the microfilm set are shown.

Ettlinger, Amrei, and Gladstone, Joan M. RUSSIAN LITERATURE, THEATRE AND ART; A BIBLIOGRAPHY OF WORKS IN ENGLISH PUBLISHED 1900-1945. London: Hutchinson, [1947]. 96 p. Reprint. Port Washington, N.Y.: Kennikat, 1971. 96 p.

> Lists nineteenth and twentieth-century English translations. Main list, under author, notes singly published works but also traces texts in collected editions and anthologies, pp. 28-91. There are lists of collections, p. 26, and of books on theater and art, pp. 14-20.

> See also INDEX TRANSLATIONUM; Line, Maurice Bernard; and THE READER'S ADVISER, below.

Evans, Charles. AMERICAN BIBLIOGRAPHY; A CHRONOLOGICAL DICTIONARY OF ALL BOOKS, PAMPHLETS, AND PERIODICAL PUBLICATIONS PRINTED IN THE UNITED STATES OF AMERICA FROM THE GENESIS OF PRINTING IN 1639 DOWN TO AND INCLUDING THE YEAR 1800. 12 vols. Chicago: Printed for the Author, 1903-34.

Volume 13, Worcester: American Antiquarian Society, 1955.

Volume 14, INDEX. Edited by Roger P. Bristol. Worcester: American Antiquarian Society, 1959.

SUPPLEMENT. Edited by Roger P. Bristol. Charlottesville: University Press of Virginia, 1970. 636 p.

> Evans groups American imprints by publishing dates and locates copies in American libraries. There are indexes of authors, printers, publishers, and subjects. Volume 14 is an author-title index for the set, but see Shipton, Clifford Kenyon, and Mooney, James E., below, for a complete index for Evans and for addenda to Evans. The SUPPLEMENT, prepared for the Bibliographical Society of America by Bristol, brings out 11,200 entries not found in Evans. Several library locations are given for some items.

Evans's work is continued to 1820 by Shaw, Ralph Robert, and Shoemaker, Richard H., see below. A further CHECKLIST by Shoemaker brings the record down to 1829. (See below.)

An interesting inclusion is a large number of theater items such as broadsides, listed by name of theater (under year of publication). Many play texts, usually listed by author, are also found under year of publication.

Most items in the original Evans work and in the Shaw and Shoemaker continuation are gradually appearing in a microprint edition, EARLY AMERICAN IMPRINTS. First series, 1956- and second series, 1964- . Edited by Clifford Kenyon Shipton (New York: Readex Microprint). A few items in fragile condition may never be reproduced.

The "Evans number" must be found in AMERICAN BIBLIOGRAPHY and its continuation in order to locate an item in the microprint series.

Farrar, Clarissa P., and Evans, Austin P. BIBLIOGRAPHY OF ENGLISH TRANS-LATIONS FROM MEDIEVAL SOURCES. Records of Civilization: Sources and Studies, no. 39. New York: Columbia University Press, 1946. 534 p.

Cites 1,500 translations into English found in separate editions or in collections. Includes modern English versions of mystery and miracle plays from various countries.

See also Coleman, Edward D., above, and Harbage, Alfred; and Stratman, Carl J., MEDIEVAL DRAMA, below.

Fidell, Estelle A., and Peake, Dorothy M.

See PLAY INDEX, Vol. II, below.

Firkins, Ina Ten Eyck, comp. INDEX TO PLAYS, 1800-1926. New York: H.W. Wilson Co., 1927. 307 p.

Guide to editions of nineteenth and twentieth-century full-length and one-act plays. Includes foreign works in English translation. Locates texts in periodicals, in collections, or in separate editions. Main entry by author. Title and subject indexes.

See also CHICOREL THEATER INDEX TO PLAYS IN ANTHOLOGIES, PERIODICALS, DISCS AND TAPES, above.

Folger Shakespeare Library. CATALOG OF MANUSCRIPTS OF THE FOLGER SHAKESPEARE LIBRARY, WASHINGTON, D.C. 3 vols. Boston: G.K. Hall, 1971.

Materials include copies of plays and masques of sixteenth and seventeenth centuries, players' parts, promptbooks, autograph letters, scores, and drawings.

See also Folger Shakespeare Library. CATALOG OF PRINTED
BOOKS, below.

_____. CATALOG OF PRINTED BOOKS OF THE FOLGER SHAKESPEARE
LIBRARY, WASHINGTON, D.C. 28 vols. Boston: G.K. Hall, 1970.

The 300,000 works listed embrace all aspects of British life in the
sixteenth and seventeenth centuries and much on drama and theater
of the two centuries that followed. As the world's most celebrated
Shakespeare library, the collection is rich in editions of Shakespeare
and other dramatists. Background material of classical, medieval,
and Renaissance periods in continental Europe also is found. For
a list of Italian plays in the library, see Clubb, Louise, in Part
IV-B, below.

See also Birmingham Shakespeare Library, above.

Freedley, George, and Nicoll, Allardyce.

See ENGLISH AND AMERICAN DRAMA OF THE NINETEENTH
CENTURY, 1801-1900, above.

French, Samuel, firm, publishers. GUIDE TO SELECTING PLAYS. London:
French, 1955?- . Annual. (Title varies.)

Plot summaries for one-act and full-length plays available from
Samuel French. Indicates required casting, costumes, and sets.

Garten, H.F. MODERN GERMAN DRAMA. London: Methuen, 1959. 272 p.

This treatise contains a list of English translations of plays, pp. 260-
65, with names of translators, publishers, etc.

See also INDEX TRANSLATIONUM, below.

Greg, Walter W. A BIBLIOGRAPHY OF THE ENGLISH PRINTED DRAMA TO
THE RESTORATION. 4 vols. London: The Bibliographical Society, 1939-62.
Illustrated.

Volume I: Records of the Stationers' Company from 1557 to 1689
and a chronology of plays to 1617, describing editions. Illustrative plates following p. 349 include facsimile title pages. Volume
II: A list of plays, 1617-89, locating copies in important libraries.
Also lost plays and plays in Latin. Illustrations. Volume III:
Lists collections of plays, with analyses of contents. Library copies
located. Play advertisements list, pp. 1141-90. Also listed are
notable prefaces; names of actors; printers' and publishers' catalogs
of plays; names of authors, with reference to year of publication
in main list (volumes I and II); dedications; prologs and epilogs;
adaptations and "drolls"; performances in London and provinces,
pp. 1462-78; producers, musicians, and choreographers; licensers;

printers; publishers and booksellers; stationers' signs and publishers' devices; artists; and mottos. Illustrations. Volume IV: Introductory essay; additions and corrections to play lists in first three volumes.

See also Chambers, Edmund K., above, and Harbage, Alfred; and Stratman, Carl J., below.

_____ . A LIST OF MASQUES, PAGEANTS, ETC., SUPPLEMENTARY TO A LIST OF ENGLISH PLAYS. London: The Bibliographical Society, 1902. xi, 35 p., cxxxi.

Author list of masques and pageants, pp. 1-28. See also: addenda, p. 29; title index, pp. 33-35; bibliographic essay, pp. i-xxi; list of stationers' advertisements, pp. xxv-xxxvii and Appendix II, "Early Play Lists", pp. xli-cxx.

Main section describes the entertainments and gives library locations of texts.

See also Chambers, Edmund K., above, and Harbage, Alfred, below.

GUIDE TO THE PERFORMING ARTS. Compiled by Sara Yancey Belknap. Metuchen, N.J.: Scarecrow Press, 1957-67. Annual.

Lists, under subject, author, and title interfiled, references to articles on all aspects of theater, musical productions, and moving pictures. Includes obituaries, reviews, musical program notes, casts, illustrations, and plays published in periodicals. Television list is separate.

Louis A. Rachow and Katherine Hartley assumed editorship, publishing in 1972 the volume which covers the performing arts activities of 1968. Their editorship resulted in a change of scope and method.

The 1968 annual indexed forty-eight publications pertaining to theater and drama; dance (ballet and modern); music; motion pictures; radio and television broadcasting; magic; and the circus. The journals scanned are mainly from the United States, with the addition of a few Canadian and major European titles.

The new editors have adopted standard subject headings, many of which are more specific than those used in earlier annual volumes.

Harbage, Alfred. ANNALS OF ENGLISH DRAMA, 975-1700; AN ANALYTICAL RECORD OF ALL PLAYS, EXTANT OR LOST, CHRONOLOGICALLY ARRANGED AND INDEXED BY AUTHORS, TITLES, DRAMATIC COMPANIES, ETC. Revised by S. Schoenbaum. Philadelphia: University of Pennsylvania, 1964. 323 p.

Plays written in England or by Englishmen abroad (some never performed). Supplies author, title, date of premiere, type of drama, name of performing company, dates of earliest text and later editions.

Note supplementary material: plays of uncertain date or identity, pp. 202-8; editions, pp. 209-15; plays edited for dissertations, pp. 216-17; dramatic companies, pp. 297-302; theaters, pp. 303-6.

The Appendix, pp. 307-21, is a bibliography of extant manuscripts of plays written between 975 and 1700. Locates manuscripts in U.S. and British research libraries.

See also Chambers, Edmund K.; and Greg, Walter W., above, and Stratman, Carl J., ENGLISH PRINTED TRAGEDY and MEDI-EVAL DRAMA, below.

_____. ANNALS OF ENGLISH DRAMA, 975-1700. SUPPLEMENT TO THE REVISED EDITION. By S. Schoenbaum. Evanston, Ill.: Northwestern University, Department of English, 1966. 19 p.

SECOND SUPPLEMENT. Evanston, Ill.: Northwestern University, Department of English, 1970. 19 p.

Hartley, Katherine

See GUIDE TO THE PERFORMING ARTS, above.

Hill, Frank Pierce, comp. AMERICAN PLAYS PRINTED 1714-1830; A BIBLIO-GRAPHICAL RECORD. Stanford, Calif.: Stanford University Press, 1934. 152 p.

Based on work by Fred W. Atkinson and by Oscar Wegelin, below. This compilation locates plays in one or more of ten large U.S. libraries. Plays are by American or foreign authors published in the United States.

Separate author and title indexes. Also a chronological grouping of titles.

Continued by Roden, Robert F., below.

Holzknecht, Karl J. OUTLINES OF TUDOR AND STUART PLAYS.

See Part II-A.

Huntington [Henry E.] Library. Larpent Plays.

See Macmillan, Dougald, below.

INDEX TO FULL-LENGTH PLAYS.

See Thomson, Ruth Gibbons; and Ireland, Norma Olin, below.

INDEX TO MONOLOGS AND DIALOGS and SUPPLEMENT.

See Ireland, Norma Olin, below.

INDEX TO ONE-ACT PLAYS.

See Logasa, Hannah, and Ver Nooy, Winifred, below.

INDEX TO PLAYS, 1800-1926.

See Firkins, Ina Ten Eyck, above.

INDEX TO PLAYS IN A SELECTED LIST OF PERIODICALS.

See Keller, Dean H., below.

INDEX TO PLAYS IN COLLECTIONS.

See Ottemiller, John H., below.

INDEX TO PLAYS, WITH SUGGESTIONS FOR TEACHING.

See Mersand, Joseph, below.

INDEX TO SKITS AND STUNTS.

See Ireland, Norma Olin, below.

INDEX TRANSLATIONUM; INTERNATIONAL BIBLIOGRAPHY OF TRANSLA-
TIONS. Paris: UNESCO, 1949-   . Annual.

Formerly quarterly, now annual. Books grouped by subject (e.g.,
literature) under country where translated, and then by author.
Titles in language of translation, followed by original title (Russian
is transliterated).

Volume 18, (1967) covers 36,000 titles published in seventy countries in 1965 as well as some titles missed earlier.

For years before 1949, consult special bibliographies such as Pane,
Remigio Ugo; and the series, THE LITERATURES OF THE WORLD
IN ENGLISH TRANSLATION, below.

A CUMULATIVE INDEX TO ENGLISH TRANSLATIONS, 1948-1968
(2 vols. Boston: G.K. Hall, 1973) is based on INDEX TRANS-
LATIONUM. See annotation above.

Ireland, Norma Olin. INDEX TO FULL-LENGTH PLAYS, 1944-1964. Boston:
F.W. Faxon, 1967. 296 p.

Selective list of plays in English. Updates the Thomson, Ruth
Gibbons. INDEX TO FULL-LENGTH PLAYS, 1895-1925; 1926-1944.

Ireland lists 775 singly published plays and also plays in 140 collections. Title, author, and subject in one alphabet, with fullest information under title. Brief notes on actors and sets. Pulitzer prizes, p. 192.

Translations, including adaptations, are under English title, with foreign title also shown.

See also Ottemiller, John H., below.

_____. AN INDEX TO MONOLOGS AND DIALOGS. Boston: F.W. Faxon, 1949. 171 p.

Analyzes collections published down to 1949. Plays listed by author, title, and subject. See also SUPPLEMENT below.

_____. INDEX TO MONOLOGS AND DIALOGS, SUPPLEMENT. New York: F.W. Faxon, 1959. 133 p.

Material published from 1948 to 1958. Entries are arranged as in basic volume. See above.

_____. AN INDEX TO SKITS AND STUNTS. Boston: F.W. Faxon, 1958. 348 p.

Skits, classified by subject, are located in collections.

Japanese P.E.N. Club.

See Nihon Pen Kurabu, below.

Keller, Dean H. INDEX TO PLAYS IN PERIODICALS. Metuchen, N.J.: Scarecrow Press, 1971. 588 p.

SUPPLEMENT. Metuchen, N.J.: Scarecrow Press, 1973. 263 p.

Includes one-act and long plays, mainly in English, found in theater and general periodicals from their first volumes on to 1969. A fuller list than the CHICOREL THEATER INDEX. (See above.) The SUPPLEMENT extends coverage to 1971 but also indexes, from Volume I on, thirty-six more periodicals, including some in foreign languages.

See also PLAYS IN PERIODICALS, below.

Kreider, Barbara. INDEX TO CHILDREN'S PLAYS IN COLLECTIONS. Metuchen, N.J.: Scarecrow Press, 1972. 138 p.

Five hundred plays and skits in English are cited by author, title, and subject. Collections analyzed are new books published in the United States between 1965 and 1969. A cast analysis by sex and number of players is added.

See also American Library Association, above.

Lewanski, Richard Casimir.

> See THE LITERATURES OF THE WORLD IN ENGLISH TRANSLA-
> TION, below.

LIBRARY OF CONGRESS AND NATIONAL UNION CATALOG AUTHOR LIST,
1942-1962; A MASTER CUMULATION. Detroit: Gale Research Co., 1969- .

> This multivolume work brings together and interfiles the entries
> from the NATIONAL UNION CATALOG and the U.S. Library of
> Congress, AUTHOR CATALOG. See NATIONAL UNION CATA-
> LOG, below.

Line, Maurice Bernard. A BIBLIOGRAPHY OF RUSSIAN LITERATURE IN EN-
GLISH TRANSLATION TO 1900 (EXCLUDING PERIODICALS). London: The
Library Association, 1963. 74 p.

> Indexed under original author's name. Lists few plays.

> See also Ettlinger, Amrei, and Gladstone, Joan M.; and INDEX
> TRANSLATIONUM, above, and THE LITERATURES OF THE WORLD
> IN ENGLISH TRANSLATION, Volume II: THE SLAVIC LITERA-
> TURES, below.

LITERARY HISTORY OF THE UNITED STATES and SUPPLEMENTS.

> Consult for basic information on editions of American authors. See
> full annotation in Part I-E2.

THE LITERATURES OF THE WORLD IN ENGLISH TRANSLATION. New York:
Ungar, 1967- .

> Volumes in this series vary in emphasis and treatment. Volume I:
> THE GREEK AND LATIN LITERATURES by George B. Parks and
> Ruth Z. Temple, 1968, 442 p., has Greek and Roman sections,
> with period subdivision. Works are listed by author. Volume II:
> THE SLAVIC LITERATURES, is by Richard Casimir Lewanski, 1967,
> 630 p. Volume III: ROMANCE LITERATURES, by Parks and Temple,
> 1970, is in two parts: Part 1: CATALAN, ITALIAN, PORTU-
> GUESE, BRAZILIAN, PROVENCAL, RUMANIAN, SPANISH, AND
> SPANISH-AMERICAN LITERATURES, 473 p. Part 2: FRENCH
> LITERATURE, 473 p.; Promised are Volume IV: THE CELTIC, GER-
> MANIC, AND OTHER LITERATURES OF EUROPE, and Volume V:
> THE LITERATURES OF ASIA AND AFRICA.

Logasa, Hannah, comp. AN INDEX TO ONE-ACT PLAYS FOR STAGE AND
STUDY.

THIRD SUPPLEMENT, 1941-1948. Boston: F.W. Faxon, 1950. 318 p.; INDEX
TO ONE-ACT PLAYS FOR STAGE, RADIO, AND TELEVISION.

FOURTH SUPPLEMENT, 1948-1957. Boston: F.W. Faxon, 1958. 245 p.

These do not cover periodicals.

_____. AN INDEX TO ONE-ACT PLAYS FOR STAGE, RADIO, AND TELEVISION.

FIFTH SUPPLEMENT, 1956-1964. Boston: F.W. Faxon, 1966. 260 p.

Similar to preceding supplements. Includes adaptations from novels; plays for children and young people, by age group.

Logasa, Hannah, and Ver Nooy, Winifred, comps. AN INDEX TO ONE-ACT PLAYS. Boston: F.W. Faxon, 1924. 327 p.

Locates more than 5,000 plays in English in collections or in periodicals from 1900 on. Main entry, under title, describes setting and characters. Also has indexes by author and subject and lists of periodicals and of books analyzed.

_____. INDEX TO ONE-ACT PLAYS. SUPPLEMENT, 1924-1931. Boston: F.W. Faxon, 1932. 432 p.;

SECOND SUPPLEMENT, 1932-1940. Boston: F.W. Faxon, 1941. 556 p.

These cover both books and periodicals.

Continued by Logasa. AN INDEX TO ONE-ACT PLAYS FOR STAGE AND STUDY. (See above.)

Macmillan, Dougald, comp. CATALOGUE OF THE LARPENT PLAYS IN THE HUNTINGTON LIBRARY. San Marino: Henry E. Huntington Library and Art Gallery, 1939. 442 p.

Chronology (1737 to 1824) of printed and manuscript plays with notes describing the Huntington Library's copies. Gives date of premiere or licensing. Plays named are available in microprint in Wells, Henry W. THREE CENTURIES OF DRAMA, 1500-1830 [New York: Readex Microprint, 1952-56. (5471 cards in 24 boxes)]. There are author and title indexes.

Mersand, Joseph. INDEX TO PLAYS, WITH SUGGESTIONS FOR TEACHING. New York: Scarecrow Press, 1966. 114 p.

Lists, by title, modern plays for radio, television, or stage and locates them in anthologies. Separate groups of one-acts and long plays. Biographical and critical notes make this useful for high school teachers.

Lacks author index.

See also National Council of Teachers of English, GUIDE TO PLAY SELECTION, below. (Mersand's selection is more sophisticated.)

Modern Language Association. American Literature Group. Committee on Manuscript Holdings. AMERICAN LITERARY MANUSCRIPTS. Austin: University of Texas, c. 1960. xxviii, 421 p.

Mainly a bibliography of literary manuscripts and authors' personal papers. Also includes documents and other special materials relating to the authors. Locates material in libraries. Important for advanced research only.

Nairn, John Arbuthnot. CLASSICAL HAND-LIST. 3d ed. Oxford: B.H. Blackwell, 1953. 164 p. Reprint. Oxford: B.H. Blackwell, 1960. 164 p.

Classified bibliography of texts, translations, and critical works on Greek and Latin classics. Unannotated. An older, standard work.

See also THE LITERATURES OF THE WORLD IN ENGLISH TRANSLATION, above, and THE READER'S ADVISER; and Smith, Frank Seymour. CLASSICS IN TRANSLATION, below.

National Council of Teachers of English. Committee on Playlists. GUIDE TO PLAY SELECTION. 2d ed. New York: Appleton-Century-Crofts, 1958. 178 p.

Main list subdivided into earlier and modern full-length and one-act plays. Under title, gives summary, setting, characters, costumes, publisher, etc.

Supplies indexes of the following: anthologies; books on play production; publishers and agents. Chapters on television and "guidance" plays.

See also Mersand, Joseph, above.

NATIONAL INDEX OF AMERICAN IMPRINTS THROUGH 1800.

See Shipton, Clifford Kenyon, below.

THE NATIONAL UNION CATALOG. Ann Arbor: Mich.: J.W. Edwards, 1953-   .

Lists books deposited for copyright at the U.S. Library of Congress and is a continuation of the U.S. Library of Congress, AUTHOR CATALOG (1942-   .) and its supplements. Works in many languages are included.

THE NATIONAL UNION CATALOG is also a finding guide for copies of books in other American libraries which report their holdings.

See also U.S. Copyright Office. CATALOG OF COPYRIGHT ENTRIES, etc., below.

NATIONAL UNION CATALOG...1942-1962; A MASTER CUMULATION.

See LIBRARY OF CONGRESS AND NATIONAL UNION CATALOG AUTHOR LIST, above.

New York Public Library. CATALOG OF THE THEATRE AND DRAMA COL-
LECTIONS. 21 vols. Boston: G.K. Hall, 1967. To be supplemented.

> Catalog of books and periodicals in a major theatrical library.
> Part I, a list of more than 120,000 plays, has two sections:
> (1) A six-volume "Cultural Origins List" groups plays by language.
> These may be singly published, in a series, or in a periodical.
> (2) The six-volume Author List brings together editions, phonodiscs,
> and promptbooks of plays, in original language or translated. Plays
> in Oriental, Hebrew, and Cyrillic alphabets are omitted but can be
> found in the New York Public Library's catalogs of the Slavonic,
> Jewish, and Oriental collections. Also excluded are children's
> plays, Christmas and morality plays.

> Part II, "Books on the Theatre," lists subjects, authors, and titles
> in one alphabet and includes periodicals and series as well as
> single titles. Note that the subject heading "Biography" is fol-
> lowed by names of biographees. These items are not repeated in
> the main alphabet under name of biographee.

> Ephemeral materials such as playbills are numerous in the New
> York collection but are not found in this catalog.

> Scripts for motion pictures, radio, and television, published or
> unpublished, are included.

Nicoll, Allardyce.

> See ENGLISH AND AMERICAN DRAMA OF THE NINETEENTH
> CENTURY, 1801-1900, above.

Nihon Pen Kurabu. (Japanese P.E.N. Club). JAPANESE LITERATURE IN
EUROPEAN LANGUAGES, A BIBLIOGRAPHY. Compiled by Japanese P.E.N.
Club. 2d ed. Tokyo: 1961. 98 p.

> Under "Classical Drama and Modern Literature-poetry and Drama,"
> the subsection "Translations" gives titles of plays in English, fol-
> lowed by Japanese characters, and locates texts in books or peri-
> odicals.

> A supplement (1964) has similar arrangement.

> See also INDEX TRANSLATIONUM, above.

NINETEENTH-CENTURY DRAMA.

> See ENGLISH AND AMERICAN DRAMA OF THE NINETEENTH
> CENTURY.

NINETEENTH-CENTURY READERS' GUIDE.

> See READERS' GUIDE TO PERIODICAL LITERATURE, below.

O'Brien, Robert Alfred. SPANISH PLAYS IN ENGLISH TRANSLATION; AN ANNOTATED BIBLIOGRAPHY. New York: Published for the American Educational Association by Las Americas Publishing Co., 1963. 70 p. and index.

> Main entry under author, with short biographical and historical notes on his plays, whether translated in full or abridged. Includes some plays printed in anthologies.

> Index of titles and authors.

> See also Pane, Remigio Ugo, below, and INDEX TRANSLATIONUM, above.

O'Mahony, Mathew. PROGRESS GUIDE TO ANGLO-IRISH PLAYS. Dublin: Progress House, 1960. 181 p.

> Five hundred plays available from publishers, mainly in acting editions, are listed, with synopses. Plays are grouped by number of acts and number of characters. Useful primarily to amateurs.

Ottemiller, John H. INDEX TO PLAYS IN COLLECTIONS. 5th ed., rev. Metuchen, N.J.: Scarecrow Press, 1971. 452 p.

> Covers plays from all periods and places if published in collections in England or the United States from 1900 to mid-1970. Analyzes 1,047 collections in which three or more authors are represented. One-acts appear only if in a collection predominantly of full-length plays. Shakespeare is excluded. Radio, television, and children's plays are represented.

> Main entry under author, with reference to list of collections. Separate title index.

> See also Ireland, Norma Olin. INDEX TO FULL-LENGTH PLAYS, above.

Pane, Remigio Ugo. ENGLISH TRANSLATIONS FROM THE SPANISH, 1484-1943; A BIBLIOGRAPHY. Rutgers University Studies in Spanish, no. 2. New Brunswick, N.J.: Rutgers University Press, 1944. 218 p.

> An author list of 2,682 items. Limited to peninsular Spain. Locates translations in single works, periodicals, and series. Has index of translators.

> See also INDEX TRANSLATIONUM; and O'Brien, Robert Alfred, above.

Parks, George B.

> See THE LITERATURES OF THE WORLD IN ENGLISH TRANSLATION, above.

Patterson, Charlotte A.

> See PLAYS IN PERIODICALS, below.

Peabody Institute Library. CATALOGUE OF THE LIBRARY OF THE PEABODY INSTITUTE OF THE CITY OF BALTIMORE. 5 vols. Baltimore: I. Friedenwald, 1883-92.

> Many entries under "Drama and the Stage." Separate author and title lists show publication of plays in American and European periodicals or in books and series.

_____. SECOND CATALOGUE OF THE LIBRARY OF THE PEABODY INSTI-TUTE OF THE CITY OF BALTIMORE, INCLUDING THE ADDITIONS MADE SINCE 1882. 8 vols. Baltimore: I. Friedenwald, 1896-1905.

> The second catalogue records additions to the library since 1882.

Peake, Dorothy M.

> See PLAY INDEX, below.

PLAY INDEX, 1949-1952; AN INDEX TO 2,616 PLAYS IN 1,138 VOLUMES. Compiled by Dorothy Herbert West and Dorothy M. Peake. New York: H.W. Wilson, 1953. 239 p.

> Plays are listed by author, title, and subject or type, in one alphabet. The author entry notes the type of drama, number of men and women in cast, etc. Plays of all lengths in the English language are shown, but new editions of Shakespeare's works are omitted.

PLAY INDEX, 1953-1960. Edited by Estelle A. Fidell and Dorothy M. Peake. New York: H.W. Wilson, 1963. 404 p.

> Covers 4,592 plays in English.

PLAY INDEX, 1961-1967. Edited by Estelle A. Fidell. New York: H.W. Wilson, 1968. 464 p.

> Covers 4,793 plays.

PLAYER'S LIBRARY.

> See British Drama League, above.

PLAYS IN PERIODICALS; AN INDEX TO ENGLISH LANGUAGE SCRIPTS IN TWENTIETH CENTURY JOURNALS. Compiled by Charlotte A. Patterson. Boston: G.K. Hall, 1970.

> Title entries for 4,000 plays, 1900-68, most of which were not separately published. Author index.

> See also Keller, Dean H., above.

Plummer, Gail. DRAMATIST'S GUIDE TO SELECTION OF PLAYS AND MUSICALS. Dubuque, Iowa: William C. Brown, 1963. 144 p.

> Plays are grouped by suitability for college, children's, community or high school use. There are lists of one-acts, plays not requiring payment of royalties, musicals, and light operas, with details on sets, actors required, royalty, etc. Lacks index.

> See also National Council of Teachers of English, above.

Pollard, Alfred William, and Redgrave, G.R., comps. SHORT TITLE CATALOGUE OF BOOKS PRINTED IN ENGLAND, SCOTLAND, AND IRELAND, AND OF ENGLISH BOOKS PRINTED ABROAD 1475-1640. London: Bibliographical Society, 1948. 609 p.

> Lists by author or, for anonymous works, title, approximately 26,000 editions and locates copies in American and British libraries. Each item is assigned, for scholarly reference, a "short title catalog (STC) number."

> Plays are listed, as well as pamphlets and contemporary criticism.

> For the texts of items cited in Pollard and Redgrave and now available on microfilm, refer to ENGLISH BOOKS, 1475-1640 and its CONSOLIDATED CROSS INDEX, above. Note, however, that not all texts listed in Pollard and Redgrave will be reproduced on microfilm.

Rachow, Louis A.

> See GUIDE TO THE PERFORMING ARTS, above.

THE READER'S ADVISER. Edited by Winifred F. Courtney. 11th ed., rev. 2 vols. New York: R.R. Bowker, 1968-69.

> See Volume I, chapters 21-27, for drama reference books, critical, historical, and theoretical studies; and modern editions of plays from all periods. Contents of play collections are given.

> See also Volume II, chapter 10, for dance, film, mime, opera, radio, and television.

READERS' GUIDE TO PERIODICAL LITERATURE. New York: H.W. Wilson, 1905- . Monthly.

> A cumulative index to 150 general magazines from 1900 to date. Although few theater magazines are scanned, the READERS' GUIDE's past coverage of THEATRE ARTS MONTHLY is useful, and its current pinpointing of articles and reviews in general magazines is vital.

Author, subject, and title entries are interfiled, but the main entry for dramas is under author. Texts or excerpts published in periodicals are shown directly after the author's name. Play reviews and other articles follow.

Under the heading "Dramas" are play titles, with reference to author entry. Other headings are "Children's Plays," "Detective and Mystery Plays," "Radio Plays," and "Television Plays."

For the years 1890 to 1899 see the NINETEENTH CENTURY READERS' GUIDE for entries under author or under "Dramas." An author citation may include both play texts and reviews, thus: Gorky, Maxim. CHILDREN OF THE SUN. Drama. or Gorky, M. CHILDREN OF THE SUN. Review.

Roden, Robert F. LATER AMERICAN PLAYS, 1831-1900. New York: The Dunlap Society, 1900.

Selected plays by American authors published or performed in the United States after 1831. Translations and poetic drama included.

Main index by author, with brief notes on him, on leading actors, and on notable productions. Anonymous titles precede author list.

Roden analyzes contents of some series.

Continues chronological coverage of Wegelin, Oscar, below.

Sakanishi, Shio, comp. A LIST OF TRANSLATIONS OF JAPANESE DRAMA INTO ENGLISH, FRENCH, AND GERMAN. Washington, D.C.: American Council of Learned Societies, 1935. 89 p.

Under author are found play titles in Japanese, romanized, followed by English title. Sakanishi locates texts or summaries and partial texts in books and periodicals.

See also Nihon Pen Kurabu, above.

Salem, James M., ed.

See Drury, Francis Keese Wynkoop. DRURY'S GUIDE, above.

Schoenbaum, S.

See Harbage, Alfred, above.

Shaw, Ralph Robert, and Shoemaker, Richard H. AMERICAN BIBLIOGRAPHY; A PRELIMINARY CHECKLIST. 22 vols. New York: Scarecrow Press, 1958-66.

A chronological checklist, 1800-20, which continues Charles Evans's AMERICAN BIBLIOGRAPHY. (See above.) Locates library copies.

Volume 20 (1965) consists of addenda and a source list for all twenty volumes. Volume 21 (1965) is a title index. Volume 22

(1966) is an author index and also lists corrections.

Texts of the Shaw and Shoemaker items are being reproduced in microprint. The reader uses the item number and year in the above work to locate the text in the microprint edition, EARLY AMERICAN IMPRINTS, SECOND SERIES, 1801-1819. This is an ongoing series; about 50,000 works will be copied over a twenty-year period.

The Shaw and Shoemaker checklist is continued chronologically by Shoemaker, Richard H., below.

Shipton, Clifford Kenyon. NATIONAL INDEX OF AMERICAN IMPRINTS THROUGH 1800: THE SHORT-TITLE EVANS. Edited by Clifford Kenyon Shipton and James E. Mooney. 2 vols. Worcester, Mass.: American Antiquarian Society, 1970.

Compilation of 40,000 Evans titles and 10,000 added items.

See Evans, Charles, above.

Shoemaker, Richard H. CHECKLIST OF AMERICAN IMPRINTS, 1820 TO DATE. New York: Scarecrow Press, 1964- .

Continues Charles Evans's AMERICAN BIBLIOGRAPHY and its Shaw and Shoemaker continuation. (See above.)

Volumes through 1829 have been completed. For later volumes see Cooper, Gayle, above.

Short title catalogs.

See Pollard, Alfred William, and Redgrave, G.R., above, and Wing, Donald Goddard, below. See also Shipton, Clifford Kenyon, above.

Smith, Frank Seymour. THE CLASSICS IN TRANSLATION; AN ANNOTATED GUIDE TO THE BEST TRANSLATIONS OF THE GREEK AND LATIN CLASSICS INTO ENGLISH. New York: Scribner's, 1930. 307 p.

Describes translations and notes book review sources for some. Works appear under classical author's name.

See also THE LITERATURES OF THE WORLD IN ENGLISH TRANSLATION; Nairn, John Arbuthnot; and THE READER'S ADVISER, above.

_____. AN ENGLISH LIBRARY; A BOOKMAN'S GUIDE. Rev. ed. London: Deutsch, 1963. 384 p.

Lists in-print editions, mainly of English literary classics. Useful in choosing best British edition. Offers wide price range, including paperbacks.

See also THE READER'S ADVISER, above.

Sonneck, Oscar George Theodore. CATALOGUE OF OPERA LIBRETTOS PRINTED BEFORE 1800. 2 vols. Washington, D.C.: Government Printing Office, 1914.

> Contains 17,000 items, mainly from seventeenth and eighteenth centuries, located in the Library of Congress. Volume I contains title entries, with publication data and time and place of first performance. Volume II contains indexes of authors, arias, and composers.

THE STAGE CYCLOPEDIA.

> See Eldredge, H.J.

Stratman, Carl J., comp. and ed. BIBLIOGRAPHY OF ENGLISH PRINTED TRAGEDY. Carbondale: University of Southern Illinois Press, 1966. 843 p.

> Finding guide for tragedy only. (See definition, p. x.) Includes plays published from 1565 to 1900, in original and later editions, excluding Shakespeare. (Only adaptations of his works are found, listed under adapter.) Stratman names at least one library location for each edition.

> This work may be compared with both Greg, Walter W., and Harbage, Alfred, above. There is some overlap with Greg, but Stratman includes more works of the later period.

> Special features are a bibliography of early bibliographies of plays, pp. xiii–xvii; a list of play collections, pp. 711–63; a chronology of first editions, pp. 765–92, which indicates whether a play was ever performed; and a final index of all plays, pp. 793–823, including popular titles and changed titles.

_____. A BIBLIOGRAPHY OF MEDIEVAL DRAMA. 2d ed., rev. and enl. 2 vols. New York: Ungar, 1972.

> The first edition of this work was published in 1954 by the University of California, Berkeley (423 p.). It included citations of single plays, printed or in manuscript, as well as books and articles on medieval drama. Festschriften, unpublished theses and dissertations, and 230 book reviews published in the twentieth century were also included. The play-index located copies in major U.S. and British libraries and also analyzed contents of seventy-one anthologies.

> The second edition adds more than 5,000 entries. Arrangement is in ten categories. Corrections have been made. There is more emphasis on Continental European drama and on Latin liturgical drama. Book reviews are no longer especially indicated.

> See also Coleman, Edward D.; Farrar, Clarissa P., and Evans, Austin P.; and Harbage, Alfred, above.

Summers, Montague. A BIBLIOGRAPHY OF THE RESTORATION DRAMA. London: Fortune Press, 1934? 94 p.

> Lists printed and manuscript plays written in England from 1660 to 1700. (Anonymous plays are grouped ahead of the main list.) Gives information on first performance, if any, on editions of the author's lifetime and some of later dates. Traces some obscure plays to sets or, in a few cases, to manuscripts found in libraries or in private hands.

> Most features of this work are superseded by THE LONDON STAGE. See annotation in Part VI-A2.

Taborski, Boleslaw. POLISH PLAYS IN ENGLISH TRANSLATIONS; A BIBLIOGRAPHY. New York: Polish Institute of Arts and Sciences in America, 1968. 79 p.

> Entered under author are synopses and brief critiques. Sources of translations are books, periodicals, manuscripts, or original typescripts, said to be available from various colleges. Coverage is from earliest times to around 1939.

> See also THE LITERATURES OF THE WORLD IN ENGLISH TRANSLATION, Volume II, above.

Temple, Ruth Z.

> See THE LITERATURES OF THE WORLD IN ENGLISH TRANSLATION, above.

Thomson, Ruth Gibbons. INDEX TO FULL-LENGTH PLAYS, 1895 TO 1925. Boston: F.W. Faxon, 1956. 172 p.

> Selective title index of plays in English. Gives author, period, setting, characters, and type of drama. Locates each play in several published collections. Author and subject indexes, the latter including types of drama, e.g., Melodrama.

> Continued by Thomson's INDEX TO FULL-LENGTH PLAYS, 1926 TO 1944, below.

_____. INDEX TO FULL-LENGTH PLAYS, 1926 TO 1944. Boston: F.W. Faxon, 1946. 306 p.

> Selective index of plays in English published in collections. Same arrangement as in Volume I, above.

> Continued by Norma Olin Ireland's INDEX TO FULL-LENGTH PLAYS, 1944 TO 1964. (See above.)

THREE CENTURIES OF DRAMA, 1500-1830.

> See Bergquist, William, above.

THREE CENTURIES OF ENGLISH AND AMERICAN PLAYS, A CHECKLIST.

See Bergquist, William, above.

U.S. Copyright Office. CATALOG OF COPYRIGHT ENTRIES. DRAMAS AND WORKS PREPARED FOR ORAL DELIVERY. Washington, D.C.: Government Printing Office, 1891-1946 and Series 3, 1947-   .

This semiannual is the continuation of U.S. Copyright Office. DRAMATIC COMPOSITIONS, etc. See below.

Scope has varied. Series three includes dramas, musicals, radio, television, and film scripts, addresses, sermons, and monologs. Entry is by author, but television and radio programs appear under title. Date and holder of copyright shown.

For reading editions, as distinct from performing editions of plays, refer to THE NATIONAL UNION CATALOG and its predecessors. (See above.)

_____. DRAMATIC COMPOSITIONS COPYRIGHTED IN THE UNITED STATES, 1870 to 1916. 2 vols. Washington, D.C.: Government Printing Office, 1918.

Enters by title 60,000 plays registered for copyright, with date and name of copyright holder. Some of these items were never published. After 1909, manuscript or printed copies of the works were deposited at the Library of Congress. Prior to that, title page only was required. There are separate indexes of authors, editors, translators, pseudonyms, alternate or translated titles, etc. Volume II has a supplement of titles registered in 1915-16.

For record of later copyright refer to U.S. Copyright Office. CATALOG OF COPYRIGHT ENTRIES. DRAMAS AND WORKS PREPARED FOR ORAL DELIVERY. (See above.)

A similar record exists for films, entitled U.S. Copyright Office. MOTION PICTURES. See Part VI-A5.

U.S. Library of Congress. AUTHOR CATALOG.

See THE NATIONAL UNION CATALOG, above.

Wegelin, Oscar. EARLY AMERICAN PLAYS, 1714-1830. New Series no. 10. Edited by John Malone. New York: The Dunlap Society, 1900. 113 p.

Wegelin's entries are by author, with biographical and historical notes.

See also Hill, Frank Pierce, above.

Wegelin is continued chronologically by Roden, Robert F., above.

Weingarten, Joseph Abraham, comp. MODERN AMERICAN PLAYWRIGHTS,

1918–1945; A BIBLIOGRAPHY. 1946. Reprint. New York: Franklin, 1967.

> Part I: authors from A to Lavery; Part II: Lawrence to Z. Play
> titles grouped under author with reference to first performance and
> to publication in books, sets, or periodicals. Note is made of
> copies found in New York Public Library, either of books or scripts,
> including some not shown in the NYPL's own catalog.

Wells, Henry W. THREE CENTURIES OF DRAMA, 1500–1830.

> See Bergquist, William, above.

West, Dorothy Herbert, and Peake, Dorothy M.

> See PLAY INDEX, above.

Wing, Donald Goddard. SHORT TITLE CATALOGUE OF BOOKS PRINTED IN
ENGLAND, SCOTLAND, IRELAND, WALES, AND BRITISH AMERICA, AND
OF ENGLISH BOOKS PRINTED IN OTHER COUNTRIES, 1641–1700. 3 vols.
New York: Printed for the Index Society by Columbia University Press, 1945.

> A revised and enlarged second edition is in progress, with Vol-
> ume I published in 1972.

> A list by author and anonymous title, briefly describing editions
> and locating library copies. Each edition is assigned a short
> title number (STC number), which is used by scholars to identify
> these books. Wing's list continues that of Pollard, Alfred William,
> and Redgrave, G.R., see above.

> For access to microfilm of many texts listed in Wing, see ENGLISH
> BOOKS, 1641–1700, above.

B. PLAYS IN FOREIGN LANGUAGES

In larger libraries the complete, collected, and selected works by a voluminous
author may consistently be grouped ahead of his single works. If the work
sought does not appear as an individual title, these various collections may
contain it, and the catalog cards may reveal the contents of single volumes.
Sometimes, however, simpler cataloging rules prevail, and titles must be found
in the books themselves, with or without the aid of a table of contents.

The search for a play text in its original language may require using more than
one library. If the reader has access to the published catalogs of major or
specialized libraries, these can be used to verify and to locate ownership of a
specific edition. Again, in such catalogs, the contents of collected works may
be shown in detail. Examples of published library catalogs useful to the drama
student are the NATIONAL UNION CATALOG and that of the New York
Public Library's Theatre and Drama Collection, one very broad, the other specialized, and both rich in works in most languages. Published catalogs of a
few large university libraries are similarly helpful. Call numbers are not

necessarily standardized, but the imprint itself can be used as a citation for most purposes, including an interlibrary loan. Notes on these major library catalogs are entered in Part IV-A.

The more specialized bibliographies of foreign-language plays which follow include a few listing plays reproduced in some microform. There are cross-references to the microform sets which include the plays (e.g., Binger, Norman. GERMAN DRAMA ON MICROCARDS). Ideally, the card catalog should also make clear the relationship of the bibliography to the microform set, but for various reasons this is not always true. Usually the reference librarian will provide the information. Such sets in the various microforms (microfilm, microfiche, or microprint) vary in quality and editorial standards but have been, by and large, welcomed by scholars since they make readily available texts hitherto inaccessible. Microform editions, including foreign-language drama, will be found in most large scholarly libraries, and individual reels of microfilm may under some circumstances be borrowed through interlibrary loan.

Naturally one would not go to this final step without first exhausting all resources in one's own local library by means of the indexes and finding lists described below.

Allgayer, Wilhelm, ed. DRAMENLEXIKON; EIN WEGWEISER ZU ETWA 10,000 URHEBERRECHTLICH GESCHUETZTEN BUEHNENWERKE DER JAHRE 1945-1957; 1957-1960. 2 vols. Cologne: Kiepenheuer & Witisch, 1958-62.

> This title list gives publication and first performance dates for copyrighted plays in German. (Some are translations.) The second volume lists new plays and some omitted earlier. Both volumes have indexes of authors. Note also addenda in Volume 2: titles, pp. 151-212; authors, pp. 213-27; drama publishers, pp. 229-36.

> See also INDEX TRANSLATIONUM in Part IV-A, above.

Arrom, Jose Juan. HISTORIA DE LA LITERATURA DRAMATICA CUBANA. Yale Romanic Studies, vol. 23. New Haven: Yale University Press, 1944. 132 p.

> Cuban plays are listed, pp. 95-127, and library copies located in Cuba and the United States.

Ashcom, Benjamin Bowles. A DESCRIPTIVE CATALOGUE OF THE SPANISH COMEDIAS SUELTAS IN THE WAYNE STATE UNIVERSITY LIBRARY AND THE PRIVATE LIBRARY OF PROFESSOR B.B. ASHCOM. Detroit: Wayne State University Libraries, 1965. 103 p.

> Approximately 600 titles are noted.

> See also North Carolina. University of. Library, and Toronto. University of. Library. (COMEDIAS SUELTAS), below.

Barrera y Leirado, D. Cayetano Alberto de. CATALOGO BIBLIOGRAFICO Y

BIOGRAFICO DEL TEATRO ANTIGUO ESPANOL. Madrid: M. Rivadeneyra, 1860. 723 p.

Brief entries, chiefly biographical, on Spanish theater through the eighteenth century. There are separate lists of play titles, pp. 523-92, and of the contents of collected editions, pp. 677-720.

See also Cotarelo y Mori, Emilio, below.

BIBLIOGRAPHY OF FRENCH PLAYS ON MICROCARDS.

See Thompson, Lawrence S., below.

Binger, Norman. GERMAN DRAMA ON MICROCARDS. Hamden, Conn.: Shoe String Press, 1970. 224 p.

Author list of nearly 4,000 plays, sixteenth to early twentieth century, published in German and reproduced in microcard edition. (See GERMAN DRAMA ON MICROCARDS, below.) For some plays more than one edition has been reproduced. Pseudonyms are cross-referenced. There is a title index.

See also FIFTY YEARS OF GERMAN DRAMA, below.

Brenner, Clarence Dietz. A BIBLIOGRAPHICAL LIST OF PLAYS IN THE FRENCH LANGUAGE, 1700-1789. Berkeley: Printed by Edwards Brothers for the Associated Students' Store, 1947. 229 p.

Names 11,000 plays singly published or in collections. An index of titles refers to an author list and to an anonymous title list. Locates some editions and manuscripts in chief libraries of Paris.

See also Thompson, Lawrence S., below.

British Museum. GENERAL CATALOGUE OF PRINTED BOOKS.

See Part IV-A, above.

Cioni, Alfredo. BIBLIOGRAFIA DELLE SACRE RAPPRESENTAZIONI. Biblioteca Bibliografica Italica, no. 22. Florence: Sansoni, 1961. 356 p.

Italian sacred dramas and folk plays of the sixteenth and seventeenth centuries. Works published singly or in sets.

See also Colomb de Batines, Paul; Clubb, Louise George; Corrigan, Beatrice; Herrick, Marvin T.; and Salvioli, Giovanni and Carlo, below.

Clubb, Louise George. ITALIAN PLAYS (1500-1700) IN THE FOLGER LIBRARY; A BIBLIOGRAPHY, WITH INTRODUCTION. Biblioteca di Bibliografia Italiana, no. 52. Florence: Olschki, 1968. 267 p.

Includes 890 items, with notes, following a long scholarly introduction.

See also Corrigan, Beatrice; Herrick, Marvin T.; and Salvioli, Giovanni and Carlo, below, and Cioni, Alfredo, above.

Colomb de Batines, Paul, Vicomte, comp. BIBLIOGRAFIA DELLE ANTICHE RAPPRESENTAZIONI ITALIANE SACRE E PROFANE STAMPATE NEI SECOLO XV E XVI. Milan: G.G. Goerlich, 1958. 92 p.

Describes editions of the fifteenth and sixteenth centuries. Mainly a title list of sacred plays and a few secular, pp. 71–85. The appendix lists the "sacred" and "profane" separately.

Locates copies in a few Italian libraries or in anthologies and collected works of dramatists.

See also Cioni, Alfredo, above.

Corrigan, Beatrice, comp. CATALOGUE OF ITALIAN PLAYS, 1500–1700, IN THE LIBRARY OF THE UNIVERSITY OF TORONTO. Toronto: University of Toronto Press, 1961. 134 p.

Bibliographic data on sixteenth and seventeenth-century Italian plays in a large collection. Contains indexes of plays by author and title, a list of published collections, and a roster of Italian printers. Note addenda, pp. 101–2.

See also Cioni, Alfredo; Clubb, Louise George; and Colomb de Batines, Paul, above, and Herrick, Marvin T.; and Salvioli, Giovanni and Carlo, below.

Cotarelo y Mori, Emilio. TEATRO ESPANOL; CATALOGO ABREVIADO DE UNA COLECCION DRAMATICA ESPANOLA HASTA FINES DEL SIGLO XIX Y DE OBRAS RELATIVAS AL TEATRO ESPANOL. Madrid: V. e H. de J. Rates, 1930. 164 p.

Lists more than 1,800 plays, operas, musical dramas, and works on Spanish theater from earliest days through the nineteenth century.

See also Barrera y Leirado, D. Cayetano Alberto de, above.

DRAMENLEXIKON.

See Allgayer, Wilhelm, above.

Duran Cerda, Julio. REPERTORIO DEL TEATRO CHILENO; BIBLIOGRAFIA, OBRAS INEDITAS Y ESTRENADAS. Publicaciones del Instituto de Literatura Chilena, series C, no. 1. Santiago: Universidad de Chile, 1962. 247 p.

Lists more than 1700 works under author. Also has title index and short list of critical studies.

See also Rela, Walter. CONTRIBUCION, below.

FIFTY YEARS OF GERMAN DRAMA; A BIBLIOGRAPHY OF MODERN DRAMA,

1880-1930. Baltimore: Johns Hopkins University Press, 1941. 111 p.

> Covers the library's Loewenberg collection of 3,000 plays in German, mostly first editions. No annotations. Dates of first performances are given.

> For plays of later date see Allgayer, Wilhelm, above. See also GERMAN DRAMA ON MICROCARDS, below.

FOUR CENTURIES OF SPANISH DRAMA: A COMPREHENSIVE COLLECTION OF SPANISH DRAMA OF THE SEVENTEENTH, EIGHTEENTH, AND NINETEENTH CENTURIES BEING PUBLISHED ON MICROCARDS OVER A PERIOD OF YEARS. Washington, D.C.: Microcard Editions; Louisville: Falls City Microcard, 1959-   .

> Around 600 titles a year are being reproduced by Falls City Microcard. Collection based mainly on Spanish, Spanish-American, and Catalan plays at the University of Kentucky. The actual range of this collection is from sixteenth to twentieth century.

> For an index of contents, see Thompson, Lawrence S., SPANISH PLAYS, below

FRENCH DRAMA SERIES.

> See THREE CENTURIES OF FRENCH DRAMA, below.

GERMAN DRAMA ON MICROCARDS; A COMPREHENSIVE COLLECTION OF GERMAN DRAMA PRIOR TO THE TWENTIETH CENTURY BEING PUBLISHED ON MICROCARDS OVER A PERIOD OF YEARS. Washington, D.C.: Microcard Editions; Louisville: Falls City Microcard, 1961-   .

> Based on Norman Binger's bibliography. (See above.)

Herrick, Marvin T., comp. ITALIAN PLAYS, 1500-1700, IN THE UNIVERSITY OF ILLINOIS LIBRARY. Urbana: University of Illinois Press, 1966. 92 p.

> Author list, giving for each drama the publisher, number of acts, type of play, etc. A title index includes anonymous works.

> See also Cioni, Alfredo; Clubb, Louise George; Colomb de Batines, Paul; and Corrigan, Beatrice, above, and Salvioli, Giovanni and Carlo, below.

Horn-Monval, Madeleine. REPERTOIRE BIBLIOGRAPHIQUE DES TRADUCTIONS ET ADAPTATIONS FRANCAISES DU THEATRE ETRANGER DU XV SIECLE A NOS JOURS. 8 vols. Paris: Centre National de la Recherche Scientifique, 1958-67. General Index.

> Volumes I through IV (bound as one volume) list, under original author, Greek, Latin, and other Romance language dramas, fifteenth to twentieth century, which have been translated into French. Library locations are given. Each volume has indexes of anonymous and other works, and of translators and librettists.

Volumes V and VI locate English and American plays in French translation. Volume VII covers the Netherlands, the Baltic, and the Scandinavian countries. Volume VIII, Part 1, dramas in Slavic and other European languages; Part 2, Asian and African dramas. An appendix consists of "Addenda to American theater."

A general index of authors appeared in 1967.

ITALIAN DRAMA ON MICROFILM. Cambridge, Mass.: General Microfilm Co., 1967-   .

Selected editions from the Middle Ages to the twentieth century. Not based on a single bibliography.

Johns Hopkins University. Loewenberg Collection.

See FIFTY YEARS OF GERMAN DRAMA, above.

Keller, Dean H. INDEX TO PLAYS IN PERIODICALS.

See Part IV-A, above.

Lamb, Ruth. BIBLIOGRAFIA DEL TEATRO MEXICANO DEL SIGLO XX. Coleccion Studium, 33. Mexico City: Claremont Colleges and Ediciones de Andrea, 1962. 143 p.

Mexican plays of the twentieth century listed under author, with editions described and first performances noted. No library locations given, but plays are traced to sets or periodicals.

See also Monterde Garcia Icazbalceta, Francisco, below.

Monterde Garcia Icazbalceta, Francisco. BIBLIOGRAFIA DEL TEATRO EN MEXICO. Monografias Bibliograficas Mexicanas, 28. Mexico City: Imp. de la Secretaria de Relaciones Exteriores, 1934. 649 p.

Finds original plays, translations, and adaptations by Mexican authors, printed in periodicals, collections, or as single titles. Also shows foreign dramas printed in Mexico and plays with Mexican themes, pp. 489-506. Dates of production are sometimes given.

See also Lamb, Ruth, above.

THE NATIONAL UNION CATALOG.

See Part IV-A, above.

New York Public Library. CATALOG OF THE THEATRE AND DRAMA COLLECTIONS.

Dramas in various languages appear in the six-volume "Cultural origins list."

See Part IV-A for full annotation.

North Carolina. University of. Library. CATALOGUE OF COMEDIAS SUELTAS IN THE LIBRARY. Library studies, no. 4. By William A. McKnight with the collaboration of Mabel Barrett Jones. Chapel Hill: University of North Carolina Press, 1965. 240 p.

> The collections of Spanish and Catalan drama in this library include more than 25,000 separately issued plays (comedias sueltas), published outside both the standard collections and the "obras" of their authors. Many plays were published in Spain in this manner from about 1674 into the 1820s.

> The texts themselves range from the Golden Age to the eighteenth century in origin and include both one-act and full-length plays. Many are rare. Entries are alphabetical under titles, with authors identified and editions described briefly. Some works previously listed as anonymous are given attributions. Author index.

> See also Toronto. University of. Library, below, and Ashcom, Benjamin Bowles, above.

Oberlin College Library. THE SPANISH DRAMA COLLECTION IN THE OBERLIN COLLEGE LIBRARY; A DESCRIPTIVE CATALOGUE. By Paul Patrick Rogers. Oberlin, Ohio: Oberlin College, 1940. 468 p. and

SUPPLEMENT, Oberlin, Ohio: Oberlin College, 1946. 157 p.

> Included in main volume are 7,530 items, from seventeenth century to 1924, arranged by author. The supplement adds anonymous plays and lists of theaters, printers, and musical composers.

Ottemiller, John H. INDEX TO PLAYS IN COLLECTIONS.

> Includes a few foreign-language plays in collections published in Great Britain or the United States. Foreign titles are cross-referenced with English translation.

> See Part IV-A for full citation.

Pennsylvania. University of. Libraries. SPANISH DRAMA OF THE GOLDEN AGE; THE COMEDIA COLLECTION IN THE UNIVERSITY OF PENNSYLVANIA LIBRARIES. New Haven: Research Publications, [1972 ?]. 86 reels on 35mm positive microfilm.

> Reproduces the primary and some secondary works in several special collections donated to the University of Pennsylvania. Many of these are rare editions. In all, 3,200 plays of the Golden Age in seventeenth through early nineteenth-century editions, as well as related nondramatic works, are included.

For an index to the microfilm set and the collections, see Regueiro, Jose M., below.

Regueiro, Jose M. SPANISH DRAMA OF THE GOLDEN AGE; A CATALOGUE OF THE COMEDIA COLLECTION IN THE UNIVERSITY OF PENNSYLVANIA LIBRARIES, New Haven: Research Publications, c. 1971. 106 p.

This catalog serves as a guide to the collection itself and to the microfilm set reproduced from the texts in the library. See Pennsylvania. University of. Libraries, above.

Rela, Walter. CONTRIBUCION A LA BIBLIOGRAFIA DEL TEATRO CHILENO, 1804-1960. Montevideo: Universidad de la Republica, 1960. 51 p.

List of historical and critical articles and books on theater. See theater periodicals list, p. 25. Author list, pp. 25-51, cites first publication of plays, whether in book or periodical.

See also Duran Cerda, Julio, above.

_____. REPERTORIO BIBLIOGRAFICO DEL TEATRO URUGUAYO, 1816-1964. Montevideo: Editorial Sintesis, 1965. 35 p.

Authors listed alphabetically, with their works as published in books or periodicals. Also a short bibliography of critical studies and a name index.

Rogers, Paul Patrick.
See Oberlin College Library, above.

Salvioli, Giovanni, and Salvioli, Carlo. BIBLIOGRAFIA UNIVERSALE DEL TEATRO DRAMMATICO ITALIANO. Venice: Carlo Ferrari, 1903. 931 p. APPENDIX, 55 p.

Only one volume, A-Cz, was published, assembling, by title, first editions of plays and musical dramas in Italian from earliest times to 1903. Some plays found in periodicals and collections. Notes concern editions, translations, and productions. The appendix in the same volume has separate pagination.

See also Cioni, Alfredo; Clubb, Louise George; Colomb de Batines, Paul; Corrigan, Beatrice; and Herrick, Marvin T., above.

Sousa, Jose Galante de. O TEATRO NO BRASIL. 2 vols. Rio de Janeiro: Minsterio da Educacao e Cultural, Instituto Nacional do Livro, 1960.

Volume I is a history of theater in Brazil, with a brief bibliography. Volume II is a bio-bibliography of Portuguese and Brazilian writers for the theater, some of whom were also actors or directors.

SPANISH DRAMA SERIES.

See FOUR CENTURIES OF SPANISH DRAMA, above.

Thompson, Lawrence S. A BIBLIOGRAPHY OF FRENCH PLAYS ON MICRO-
CARDS. Hamden, Conn.: Shoe String Press, 1967. 689 p.

Guide to plays reproduced in the series THREE CENTURIES OF
FRENCH DRAMA. (See below.)

Future editions of the Thompson work are planned as the microcard
series is augmented over a number of years.

See also Brenner, Clarence Dietz, above.

_____. A BIBLIOGRAPHY OF SPANISH PLAYS ON MICROCARDS. Hamden,
Conn.: Shoe String Press, Archon, 1968. 490 p.

Listing items by author or anonymous title, Thompson's bibliography
ranges from sixteenth into twentieth century. Plays are Spanish,
Spanish-American, and Catalan works found mainly in the University of Kentucky Library and available also on microcards in the
series FOUR CENTURIES OF SPANISH DRAMA. (See above.)

See also Cotarelo y Mori, Emilio, above.

THREE CENTURIES OF FRENCH DRAMA: A COMPREHENSIVE COLLECTION
OF FRENCH DRAMA OF THE SEVENTEENTH, EIGHTEENTH, AND NINE-
TEENTH CENTURIES BEING PUBLISHED ON MICROCARDS OVER A PERIOD
OF YEARS. Washington, D.C.: Microcard Editions; Louisville: Falls City
Microcard.

About 600 titles a year reproduced on microcards from copies of
plays in the Library of Congress and at the University of Kentucky.
(Other institutions will also contribute.)

For an index to plays reproduced up to 1967, see Thompson,
Lawrence S., above.

Toronto. University of. Library. A BIBLIOGRAPHY OF COMEDIAS SUELTAS
IN THE UNIVERSITY OF TORONTO LIBRARY. Compiled by J.A. Molinaro
et al. Toronto: University of Toronto Press, 1959. 149 p.

Titles in a collection of rare editions of seventeenth and eighteenth-
century Spanish plays. Author list, pp. 143–49. Index of publishers and bookdealers, pp. 139–42.

See also Ashcom, Benjamin Bowles; and North Carolina. University
of. Library, above.

_____. CATALOGUE OF ITALIAN PLAYS, 1500-1700.

See Corrigan, Beatrice, above.

Part V

SOURCES FOR REVIEWS OF PLAYS

AND MOTION PICTURES

The bibliographies and indexes in Part V list play and motion picture reviews, mainly in English-language periodicals. Some include reviews of dance and musical events, as well as those "staged" occasions called "happenings."

Many of the indexes for play reviews also yield drama criticism of a retrospective and literary nature. It is, of course, impossible to draw a firm line, since often a critic will make his review of a production the occasion for far-ranging literary criticism.

A few of the works which follow include only criticism or interpretation of published works as distinct from reviews of productions (e.g., the two volumes, DRAMA CRITICISM, by Arthur Coleman and Gary R. Tyler), and at least one (MODERN DRAMA, by Irving Adelman and Rita Dworkin) has more references to criticism than to reviews. They are listed here for the sake of breadth and because of their demonstrated usefulness to students of either theater history or of the drama as literature. For purely literary evaluations, particularly of established authors, see also Part VI-B.

Adelman, Irving, and Dworkin, Rita. MODERN DRAMA; A CHECKLIST OF CRITICAL LITERATURE ON TWENTIETH CENTURY PLAYS. Metuchen, N.J.: Scarecrow Press, 1967. 370 p.

> Refers to criticism of special merit, mainly in English, in more than 800 books and periodicals. Lists, under author, general criticism, and comment on single plays. Titles are cited in original language, followed by English versions. Bibliographies are given for some playwrights.

> See also Breed, Paul Francis, and Sniderman, Florence M.; Coleman, Arthur, and Tyler, Gary R.; Palmer, Helen H., and Dyson, Anne Jane; and Salem, James M. A GUIDE TO CRITICAL REVIEWS (Parts I and III), all below.

ART INDEX. New York: H.W. Wilson, 1933-   .

> Although mainly concerned with the visual arts, this index also

refers to reviews of some motion pictures, of dance performances, and of "happenings." Coverage begins from 1929.

Seek entries under names of individuals or under subject, e.g., "Choreography," "Moving Pictures—Criticisms, Plots," etc.

ART INDEX scans major art periodicals and a few other scholarly journals.

See also MUSIC INDEX, below, and GUIDE TO THE PERFORMING ARTS, annotated in Part IV-A.

Bacon, Jean C.

See POOLE'S INDEX. DATE AND VOLUME KEY.

Belknap, Sara Yancey.

See GUIDE TO DANCE PERIODICALS; GUIDE TO THE MUSICAL ARTS; and GUIDE TO THE PERFORMING ARTS.

Bell, Marion V.

See POOLE'S INDEX. DATE AND VOLUME KEY.

Bonin, Jane F. PRIZE-WINNING DRAMA: A BIBLIOGRAPHICAL AND DE-SCRIPTIVE GUIDE. Metuchen, N.J.: Scarecrow Press, 1973. 222 p.

Chronological record of dramas which won major American theater prizes from 1917 through 1971. Brief historical notes; synopses; statements on critical reception and performance history; short, not definitive bibliographies of criticism.

See also Toohey, John L., below.

Breed, Paul Francis, and Sniderman, Florence M., comps. DRAMATIC CRITI-CISM INDEX; A BIBLIOGRAPHY OF COMMENTARIES ON PLAYWRIGHTS FROM IBSEN TO THE AVANT-GARDE. Detroit: Gale Research Co., 1972. 1022 p.

Citing books and periodicals, Breed and Sniderman have nearly 12,000 entries in English on American and foreign playwrights, chiefly of the twentieth century. The author list cites general criticism followed by criticism and reviews of specific plays. An index of critics and a list of the books indexed are added.

See also Adelman, Irving, and Dworkin, Rita, above, and Coleman, Arthur, and Tyler, Gary R.; Palmer, Helen H., and Dyson, Anne Jane; and Salem, James M. A GUIDE TO CRITICAL REVIEWS (Parts I and III), all below.

British Film Institute. MONTHLY FILM BULLETIN. London, 1934- .

Prints reviews of films worldwide. Entries are under original title, with English translation. Entertainment films and current non-fiction and short films are reviewed separately. These reviews have a single source and perhaps a limited point of view.

The BULLETIN also prints many checklists of directors' and actors' careers on film, radio, and stage. There is an annual index.

BRITISH HUMANITIES INDEX, 1962- . London: Library Association, 1963- . Quarterly.

Successor to SUBJECT INDEX TO PERIODICALS. (See below.) Indexes British journals, many with local emphasis. Entry is by subject, but the annual cumulation has separate author index.

Few reviews; many survey articles. Film reviews found under "Cinema."

BULLETIN OF BIBLIOGRAPHY AND MAGAZINE NOTES. Boston: F.W. Faxon, 1897- . (Title varies.)

From April 1912 to May/August 1953 this was known as BULLETIN OF BIBLIOGRAPHY AND DRAMATIC INDEX. The "Dramatic Index" listed reviews of stage, screen, and television shows. The BULLETIN is especially useful from 1949 through 1953, to supplement the CUMULATED DRAMATIC INDEX. In its present form, the BULLETIN prints bibliographies on many subjects including playwrights and theater. These are best approached through BIBLIOGRAPHIC INDEX   See Part VI A.

BULLETIN SIGNALETIQUE. SCIENCES HUMAINES. PHILOSOPHIE. Paris: Centre National de la Recherche Scientifique, 1961- . Quarterly.

Annotated list of articles and book reviews. See sections "Theatre" and "Cinema" under "Litterature et Arts du Spectacle." No play reviews are listed, but for film reviews see "Cinema" with the subheadings "Festivals" and "Realisations," in which films are grouped by country of origin. Compte rendu indicates a review and is abbreviated as c.r.

Coleman, Arthur, and Tyler, Gary R. DRAMA CRITICISM: A CHECKLIST OF INTERPRETATION SINCE 1940 OF ENGLISH AND AMERICAN PLAYS. Vol. I. Denver: Alan Swallow, 1966. 457 p.

Volume I lists, by author, criticism of drama (not of performance). The items appeared in books and periodicals from 1940 to 1964, including American, British, Canadian, Irish, Australian, and New Zealand drama. Analyzes collections only if they treat more than one playwright. Separate list of Shakespearean criticism, pp. 236-392.

See also Adelman, Irving, and Dworkin, Rita; and Breed, Paul

Francis, and Sniderman, Florence M., above; and Palmer, Helen H., and Dyson, Anne Jane; and Salem, James M. A GUIDE TO CRITICAL REVIEWS (Parts I and III), below.

_____. A CHECKLIST OF INTERPRETATION SINCE 1940 OF CLASSICAL AND CONTINENTAL PLAYS. Vol. II. Denver: Alan Swallow, 1971. 446 p.

Cornyn, Stan. A SELECTIVE INDEX TO 'THEATRE MAGAZINE.' New York: Scarecrow Press, 1964. 289 p.

Index to a periodical published from 1900 to 1931. Scope: theater and motion pictures, worldwide. Lists items by subject, title, and author. Includes theatrical reviews, book reviews, synopses, and articles, with cross-reference to a table showing volume and year.

Cowie, Peter, ed.

See INTERNATIONAL FILM GUIDE, below.

CRITICS' GUIDE TO FILMS AND PLAYS. New York: Critics' Guide, 1967–69. Monthly. Ceased with Vol. II, no. 6.

Excerpts from current reviews in New York newspapers and in a few periodicals not indexed elsewhere.

See also FILMFACTS; NEW YORK THEATRE CRITICS' REVIEWS; READERS' GUIDE TO PERIODICAL LITERATURE; and the several NEW YORK TIMES entries, below.

CRITICS' GUIDE TO MOVIES AND PLAYS.

See CRITICS' GUIDE TO FILMS AND PLAYS, above.

CUMULATED DRAMATIC INDEX, 1909-1949.

See Part I-A.

Curley, Dorothy Nyren, and Curley, Arthur, eds. A LIBRARY OF LITERARY CRITICISM: MODERN ROMANCE LITERATURES. New York: Ungar, 1967. 510 p.

Excerpts from literary reviews, arranged under author. A few playwrights of the twentieth century are included.

Doak, Wesley A.

See FILM REVIEW INDEX, below.

Dworkin, Rita.

See Adelman, Irving, above.

Dyson, Anne Jane.

    See Palmer, Helen H., below.

EDUCATIONAL THEATRE JOURNAL: A TEN YEAR INDEX.

    See Welker, David, below.

ESSAY AND GENERAL LITERATURE INDEX, 1900- . New York: H.W. Wilson, 1934- .

    Cumulative subject and author index to essays, play reviews, etc., published in collections. Under each author's name are listed (1) his own essays, if any; (2) essays of which he is the subject; and (3) those dealing with his individual works, grouped by title. The essays on dramas are often reviews of productions, including revivals.

    Within the Shakespeare section, arrangement is elaborate, but reviews are grouped under title of play.

    A few film reviews under heading "Moving Picture Plays--Plots, Criticisms."

Fawcett, Marion.

    See AN INDEX TO 'FILMS IN REVIEW,' below.

THE FILM INDEX.

    See Writers' Program (New York), below.

FILM REVIEW INDEX. Edited by Wesley A. Doak and William J. Speed. Monterey Park, Calif.: Audio-Visual Associates, 1970-72. Quarterly.

    This publication indexed critical reviews in thirty educational and film periodicals. It is continued by INTERNATIONAL INDEX TO MULTI-MEDIA INFORMATION. (See below.)

FILMFACTS. New York, 1958- . Semimonthly.

    Associated with the American Film Institute, FILMFACTS lists U.S. and foreign feature films, with synopses and excerpts from reviews in American newspapers and magazines. An international roster of film festivals and awards, "Film Praise," precedes the annual index in January.

    See also INTERNATIONAL FILM GUIDE, below.

FILMS IN REVIEW. New York: National Board of Review of Motion Pictures,

1950- . Monthly.

> Emphasizes Hollywood feature films. Prints reviews, articles, and letters. All the reviews originate with FILMS IN REVIEW and perhaps share a limited point of view.

> For a separate index to this publication, see INDEX TO 'FILMS IN REVIEW', below.

Goode, Stephen H.

> See INDEX TO COMMONWEALTH LITTLE MAGAZINES.

Gregor, Joseph. DER SCHAUSPIELFUEHRER.

> See Part II-A.

GUIDE TO DANCE PERIODICALS. Edited by Sara Yancey Belknap. Vol. I: 1931/35 to Vol. X: 1962. Issued irregularly. (Has ceased publication.)

> Publisher and frequency varied. Fifteen or more dance periodicals were indexed, with author and subject entries. From Volume V on, illustrations in the periodicals scanned were listed.

> See also GUIDE TO THE MUSICAL ARTS and GUIDE TO THE PERFORMING ARTS, below.

GUIDE TO THE MUSICAL ARTS. Compiled by Sara Yancey Belknap. New York: Scarecrow Press, 1957. Unpaged.

> Published in one volume, this index cites 15,000 articles on music, opera, dance, and theater appearing in periodicals from 1953 through 1956, with a few earlier items. Based on ten music periodicals, two for theater, and one for the dance.

> The second part of the volume, approximately one-third of the text, lists illustrations in periodicals.

> Continued by GUIDE TO THE PERFORMING ARTS.

> See also MUSIC INDEX, below.

GUIDE TO THE PERFORMING ARTS.

> See Part IV-A.

INDEX TO COMMONWEALTH LITTLE MAGAZINES, 1964-65. By Stephen H. Goode. New York: Johnson Reprint Co., 1966. 187 p. Vol. II, 1966-67. New York: Johnson Reprint Co., 1968. 253 p.

> An author-subject index of English-language "little magazines" published in Commonwealth and ex-Commonwealth countries. Reviews of published plays (including translations) are noted thus:

Brecht, Bertolt. ST. JOAN OF THE STOCKYARDS, a.r. by
John Russell Taylor.

Reviews of productions are noted thus: Weiss, Peter. THE MARAT/
SADE, a prod. r. by Steve Vinaver.

Future biennial volumes are promised as well as retrospective volumes to 1900. The 1968-69 volume was published in 1970 by
Whitston Publishing Co., Troy, New York. The 1970-71 volume
is currently being prepared by Whitston.

AN INDEX TO 'FILMS IN REVIEW,' 1950-1959. By Marion Fawcett. New
York: National Board of Review of Motion Pictures, 1961. 105 p.

Index to articles and book reviews in the periodical FILMS IN
REVIEW. (See above.) The index consists of several lists, as follows:
articles (by title); subjects; book reviews; film titles with references
to reviews; illustrations; authors of reviews; directors; actors.

AN INDEX TO 'FILMS IN REVIEW,' 1960-1964. By Marion Fawcett. New
York: National Board of Review of Motion Pictures, 1966. 196 p.

INTERNATIONAL FILM GUIDE. Edited by Peter Cowie. London: Tantivy
Press; New York: A.S. Barnes, 1964- . Illustrated. Annual.

Contents have varied. The 1968 volume includes film reviews,
under nation; capsule book reviews; critiques of film periodicals
(with digest of special issues); notes on new continental and British
theaters; articles on directors. Also lists archives, equipment suppliers, services, schools, films for loan, festivals, and awards.

See also FILMFACTS, above.

INTERNATIONAL INDEX.

See SOCIAL SCIENCES AND HUMANITIES INDEX.

INTERNATIONAL INDEX TO MULTI-MEDIA INFORMATION. Edited by
Wesley A. Doak and William J. Speed. Pasadena, Calif.: Audio-Visual
Associates, Spring 1973- . Quarterly.

Begins with Volume 4, continuing the numbering of its predecessor
FILM REVIEW INDEX. Indexes reviews of all media, such as
films, filmstrips, cassette tapes, slides, and recordings, as found
in 110 general, educational, and audiovisual periodicals. Among
them are SIGHTLINES, MONTHLY FILM BULLETIN (London),
SIGHT AND SOUND, LANDERS FILM REVIEWS, SATURDAY RE-
VIEW/WORLD, and TIME. Cites reviews of approximately 490
films in each issue, including documentaries, short subjects, and
feature films on 16mm. Also refers to articles on film making.

In the main alphabet films are entered by title, with references to reviews, as well as technical information, name of distributor, price. Subject index. List of distributors, with addresses.

International Theatre Institute. WORLD PREMIERES.

See WORLD PREMIERES.

A LIBRARY OF LITERARY CRITICISM.

See Curley, Dorothy Nyren, and Curley, Arthur, above; also Nyren, Dorothy; and Temple, Ruth Z., below.

Melchinger, Siegfried. CONCISE ENCYCLOPEDIA OF MODERN DRAMA.

See Part II-A.

LE MONDE. INDEX ANALYTIQUE. Paris: Le Monde, 1965 (c. 1967)- . Annual.

Index to articles, news items, and reviews printed in LE MONDE during the year covered. For reviews see "Theatre," with sub-heading "Comptes rendus," where plays are listed by author and title separately. Shows openings, in European theaters but mainly in France, for drama, opera, and musicals. See also items under "Films, critiques," where films are listed by title, with date of review.

In addition to annual volumes, retrospective volumes have appeared, beginning with 1944-45.

See also BULLETIN SIGNALETIQUE, above, and WORLD PRE-MIERES, below.

MUSIC INDEX. Detroit: Information Coordinators, 1949- . Monthly, cumulating annually.

Guide to music periodical literature. For reviews of dance, operas, liturgical music dramas (e.g., THE PLAY OF DANIEL), etc., see entries under name of performer or organization. All first performances of works are indexed.

See also GUIDE TO THE MUSICAL ARTS, above.

NEW YORK CRITICS' GUIDE TO FILMS AND PLAYS.

See CRITICS' GUIDE TO FILMS AND PLAYS, above.

NEW YORK THEATRE CRITICS' REVIEWS. New York: Critics' Theatre Reviews, 1940- . Biweekly.

Reprints reviews from New York newspapers. An index in each issue lists all plays current in New York and refers to the issue of the N.Y.T.C. REVIEWS in which a play was discussed.

A cumulated annual index shows authors, casts, directors, producers, designers, and composers, as well as titles. A cumulated index covers Volumes I–XXI (1940–60).

See also CRITICS' GUIDE TO FILMS AND PLAYS, above, and NEW YORK TIMES THEATER REVIEWS, 1920–1970, below.

NEW YORK TIMES DIRECTORY OF THE FILM. New York: Arno Press, Random House, 1971. 1243 p.

Reprints NEW YORK TIMES reviews of each year's "ten best films," 1924–70. Name and corporate indexes.

See also NEW YORK TIMES FILM REVIEWS, 1913–1968, below.

NEW YORK TIMES FILM REVIEWS, 1913–1968. 6 vols. New York: Arno Press and the NEW YORK TIMES, 1970. To be supplemented.

Compilation of reviews in the NEW YORK TIMES. Films cross-indexed by title, actor, director, writer, etc.

See also NEW YORK TIMES DIRECTORY OF THE FILM, above, and NEW YORK TIMES INDEX, below.

NEW YORK TIMES INDEX. New York: New York Times, 1851–   . Issued irregularly.

A subject index based on the late city edition. Frequency has varied. Cumulated annually. From its earliest issues, the INDEX has pinpointed play reviews, but the subject heading has varied, including the following: "Dramas"; "Dramatic"; "Metropolitan Area--Reviews and Notes"; "Miscellaneous: Dramatic"; "Plays and Operas"; "Play Reviews and Notes"; "Theater Reviews and Notes." New York performances are meant unless otherwise noted. In recent volumes the asterisk means an Off-Broadway New York performance. Film reviews also are indicated under "Motion pic-tures--Reviews" and similar headings.

Two new compilations from the INDEX are easier to use, namely THE NEW YORK TIMES FILM REVIEWS, 1913–1968. (See above.) and the NEW YORK TIMES THEATER REVIEWS, 1920–1970, below.

NEW YORK TIMES THEATER REVIEWS, 1920–1970. 10 vols. New York: New York Times, 1971. To be supplemented.

Compiled from the daily and Sunday TIMES are these entries for reviews and background articles on theater, drama, authors, actors, and directors. Motion pictures, radio, and television are excluded.

A two-volume index lists persons, titles, and companies. Easier to use than the NEW YORK TIMES INDEX, above.

See also NEW YORK TIMES FILM REVIEWS, 1913-1968, above, for some acting and directing careers.

NINETEENTH CENTURY READERS' GUIDE TO PERIODICAL LITERATURE, 1890-1899, WITH SUPPLEMENTARY INDEXING 1900-1922. 2 vols. Edited by Helen Grant Cushing and Adah V. Morris. New York: H.W. Wilson, 1944.

See READERS' GUIDE TO PERIODICAL LITERATURE in Part IV-A.

See also POOLE'S INDEX, below.

Nyren, Dorothy, comp. A LIBRARY OF LITERARY CRITICISM: MODERN AMERICAN LITERATURE. 3d ed. New York: Ungar, 1964. 620 p.

Excerpts from literary reviews arranged by author. Few dramatists are included.

Note "Supplement," pp. 555-92, and "Index to Critics", pp. 593-617.

Palmer, Helen H., and Dyson, Anne Jane, comps. AMERICAN DRAMA CRITICISM; INTERPRETATIONS, 1890-1965 INCLUSIVE, OF AMERICAN DRAMA SINCE THE FIRST PLAY PRODUCED IN AMERICA. Hamden, Conn.: Shoe String Press, Archon, 1967. 239 p.

Entry is by playwright, with pseudonyms and joint authors shown. Gives date of first performance and sources of reviews in books or American journals.

See also Adelman, Irving, and Dworkin, Rita; Breed, Paul Francis, and Sniderman, Florence M.; and Coleman, Arthur, and Tyler, Gary R.; above, and Salem, James M. A GUIDE TO CRITICAL REVIEWS (Part I), below.

_____. AMERICAN DRAMA CRITICISM: SUPPLEMENT I. TO JANUARY 1969. Hamden, Conn.: Shoe String Press, Archon, 1970. 101 p.

Added are items through 1968. Also has lists of books and periodicals indexed in basic volume and supplement.

_____. EUROPEAN DRAMA CRITICISM. Hamden, Conn.: Shoe String Press, 1968. 460 p.

Covers criticism, mainly in English, of European and British plays from early times to the 1960s. Omits Shakespeare.

Main list, under playwright, gives play titles in English. An index includes the foreign titles.

SUPPLEMENT I, to January 1970. Hamden, Conn.: Shoe String

Press, Archon, 1970. 243 p. SUPPLEMENT II, to January 1973. Hamden, Conn.: Shoe String Press, 1974. 209 p.

See also Adelman, Irving, and Rita Dworkin; Breed, Paul Francis, and Sniderman, Florence M.; and Coleman, Arthur, and Tyler, Gary R., Volume II., all above.

PALMER'S INDEX TO THE 'TIMES' NEWSPAPER, 1790-JUNE 1941. London: Palmer, 1868-1943. Quarterly.

For reviews, see play-titles under "Theatres."

See also The Times. INDEX TO 'THE TIMES' (official index), below.

Pence, James Harry, comp. THE MAGAZINE AND THE DRAMA: AN INDEX. New York: The Dunlap Society, c. 1896. 190 p.

Subject index of British and American periodical articles on acted drama. Begins with early nineteenth century but is most useful from 1870 to 1890. Some reviews are entered under author of play, some under a performer's name; reviews of Shakespeare's plays are under titles.

POOLE'S INDEX TO PERIODICAL LITERATURE. Boston: Houghton Mifflin, 1802-1906. Reprint. 6 vols. in 7. New York: Peter Smith, 1938-59.

Subject index to English and American periodicals. For drama there is some irregularity of entry; for example, some reviews of HAMLET productions may occur under title, others under playwright's name, e.g., Shakespeare, HAMLET, followed by a phrase, "acted by," "revival of," "at Princess's [Theatre]," etc. Other items may be grouped under "Shakesperian Revivals, Recent."

Gives abbreviated page reference and volume number only. To find year of periodical, consult POOLE'S INDEX. DATE AND VOLUME KEY. (See below.)

See also NINETEENTH CENTURY READERS' GUIDE, found under READERS' GUIDE TO PERIODICAL LITERATURE in Part IV-A.

POOLE'S INDEX. DATE AND VOLUME KEY. A.C.R.L. Monograph no. 19. By Marion V. Bell and Jean C. Bacon. Chicago: Association of College and Research Libraries, 1957. 61 p.

This separately published key correlates volume number and year of publication for periodicals cited in POOLE'S INDEX, above.

POOLE'S INDEX TO PERIODICAL LITERATURE. CUMULATIVE AUTHOR INDEX, 1803-1906. Compiled and edited by C. Edward Wall. Cumulative Author Index Series, no. 1. Ann Arbor, Mich.: Pierian Press, 1971. 488 p.

READERS' GUIDE TO PERIODICAL LITERATURE.

See Part IV-A.

Salem, James M. A GUIDE TO CRITICAL REVIEWS. PART I: AMERICAN DRAMA FROM O'NEILL TO ALBEE. Metuchen, N.J.: Scarecrow Press, 1966. 183 p. AMERICAN DRAMA, 1909-1969. 2d ed. Metuchen, N.J.: Scarecrow Press, 1973. 591 p.

The second edition cites reviews of over 1,700 plays by 290 playwrights.

See also Adelman, Irving, and Dworkin, Rita; Breed, Paul Francis, and Sniderman, Florence M.; Coleman, Arthur, and Tyler, Gary R.; Palmer, Helen H., and Dyson, Anne Jane, above.

_____. A GUIDE TO CRITICAL REVIEWS. PART II: THE MUSICAL FROM RODGERS-AND-HART TO LERNER-AND-LOEWE. Metuchen, N.J.: Scarecrow Press, 1967. 353 p.

Separate indexes of authors, composers, choreographers, lyricists, directors, and designers; titles of musicals, pp. 338-53; original works on which these were based, pp. 330-37.

Main list consists of titles of musicals in chronological order, with date, number of performances, and the usual credits, followed by references to New York reviews.

_____. A GUIDE TO CRITICAL REVIEWS. PART III: MODERN BRITISH AND CONTINENTAL DRAMA FROM IBSEN TO PINTER. Metuchen, N.J.: Scarecrow Press, 1968.

_____. A GUIDE TO CRITICAL REVIEWS. PART IV: THE SCREENPLAY. 2 vols. Metuchen, N.J.: Scarecrow Press, 1971.

DER SCHAUSPIELFUEHRER

See Gregor, Joseph, in Part II-A.

SOCIAL SCIENCES AND HUMANITIES INDEX. New York: H.W. Wilson, 1916-   . Quarterly. Cumulates annually and at longer intervals.

Successor to INTERNATIONAL INDEX. Coverage has varied but is now limited to about 175 English and American journals, with entries by subject and author.

Reviews are noted under playwright's name. Lacking that, see "Drama--Criticism." See also "Shakespeare--Stage Presentation," "--Adaptations," and "-- Moving Picture Versions."

Film reviews are grouped under "Moving Picture Reviews" with separate lists for documentaries and foreign films.

See also BRITISH HUMANITIES INDEX and READERS' GUIDE TO
PERIODICAL LITERATURE, above, and SUBJECT INDEX TO PERI-
ODICALS, below.

SUBJECT INDEX TO PERIODICALS. London: Library Association, 1915/16-61.

Has entries under "Theatre" and also "Cinema."

Continued by BRITISH HUMANITIES INDEX. (See above.)

Temple, Ruth Z., ed. A LIBRARY OF LITERARY CRITICISM: MODERN
BRITISH LITERATURE. 3 vols. New York: Ungar, 1966.

Excerpts from literary reviews, arranged under author, including a
few twentieth-century playwrights. Bibliography.

THEATRE MAGAZINE. A SELECTIVE INDEX.

See Cornyn, Stan, above.

The Times (London). INDEX TO THE 'TIMES,' 1906-   . London: Times,
1907-   .

Title and frequency have varied. Indexes final edition mainly.
After December 1949 see heading "Drama"; before that date, see
"Theatrical Productions."

See also PALMER'S INDEX TO THE 'TIMES,' above.

Toohey, John L. A HISTORY OF THE PULITZER PRIZE PLAYS. New York:
Citadel Press, 1967. 344 p. Illustrated.

Each entry summarizes a play and tells cast, length of run, and
sources of reviews, with excerpts. There is a list of the year's
"also rans." Index.

Wall, C. Edward.

See POOLE'S INDEX TO PERIODICAL LITERATURE. CUMULATIVE
AUTHOR INDEX, 1803-1906, above.

Welker, David, ed. EDUCATIONAL THEATRE JOURNAL: A TEN-YEAR
INDEX, 1949-1958. East Lansing, Mich.: American Educational Theatre
Association, 1959. 84 p.

Indexes this journal only. Reviews and articles on stage, radio,
television, and film are listed by subject, title, and author,
interfiled.

WORLD PREMIERES. Paris: International Theatre Institute, 1949-   . Monthly.
(Title has varied.)

Successor to BULLETIN OF THE INTERNATIONAL THEATRE IN-
STITUTE. Surveys theater in fifty countries. A section which
reports on premieres has had various titles. Items typically include
plot summaries, place and date of first performance, and reference
to reviews in periodicals. Some years had annual indexes.

Continued by INTERNATIONAL THEATRE INFORMATIONS (Paris:
International Theatre Institute). The review feature has been continued in this bilingual (French and English) quarterly from 1964 on.

Writers' Program of the Works Progress Administration (New York). THE FILM
INDEX, A BIBLIOGRAPHY. Edited by Harold Leonard. New York: The
Museum of Modern Art and H.W. Wilson Co., 1941. Vol. I: THE FILM AS
ART. 723 p. (No more published.)

Annotations for more than 8,000 books and periodical articles.
Part I, "History and Technique"; Part II, "Types of Film." The
latter includes both documentary and entertainment films. A
section on adaptations shows sources in drama, fiction, etc.
See also Enser, A.G.S., in Part II-A of this Guide.

Reviews are cited in Part II of THE FILM INDEX, but see also
Part I for volumes of collected film criticism.

Part VI

BIBLIOGRAPHIES, INDEXES, AND ABSTRACTS

The general reader, as well as the student of the performing arts, may at some time want numerous references to esthetic, biographical, historical, or technical material. Such information possibly is too recent or too specialized to be found in encyclopedias and surveys. Usually, then, the reader should consult bibliographies, old or new, pertaining to some aspect of the performing arts. He will use periodical indexes, especially for recent material; and sometimes abstracts will shorten his path.

Part VI of this volume describes such aids. In Section A (which has five subdivisions) are listed those works which pertain to the stage, motion pictures, musical theater, and related arts; in Section B, those concerned with literature. (Items treating both subjects are assigned to Section A.) Section C, listing only bibliographies of dissertations and theses on drama, theater, and related subjects, will interest the advanced graduate student.

Some of the following items were described earlier; for example, a work leading to play reviews is annotated in Part V and, if useful in other ways, now reappears as a cross-reference.

Because of the recent upsurge of publication on the performing arts, Part VI must be selective. The attempt has been made to include the most useful indexes and abstracts, regardless of their starting date. Bibliographies, however, are limited to a few older works and to a much larger number published between 1952 and 1973. For further information about older works, consult Blanch M. Baker and others. (See Part I.)

The situation is enriched and complicated by the interrelationships of theater and such subjects as art, architecture, archaeology, music, literature, rhetoric, and social history, all with intricacies of their own. The reader in these fringe areas must explore, first referring to major guides for these subjects, as suggested in Part I. Beyond the help they give, some of the bibliographies, indexes, and abstracts discussed below will open broad new roads.

A. THEATER AND RELATED ARTS

BIBLIOGRAPHIES

The five-volume work of Theodore Besterman is a master key to bibliographies, old and new. Current issues and cumulated volumes of BIBLIOGRAPHIC IN-DEX carry the record forward. See the annotations below.

FESTSCHRIFTEN

For a discussion of the bibliographic control of these publications (also known as homage studies or melanges), see the headnote in Part VI-B.

JOURNAL ARTICLES

There is no one entirely satisfactory index to current periodical publication on the performing arts. The best general access is available through use of the GUIDE TO THE PERFORMING ARTS, together with MUSIC INDEX, supplemented, for coverage of popular magazines, by the READERS' GUIDE TO PERIODICAL LITERATURE. International indexing in the English language needs to be improved. The INTERNATIONAL INDEX TO FILM PERIODICALS (1972-   .) is a welcome addition, and the new FILM LITERATURE INDEX looks promising. See the annotations below.

NEW BOOKS AND BOOK REVIEWS

There are many approaches to new and forthcoming books, such as the "trade bibliographies" in Great Britain, the United States, and other language areas. These do not evaluate, nor are they selective. The scholar will seek a selective list such as the "Bibliographie," an annual checklist in the journal REVUE D'HISTOIRE DU THEATRE or, perhaps, one limited to English-language books, in MODERN DRAMA. From 1948 on, the SHAKESPEARE SURVEY has included "The Year's Contributions to Shakespeare Studies." Similarly, the YEAR'S WORK IN MODERN LANGUAGE STUDIES (MHRA) and the YEAR'S WORK IN ENGLISH STUDIES (English Association) evaluate new work in those fields. (See Part VI-B, below.)

The Music Library Association's journal NOTES carries in each quarterly issue an extensive checklist of recent books on music, musical theater, dance, and related matters. Also broad in scope is the ANNOTATED BIBLIOGRAPHY OF NEW PUBLICATIONS IN THE PERFORMING ARTS. See below.

As some of these annotate briefly or not at all, book reviews are needed, too. Some are cited in indexes such as GUIDE TO THE PERFORMING ARTS, ART INDEX, MUSIC INDEX, and EDUCATION INDEX. The ANNUAL BIBLIOG-

RAPHY OF ENGLISH LANGUAGE AND LITERATURE (MHRA) mentions some reviews along with notice of a book's publication.

The NEW YORK TIMES BOOK REVIEW INDEX, 1896-1970, edited by Wingate Froscher in five volumes (New York: Arno, 1973) cites reviews from the NEW YORK TIMES only.

It is usually efficient to consult first the general book review indexes, of which BOOK REVIEW DIGEST is most current. Its usefulness is enhanced by the printing of excerpts from reviews. This index is limited to English-language books distributed in the United States. BOOK REVIEW INDEX and the INDEX TO BOOK REVIEWS IN THE HUMANITIES point out reviews in a wide variety of periodicals, without excerpts. The last-mentioned is especially helpful to scholars, as it shows reviews in selected foreign journals. An extensive international index to book reviews is the INTERNATIONALE BIBLIOGRAPHIE DER REZENSIONEN. However, entries are in German, and the journals cited range from general to special and very obscure. This tool is practical mainly for scholars with access to interlibrary loan or to a major library.

Most of these general book review indexes are available in reference collections of large libraries and are not further described in this guide.

1. General

American Community Theatre Association.

> See Biddulph, Helen R., below.

American Educational Theatre Association. A BIBLIOGRAPHY OF THEATRE ARTS PUBLICATIONS IN ENGLISH. Washington, D.C.: A.E.T.A., 1937-65. (Title has varied.)

> By various compilers, listed in order of publication, titles are as follows:

> McDowell, John, and McGaw, Charles J., comps. A BIBLIOGRAPHY ON THE THEATER AND DRAMA IN AMERICAN COLLEGES AND UNIVERSITIES, 1937-1947. New York: Speech Association of America, 1949. 124 p.

> > Annotations for books, articles, dissertations, and theses.

> Melnitz, William W., comp. THEATRE ARTS PUBLICATIONS IN THE UNITED STATES, 1947-1952; A FIVE-YEAR BIBLIOGRAPHY. A.E.T.A. Monograph, no. 1, Washington, D.C.: A.E.T.A., 1959. 91 p.

An unannotated checklist of 4,000 books, articles, and newspaper items. Excludes play reviews and unpublished dissertations.

Mauk, E.P. "Addenda to A.E.T.A. Monograph no. 1." EDUCA-TIONAL THEATRE JOURNAL 14 (1962): 324-31.

Covers the same years as Melnitz, William W., above, but shows articles only.

Busfield, Roger M., ed. THEATRE ARTS PUBLICATIONS AVAIL-ABLE IN THE UNITED STATES, 1953-1957; A FIVE-YEAR BIBLIOG-RAPHY. Washington, D.C.: A.E.T.A. Bibliography Project, 1964. 188 p.

Unannotated list of books and articles in English pub-lished in Canada, Great Britain, and the United States.

Dukore, Bernard F., ed. BIBLIOGRAPHY OF THEATRE ARTS PUBLICATIONS IN ENGLISH, 1963. Washington, D.C.: A.E.T.A. Bibliography Project, 1965. 82 p.

Unannotated list of books, including single plays and anthologies, as well as articles in forty-two periodicals. This publication was intended as an annual under varied editorship, but was not continued.

See also ANNOTATED BIBLIOGRAPHY OF NEW PUB-LICATIONS IN THE PERFORMING ARTS, below.

Angotti, Vincent L. SOURCE MATERIALS IN THE FIELD OF THEATRE; AN ANNOTATED BIBLIOGRAPHY AND SUBJECT INDEX TO THE MICROFILM COLLECTION. Ann Arbor, Mich.: University Microfilms Library Service, [1967]. 73 p.

A complementary guide to the microfilm collection, compiled by University Microfilms. Eighty books, periodicals, manuscripts, journals, and diaries are contained in the microfilm collection, SOURCE MATERIALS IN THE FIELD OF THEATRE (twenty-two reels reproducing primary and secondary materials found in private collec-tions and American and foreign libraries).

Annotations consist of a summary and critical interpretation of each text. Incorrect pagination and other bibliographic errors or omis-sions in the original texts are clarified. Reel numbers are given. Subject index, pp. 69-73.

ANNOTATED BIBLIOGRAPHY OF NEW PUBLICATIONS IN THE PERFORMING ARTS. New York: Drama Book Shop, 1970- . Quarterly.

Classified, briefly annotated list of books published in England and the United States. Treats theater, with some coverage of costume, dance, motion pictures, radio, and television. Has a supplementary list of drama recordings.

Baker, Blanch M. THEATRE AND ALLIED ARTS.

See Part I-A.

_____, comp. DRAMATIC BIBLIOGRAPHY; AN ANNOTATED LIST OF BOOKS ON THE HISTORY AND CRITICISM OF THE DRAMA AND STAGE AND ON THE ALLIED ARTS OF THE THEATER. New York: H.W. Wilson, 1933. xvi, 320 p.

Classified, critically annotated bibliography, still useful for items omitted from Blanch M. Baker's THEATRE AND ALLIED ARTS, such as most works printed before 1885. Lists books and some monographs in series; also play collections and anthologies, a category omitted from THEATRE AND ALLIED ARTS. (See Part III, "Pageantry, Religious Drama, Entertainment," and Part IV, "Anthologies.")

Beaumont, Cyril William, comp. A BIBLIOGRAPHY OF DANCING. London: Dancing Times, 1929. Reprint. New York: Blom, 1963. 228 p.

Selective annotated list of books in the British Museum. Includes many rare ballet librettos and technical treatises. Has detailed notes on books which show dance steps. Subject index.

See also Leslie, Serge, below.

Besterman, Theodore. A WORLD BIBLIOGRAPHY OF BIBLIOGRAPHIES AND OF BIBLIOGRAPHICAL CATALOGUES, CALENDARS, ABSTRACTS, DIGESTS, INDEXES, AND THE LIKE. 4th ed., rev. and enl. 5 vols. Lausanne: Societas Bibliographica, 1965-66.

Major guide to bibliographies of all periods and on most subjects, in various languages. Most references are to books published through 1963, but some documents, society publications, and library book catalogs are shown. Also included are bibliographies of dissertations, found under the heading "Academic Writings."

Besterman's classification of subjects is helpful. Under such headings as "Drama and Stage," "Music," or "Opera," there are geographical and other subdivisions. Most entries are annotated. The fifth volume is an index of authors, editors, and translators.

See also BIBLIOGRAPHIC INDEX, below.

BIBLIOGRAPHIC INDEX; A CUMULATIVE BIBLIOGRAPHY OF BIBLIOGRAPHIES. New York: H.W. Wilson, 1938-   . Semiannual, with bound cumulation. (Frequency has varied.)

Under subjects are listed bibliographies separately issued or occurring as part of a book or pamphlet; also those found in more than 1,900 periodicals. Items contain at least fifty references. The scope is international, but material in East European languages is scant.

Bibliographies of dissertations appear under the heading "Dissertations, Academic." Note also the subheading "Research in Progress." Some entries refer to journals where dissertations are regularly listed.

See also Besterman, Theodore, above.

Biddulph, Helen R., and Mailer, Julia H., comps. BIBLIOGRAPHY OF BOOKS, PAMPHLETS, AND MAGAZINES RELATING TO COMMUNITY THEATRE. For the American Community Theatre Association. Washington, D.C.: A.E.T.A.?, 1966. 21 p.

This is a practical reference tool, with emphasis on ways and means in publicity, directing, acting, costume, stagecraft, and theater architecture. There are brief evaluations of current and out-of-print books and pamphlets in English. Periodicals list, pp. 20-21, also is limited to English.

BIOGRAPHY INDEX; A CUMULATIVE INDEX TO BIOGRAPHICAL MATERIAL IN BOOKS AND MAGAZINES. New York: H.W. Wilson, 1947-   . Quarterly, with annual and triennial cumulations.

Cites English-language biographies in book or chapter form, as well as prefaces in otherwise nonbiographical books; also journal entries derived from 1,700 periodicals scanned by the Wilson indexes and from other selected journals; NEW YORK TIMES obituaries are entered also.

Entries found under name of biographee. There is an occupational index.

See also NEW YORK TIMES OBITUARIES INDEX, 1858-1968, below.

Boston Public Library.   Allen A. Brown Collection.

See Part IV-A.

British Drama League.   The Players' Library.

See Part IV-A.

BRITISH HUMANITIES INDEX.

See Part V.

British Museum.   Department of Printed Books.   GENERAL CATALOGUE.

See Part IV-A.

BULLETIN OF BIBLIOGRAPHY AND MAGAZINE NOTES.

See Part V.

Chicorel, Marietta. CHICOREL BIBLIOGRAPHY TO THE PERFORMING ARTS. Chicorel index series, vol. 3A. Edited by Marietta Chicorel. New York: Chicorel Publishing Corp., 1972. 498 p.

Unannotated bibliography of books, mainly those published in the English language on drama and theater, but including also costume, dance, motion pictures, opera, puppets, and television. Arrangement is alphabetical under subject headings from "Acting" to "Tragedy." As some classifications have many subdivisions and one may question the classification, browsing is necessary. There is a specific table of contents, but no author-title index.

CIRCUS AND ALLIED ARTS.

See Part I-A.

CONTEMPORARY AUTHORS.

See the headnote in Part III.

CONTEMPORARY DRAMATISTS OF THE ENGLISH LANGUAGE. By James Vinson.

A bio-bibliography for 300 living playwrights, some of whom have also acted or directed.

For full annotation, see Part II-A.

Cornyn, Stan. A SELECTIVE INDEX TO 'THEATRE MAGAZINE.'

See Part V.

Crothers, J. Francis. PUPPETEER'S LIBRARY GUIDE; THE BIBLIOGRAPHIC INDEX TO THE LITERATURE OF THE WORLD PUPPET THEATRE.

See Part I-A.

CUMULATED DRAMATIC INDEX.

See Part I-A.

CURRENT BIOGRAPHY.

See the headnote in Part III.

Dodrill, Charles W. THEATRE MANAGEMENT: SELECTED BIBLIOGRAPHY. Washington, D.C.: American Educational Theatre Association, 1966. 10 p. Mimeographed.

>Entries, with short summaries, for various publications on front-of-the house management. (Not examined.)

>See also Georgi, Charlotte, below.

Du Bois, William R., comp. ENGLISH AND AMERICAN STAGE PRODUCTIONS: AN ANNOTATED CHECKLIST OF PROMPT BOOKS, 1800-1900, FROM THE NISBET-SNYDER DRAMA COLLECTION, NORTHERN ILLINOIS UNIVERSITY LIBRARIES. Boston: G.K. Hall, 1973. xiv, 524 p.

>A checklist of 2,000 editions of plays from late eighteenth to late nineteenth century, chiefly American or British, about 700 of which have additions handwritten by directors or players. Many of these are acting editions. Some are opera librettos.

>Both this compiler and Charles H. Shattuck (THE SHAKESPEARE PROMPTBOOKS, see below) define promptbooks loosely rather than in the ordinary theatrical meaning. Alphabetized under author, entries have bibliographical description and historical notes on licensing, productions, library editions, etc. Actors associated with the parts are named and the extent of written interpolations shown. Index of titles, authors, and other names.

EDUCATION INDEX; A CUMULATIVE AUTHOR AND SUBJECT INDEX TO A SELECTED LIST OF EDUCATIONAL PERIODICALS, BOOKS, AND PAMPHLETS. New York: H.W. Wilson, 1932- . Monthly, except July and August, with annual and biennial cumulations.

>Actual coverage begins with 1929 and is restricted to English-language materials. Scope has varied. Now primarily a periodical index. Volumes before 1961 included also books, pamphlets, and extensive analytics for material in books and society proceedings.

>Among journals indexed are EDUCATIONAL THEATRE JOURNAL and SPEECH TEACHER.

>See such subject headings as "Drama(s)," "Musical Comedies," "Operas," and "Theater(s)."

ESSAY AND GENERAL LITERATURE INDEX.

>See Part V.

Folger Shakespeare Library. CATALOG OF MANUSCRIPTS.

>Records numerous letters to and from theatrical celebrities, e.g., Augustin Daly, in addition to literary manuscripts held by the library.

>For full annotation of this catalog, see Part IV-A.

_____. CATALOG OF PRINTED BOOKS.

　　See Part IV-A.

Fuhrich, Fritz.

　　See Schindler, Otto G., below.

Georgi, Charlotte. THE ARTS AND THE WORLD OF BUSINESS; A SELECTED BIBLIOGRAPHY. Metuchen, N.J.: Scarecrow Press, 1973. 123 p.

　　Classified list treating business, legal, governmental, and social aspects of arts management, as pertaining to music, visual arts, and theater. Unannotated except for the list of journals and the helpful data on associations.

　　See also Dodrill, Charles W., above.

Gilder, Rosamond. A THEATRE LIBRARY; A BIBLIOGRAPHY OF ONE HUNDRED BOOKS RELATING TO THE THEATRE. New York: Theatre Arts, for the National Theatre Conference, 1932. 74 p.

　　Still useful for its evaluation of standard histories, reference books, and pictorial resources for theater research.

Griffin, Diane.

　　See Sumner, Mark Reese, below.

GUIDE TO DANCE PERIODICALS.

　　See Part V.

GUIDE TO THE PERFORMING ARTS.

　　See Part IV-A.

Leslie, Serge. A BIBLIOGRAPHY OF THE DANCE COLLECTION OF DORIS NILES AND SERGE LESLIE; ANNOTATED BY SERGE LESLIE AND EDITED BY CYRIL BEAUMONT. 2 vols. London: C.W. Beaumont (Dancing Times, Ltd.), 1966-68. (A third volume: A-Z, twentieth-century publications, is in preparation, 1973.)

　　Volume I: A-K; Volume II: L-Z. Evaluative notes on about 2,000 books in an important private collection. Entries include obscure ballet librettos, with synopses. Each volume has a subject index.

　　See also Beaumont, Cyril W. A BIBLIOGRAPHY OF DANCING, above.

Magriel, Paul David. A BIBLIOGRAPHY OF DANCING.

See Part I-B.

Nationalbibliothek, Vienna. KATALOGE DER THEATERSAMMLUNG DER NATIONALBIBLIOTHEK IN WEIN. 4 vols. in 2. Vienna: O. Hoefels, 1928-42. Illustrated.

Catalog of special theater collections in the Austrian national library in Vienna. Volume I: DIE ALTE BIBLIOTHEK, lists by title the first editions of plays in the "Old Library." Volume II is a catalog of drawings in the theater collection. This is illustrated with a few reproductions of designs by the Bibienas and others. Volume II also describes collections of silhouettes and figurines, indexed by persons and scenes depicted. Volume III is a history of the Theater in der Wiener Leopoldstadt, 1781-1860, followed by a list of the theater collections in the Nationalbibliothek. Volume IV is a catalog of the Josef Kainz bequest in the same library.

THE NATIONAL UNION CATALOG.

See Part IV-A.

NATIONAL UNION CATALOG OF MANUSCRIPT COLLECTIONS; BASED ON REPORTS FROM AMERICAN REPOSITORIES OF MANUSCRIPTS. Ann Arbor, Mich.: J.W. Edwards, 1962- .

Compiled by the Library of Congress. The first volume reproduced catalog cards for nearly 7,300 manuscript collections located in the United States as of 1959-61. Only collections with a large group of papers, usually having a common source and formed around an individual or a family, have been listed, with the exception of some "artificial collections" which group various materials under an appropriate theme. Archives were included only if found outside of normal repositories. Collections of transcripts or photocopies were usually excluded. All collections listed must be in public or quasi-public places that regularly admit researchers.

Entries are arranged in sequence by an assigned card number. Access to specific information is gained through use of the name, subject, and repository indexes. Papers of individuals are found in the name index. The subject index has entries for drama, dramatists, theater, and theaters, with city subdivision under "Theater."

Later volumes continue the plan, some also adding entries for holders of large collections of photocopies.

See also United States. National Historical Publications Commission, and Young, William C. AMERICAN THEATRICAL ARTS, both in Part III.

New York Public Library. CATALOG OF THE THEATRE AND DRAMA COL-
LECTIONS.

    See Part IV-A.

_____. DICTIONARY CATALOG OF THE DANCE COLLECTION. 10 vols.
Boston: G.K. Hall, 1974. To be supplemented.

    This work reflects all aspects of the dance and shows all forms of
materials on the dance in a major collection. The materials listed
include books, manuscripts, pamphlets, periodicals, motion picture
films, photographs, prints, original drawings and designs, scrap-
books, programs, playbills, notated dance scores, and taped interviews, as well as numerous entries for important articles in journals
and annuals. Author, title, and subject entries are arranged in one
alphabet and include both book and nonbook materials.

    The catalog will be found useful not only as a bibliographical
aid in identifying editions, but also for many quick reference
searches. For example, under a typical heading for a ballet,
APOLLO (Balanchine), there are notes concerning various productions, with dates, names of designers, etc.

NEW YORK TIMES DIRECTORY OF THE THEATER. Introduction by Clive
Barnes. New York: Arno Press, 1973. 1,009 p.

    A one-volume edition which includes the index and appendix from
the eight-volume set of NEW YORK TIMES THEATER REVIEWS
and some preliminary unpaged illustrated material (news clippings)
on awards. The main lists are a title index and a personal name
index, both showing where TIMES reviews occurred.

    See also NEW YORK TIMES THEATER REVIEWS, 1920-1970 in
Part V.

NEW YORK TIMES INDEX.

    See Part V.

    See also NEW YORK TIMES OBITUARIES INDEX, below, and
NEW YORK TIMES DIRECTORY OF THE THEATER, above.

NEW YORK TIMES OBITUARIES INDEX, 1858-1968. New York: New York
Times, 1970. 1,136 p.

    Name entries refer to news stories in the NEW YORK TIMES.
Some exclusions have been noted.

NINETEENTH-CENTURY READERS' GUIDE.

    See READERS' GUIDE TO PERIODICAL LITERATURE in Part IV-A.

Nisbet-Snyder Collection.

See DuBois, William R., above.

Northern Illinois University. DeKalb Library. Nisbet-Snyder Collection.

See Du Bois, William R., above.

POOLE'S INDEX.

Has numerous subject entries for drama, theater, theaters, and for authors, actors, and other celebrities. Of special interest for nineteenth-century studies.

See Part V.

THE READER'S ADVISER.

See Part IV-A.

READERS' GUIDE TO PERIODICAL LITERATURE.

See Part IV-A.

Rigdon, Walter, ed. THE BIOGRAPHICAL ENCYCLOPEDIA AND WHO'S WHO OF THE AMERICAN THEATRE.

Includes a long bibliography.

See Part II-A.

Schindler, Otto G. THEATERLITERATUR. EIN BIBLIOGRAPHISCHER BEHELF FUER DAS STUDIUM DER THEATERWISSENSCHAFT...MIT EINEM ANHANG: BIBLIOGRAPHIE ZUR OESTERREICHISCHEN THEATERGESCHICHTE, ZUGEST. VON FRITZ FUHRICH. 3 vols. Vienna: Institut fuer Theaterwissenschaft, 1973. 135 p.

Unannotated international bibliography, ambitious and up-to-date, marred by many misspellings. Intended as a guide for an introductory course in theater bibliography at the Institut. The classified arrangement proceeds from special to general problems, ending with current periodicals in Germany and abroad.

Focus is on legitimate theater, but dance, circus, musical theater, motion pictures, and radio are also treated, as well as psychology, education, and sociology.

The Anhang (appendix), a bibliography of Austrian theater history compiled by Fritz Fuhrich, deals with that country in general and then with its regions. Material from the preceding German work is not repeated.

Books, articles, and dissertations are included in both sections.

Secondary School Theatre Conference. SELECTED AND ANNOTATED BIBLIOG-
RAPHY FOR THE SECONDARY SCHOOL THEATRE TEACHER AND STUDENT.
Washington, D.C.: American Educational Theatre Association, 1968. 70 p.

(Not examined.)

Shattuck, Charles Harlen. THE SHAKESPEARE PROMPTBOOKS: A DESCRIPTIVE
CATALOGUE. Urbana, Ill.: University of Illinois Press, 1965. 553 p.

About 2,000 "promptbooks" are described in detail, with notes on
their ownership, use, and special features. The term "promptbook"
is defined loosely as "all marked copies of Shakespeare used in
English-language professional theater productions from the 1620's
to 1961, found in public collections or ... (at) the Old Vic or
the Festival Theatres at the three Stratfords."

Arrangement is under play titles. Note addenda. Library locations are shown. There is a register of U.S., British, and Canadian libraries with promptbook holdings, pp. 24-28. Pages 14-24
explain the symbols and abbreviations used in older promptbooks.

Index of actors, authors, designers, directors, managers, and
prompters.

SOCIAL SCIENCES AND HUMANITIES INDEX.

See Part V.

Soleinne, Martineau de. BIBLIOTHEQUE DRAMATIQUE DE M. DE SOLEINNE.
CATALOGUE. Edited by P.L. Jacob. Paris: Administration de l'Alliance
des Arts, 1843-45. Reprint. 6 vols. in 5. New York, Franklin, 1967.

Catalog of an important theater collection, with its greatest
strength in French, and secondly, European theater. Ancient
and Oriental theater also are represented.

The French material includes ballet, court theater, educational
theater, burlesques, satires, etc. Treats provincial as well as
Parisian theater and ranges from olden times to Victor Hugo's day.

The catalog is difficult to use. Charles Brunet's list of theatrical
pieces described in the catalog (Paris: D. Morgand, 1914. 491 p.)
includes 5,000 titles and relates each to a number in the Soleinne
catalog.

SOURCE MATERIALS IN THE FIELD OF THEATRE.

See Angotti, Vincent L., above.

SUBJECT INDEX TO PERIODICALS.

See Part V.

Sumner, Mark Reese. A SELECTED BIBLIOGRAPHY ON OUTDOOR DRAMA. Institute of Outdoor Drama Bulletin no. 31. Revised by Diane Griffin. Chapel Hill, N.C.: Institute of Outdoor Drama, University of North Carolina, 1971. 16 p.

> Revised in 1971 by Diane Griffin. Shows books, articles, conference reports, theses, published scripts, as well as sources for souvenir programs. Limited to U.S. theater, except for one Canadian item.

TANZBIBLIOGRAPHIE; VERZEICHNIS DES DEUTSCHSPRACHIGEN SCHRIFT-TUMS UEBER DEN VOLKS-GESELLSCHAFTS-UND BUEHNENTANZ. Leipzig: Bibliographisches Institut, 1966- . (To be completed in fifteen to eighteen parts.)

> Shows books and periodical articles in German on the dance, folk, social, and theatrical. Items are classified and briefly annotated. Library locations are given.

> Music, costume, decor, pantomime, and theatrical dance will be treated, and indexes of authors and subjects will be provided.

TEATRAL'NAIA ENTSIKLOPEDIA.

> Includes bibliographies, in Russian.

> See annotation in Part II-A.

THEATRE DOCUMENTATION. Vols. 1-4. New York: Theatre Library Association, Fall 1968-1971/72. Semiannual.

> Volume 1, number 2 included a "Checklist of Current Theatre Arts Publications," which was a list of serial holdings in the New York Public Library, pertaining to theater in the broad sense.

THEATRE, DRAMA, AND SPEECH INDEX. Crete, Nebr.: Drama and Speech Information Center, April 1974- . Triannual, with annual cumulations.

> Available in a combined form or in separate editions devoted respectively to speech and to drama and theater.

> The intent is to index approximately sixty journals from various countries. The editors plan to add references to bibliographies, pamphlets, and unpublished research.

THE TIMES (London). INDEX TO THE 'TIMES.'

> See Part V.

U.S. Copyright Office. CATALOG OF COPYRIGHT ENTRIES. DRAMAS AND WORKS PREPARED FOR ORAL DELIVERY.

> See Part IV-A.

Welker, David, ed. EDUCATIONAL THEATRE JOURNAL: A TEN-YEAR INDEX, 1949-1958.

See Part V.

WHO'S WHO.

See the headnote in Part III.

WHO'S WHO IN AMERICA.

See the headnote in Part III.

2. Special: National, Ethnic, Historical

African Bibliographic Center. THE BEAT GOES ON; A SELECTIVE GUIDE TO RESOURCES ON AFRICAN MUSIC AND DANCE, 1965-1967. Current Reading List Series, vol. 6, no. 2. New York: African Bibliographic Center, 1967. 14 p.

Not examined.

_____. PHASE 2 OF THE BEAT GOES ON; A SELECTIVE GUIDE TO RESOURCES ON AFRICAN MUSIC AND DANCE, 1968. New York: African Bibliographic Center, 1969. 71 p.

Not examined.

See also East, N.B., AFRICAN THEATRE, below.

Allevy, Marie-Antoinette. LA MISE EN SCENE EN FRANCE DANS LA PREMIERE MOITIE DU XIXe SIECLE. Bibliotheque de la Societe des Historiens du Theatre, no. 10. Paris: Droz, 1938. 245 p.

Treatise on theater in France in the first half of the nineteenth century, with a classified bibliography, partly annotated. Relates to production, settings, artists, and the Parisian social milieu.

AMERICAN PERIODICAL SERIES, EIGHTEENTH CENTURY. Ann Arbor, Mich.: University Microfilms, 1942?. 33 reels.

This microfilm series reproduces contents of selected American periodicals and is continued by AMERICAN PERIODICAL SERIES--1800-1850. (Ann Arbor: University Microfilms, 1946-   ).

An index on microcards covers both series. See EARLY AMERICAN PERIODICALS. INDEX TO 1850, below.

ANNALS OF THE NEW YORK STAGE.

See Odell, George Clinton Densmore, below.

L'ANNEE PHILOLOGIQUE; BIBLIOGRAPHIE CRITIQUE ET ANALYTIQUE DE L'ANTIQUITE GRECO-LATINE. Paris: Societe d'Edition "Les Belles Lettres," 1928- . Annual.

> References to books, articles, and dissertations on classical antiquity, some of which relate to theater or drama. A section concerned with literary authors, alphabetically listed, is followed by a classified section including such subjects as "Archaeology," "Civilization," and "Religion," where theater-related entries can be found. Most entries are in French. Some are for publications earlier than the current year. There are indexes.
>
> See also Rounds, Dorothy, below.

Arnold, Robert Franz. BIBLIOGRAPHIE DER DEUTSCHEN BUEHNEN SEIT 1830. Strassburg: K.J. Truebner, 1909. 57 p.

> Under names of cities, Arnold lists works pertaining to theater buildings, theatrical seasons, or personalities of the theater throughout Germany from 1830 to 1909. Exluded are documents, municipal histories, travel diaries, and most almanacs or yearbooks. Name index.

Arnott, James Fullerton, and Robinson, John W., eds. ENGLISH THEATRICAL LITERATURE, 1559-1900: A BIBLIOGRAPHY. London: Society for Theatre Research, 1970. 486 p.

> Arnott and Robinson have revised and augmented Robert W. Lowe's A BIBLIOGRAPHICAL ACCOUNT OF ENGLISH THEATRICAL LITERATURE FROM THE EARLIEST TIMES TO THE PRESENT DAY (London: Nimmo, 1888. 384 p.). There are more than 4,500 entries for books, pamphlets, broadsides, manuscript letters, legal documents, society reports, etc., in classified arrangement, and a separate list of periodicals. Library locations for these materials in Great Britain and the United States are given.

Bentley, Gerald Eades. THE JACOBEAN AND CAROLINE STAGE.

> See Part IV-A.

Bergeron, David Moore. TWENTIETH-CENTURY CRITICISM OF ENGLISH MASQUES, PAGEANTS, AND ENTERTAINMENTS: 1558-1642...WITH A SUPPLEMENT ON THE FOLK-PLAY AND RELATED FORMS. By Harry B. Caldwell. Checklists in Humanities and Education. San Antonio, Tex.: Trinity University Press, c.1972. 67 p.

> Unannotated references to selected books and journal articles. Fullest treatment of Jonson and of Milton's COMUS. Supplement, pp. 41-49. Author index.
>
> See also Sibley, Gertrude Marian; and Steele, Mary Susan, below.

Birmingham Shakespeare Library. CATALOG.

See Part IV-A.

Caldwell, Harry B.

See Bergeron, David Moore, above.

Chambers, Edmund K. THE ELIZABETHAN STAGE.

See Part IV-A.

Coleman, Edward D. THE JEW IN ENGLISH DRAMA; AN ANNOTATED BIB-
LIOGRAPHY. WITH A PREFACE BY JOSHUA BLOCH. THE JEW IN WESTERN
DRAMA: AN ESSAY AND CHECKLIST (1968) BY EDGAR ROSENBERG. New
York: New York Public Library, 1970. 50 p. xx, 265 p.

Edgar Rosenberg's essay, "The Jew in Western civilization," is
followed by a preface and by Coleman's bibliography, which is
a classified, annotated list in three parts: Earliest times to 1837;
1838-1914; 1915-38. Author entries show first editions and performances, selected reviews, and locations of published plays and
typescripts in British libraries. All plays involve Jewish characters
or are translations from Hebrew or Yiddish.

Cotarelo y Mori, Emilio. Teatro ESPANOL.

See Part IV-B.

Dahlmann, Friedrich Christoph. QUELLENKUNDE DER DEUTSCHEN GESCHICHTE;
BIBLIOGRAPHIE DER QUELLEN UND DER LITERATUR ZUR DEUTSCHEN GESCH-
ICHTE. 10th ed. Edited by Hermann Heimpel and Herbert Geuss. Stuttgart:
Hiersemann, 1965- .

Includes a nineteen-page unannotated bibliography, edited by
Alexander and Baerbel Rudin, which pertains to theater and dance
and has excellent retrospective coverage of books, articles and
dissertations. Most items refer to German theater.

There are also short lists (under section 54) for motion pictures and
(under section 55) for radio.

Delannoy, J.C. BIBLIOGRAPHIE FRANCAISE DU CIRQUE. Paris: Odette
Lieutier, 1944. 74 p.

Lists published plays and pantomimes as well as books and articles
on the circus and the "theatre de la foire."

See also CIRCUS AND ALLIED ARTS in Part I-A.

DRAMA CYCLOPEDIA.

See Sherman, Robert L., below.

EARLY AMERICAN PERIODICALS. INDEX TO 1850. New York: Readex Microprint, 1964.

> This index contains 1,074 microcards reproducing the 650,000 catalog cards of an index at New York University Library. This special catalog lists contents of a group of American periodicals, 1728 to 1850, in a classified arrangement. Under "General Prose" and "Subjects," some interesting background material may be found.

> The periodicals themselves are being made available on microfilm. See AMERICAN PERIODICAL SERIES, EIGHTEENTH CENTURY, etc., above.

East, N.B., ed. AFRICAN THEATRE; A CHECKLIST OF CRITICAL MATERIALS. New York: Africana Publishing Corp., 1970. 47 p.

> Updated from a similar list in the spring 1969 issue of AFRO-ASIAN THEATRE BULLETIN. References, which are unannotated, extend from the 1920s to the late 1960s, emphasizing the last two decades. Journals referred to are mainly in English or French. Some materials mentioned treat African dance or motion pictures, but most deal with the stage, including drama in the marketplace but excluding rituals and festival drama.

> See also African Bibliographic Center. THE BEAT GOES ON, above.

Ettlinger, Amrei. RUSSIAN LITERATURE, THEATRE, AND ART.

> See Part IV-A.

Evans, Charles, AMERICAN BIBLIOGRAPHY.

> See Part IV-A.

Forrester, Felicitee Sheila. BALLET IN ENGLAND: A BIBLIOGRAPHY AND SURVEY, c. 1700–JUNE 1966. Library Association Bibliographies, no. 9. London: Library Association, 1968. 224 p. Illustrated.

> Annotated, illustrated guide to books and articles.

> Includes a directory of libraries and collections and a list of exhibitions. Indexes.

Gohdes, Clarence. LITERATURE AND THEATER OF THE STATES AND REGIONS OF THE U.S.A.; AN HISTORICAL BIBLIOGRAPHY. Durham, N.C.: Duke University Press, 1967. 276 p.

> Selective checklist of books, articles, and some newspaper items and pamphlets dealing with local theater and literature. Arrangement is geographical. No entries for individual authors or productions.

See also Stratman, Carl J. BIBLIOGRAPHY OF THE AMERICAN THEATER, below.

Hatch, James Vernon. THE BLACK IMAGE ON THE AMERICAN STAGE; A BIBLIOGRAPHY OF PLAYS AND MUSICALS, 1770-1970. New York: D.B.S. Publications, 1970. 162 p.

> Plays by or about blacks, written or produced in America from 1767 to 1970. Includes singly published plays as well as those in collections, series, or periodicals. Arrangement is roughly chronological. Title and author indexes.

Hebblethwaite, Frank P., comp. A BIBLIOGRAPHICAL GUIDE TO THE SPANISH AMERICAN THEATER. Basic Bibliographies, no. 6. Washington, D.C.: Pan American Union, Division of Philosophy and Letters, 1969. 84 p.

> References to materials in the Library of Congress and at the Pan American Union. Books and articles listed separately, with critical comment. Author index.

> See also Grismer, Raymond L., in Part VI-B, below.

Hogan, Charles Beecher. SHAKESPEARE IN THE THEATRE, 1701-1800. 2 vols. Oxford: Clarendon Press, 1952-57.

> Each volume has a chronological list of performances in London, Volume I: 1701-50; Volume II: 1751-1800. Also, each has an alphabetical list of plays, showing casts for all performances, based on available records. Appendices show London theaters in use, charts of Shakespeare's popularity and of the relative popularity of his various plays. Gives box office receipts.

> There are indexes of actors (naming parts) and of characters (naming actors who played them). No reviews are shown.

Huerta, Jorge A., ed. A BIBLIOGRAPHY OF CHICANO AND MEXICAN DANCE, DRAMA, AND MUSIC. Oxnard, Calif.: Colegio Quetzalcoatl, 1972. 59 p.

> Contains three unannotated lists, dance, drama, and music, with the subheadings pre-Columbian, Mexican, and Aztlan. Includes books, journal articles, and a few recordings.

Loewenberg, Alfred, comp. THE THEATRE OF THE BRITISH ISLES, EXCLUDING LONDON; A BIBLIOGRAPHY. Society for Theatre Research Annual for 1948-49. London: Society for Theatre Research, 1950. 75 p.

> About 1,500 classified entries for books, articles, and library collections of playbills, manuscripts, etc. All items concern British regional theater. Play reviews are excluded. Indexes.

> See also Arnott, James Fullerton, and Robinson, John W., above.

THE LONDON STAGE, 1660-1800: A CALENDAR OF PLAYS, ENTERTAIN-
MENTS, AND AFTERPIECES, TOGETHER WITH CASTS, BOX-RECEIPTS, AND
CONTEMPORARY COMMENT. COMPILED FROM THE PLAYBILLS, NEWS-
PAPERS, AND THEATRICAL DIARIES OF THE PERIOD. 11 vols. Carbondale:
Southern Illinois University Press, 1960-70. Illustrated.

> Planned to correct and supplement John Genest's SOME ACCOUNT
> OF THE ENGLISH STAGE, FROM THE RESTORATION IN 1660 TO
> 1830. (10 vols. Bath, Eng.: H.E. Carrington, 1832).

> A chronology of London theatrical seasons, 1660-1800, listing
> plays, with casts, etc. Each volume has an index.

> See also Summers, Montague, in Part IV-A.

Lowe, Robert W. A BIBLIOGRAPHICAL ACCOUNT OF ENGLISH THEATRICAL
LITERATURE FROM THE EARLIEST TIMES TO THE PRESENT DAY. London:
John C. Nimmo, 1888. 384 p.

> This respected older work has been revised and updated. See
> Arnott, James Fullerton, above.

McCready, Warren T. BIBLIOGRAFIA TEMATICA DE ESTUDIOS SOBRE EL
TEATRO ESPANOL ANTIGUO. Toronto: University of Toronto Press, 1966.
445 p.

> Primarily an unannotated classified list of journal articles, essays
> in Festschriften, and scholarly book reviews, all concerned with
> theater and drama in Spain from earliest times through the Golden
> Age. Also cited are plays found in periodicals as well as separate
> editions of dramatic works, with references to reviews.

McPharlin, Marjorie Batchelder.

> See McPharlin, Paul, below.

McPharlin, Paul. THE PUPPET THEATRE IN AMERICA: A HISTORY, 1524-
1948, WITH A SUPPLEMENT, PUPPETS IN AMERICA SINCE 1948. Supplement
by Marjorie Batchelder McPharlin. Boston: Plays, Inc., 1969. 734 p.
Illustrated.

> Historical treatise, with an extensive list of puppeteers from 1524
> to 1948.

> The SUPPLEMENT (pp. 485-734) contains a selective classified list
> (pp. 655-89) of books in various languages but mainly in English,
> not limited to post-1948 works. Stresses relationship of puppetry
> to the fine arts.

Mikhail, E.H. BIBLIOGRAPHY OF MODERN IRISH DRAMA, 1899-1970.
London: Macmillan, 1972. 51 p.

> A checklist of approximately 600 items under headings for bibliog-

raphies, books, periodical articles, and unpublished material. Items have both literary and theatrical interest.

Nicoll, Allardyce. ENGLISH DRAMA, 1900-1930; THE BEGINNINGS OF THE MODERN PERIOD. Cambridge, Eng.: At the University Press, 1973. 1,083 p.

A history followed by a handlist of plays from 1900 to 1930, on pp. 451-1048; addenda, pp. 1049-53. The list shows theater where first performance occurred. Unannotated. No editions shown.

Odell, George Clinton Densmore. ANNALS OF THE NEW YORK STAGE. 15 vols. New York: Columbia University Press, 1927-49. Illustrated. Reprint. New York: AMS Reprint, 1970.

The period treated is from about 1699 to 1894. Detailed account of plays, actors, and theaters in historical context. Index of names and titles.

In 1963 the American Society for Theatre Research published a separate INDEX TO THE PORTRAITS IN ODELL'S 'ANNALS OF THE NEW YORK STAGE.'

Rela, Walter. CONTRIBUCION A LA BIBLIOGRAFIA DEL TEATRO CHILENO.

See Part IV-B.

RESTORATION AND EIGHTEENTH-CENTURY THEATRE RESEARCH.

See Stratman, Carl J., et al., below.

Rosenberg, Edgar.

See Coleman, Edward D., above.

Rounds, Dorothy. ARTICLES ON ANTIQUITY IN FESTSCHRIFTEN, AN INDEX; THE ANCIENT NEAR EAST, THE OLD TESTAMENT, GREECE, ROME, ROMAN LAW, BYZANTIUM. Cambridge, Mass.: Harvard University Press, 1962. 560 p.

International list extending through 1954. Subject and author entries are interfiled. Library locations are given.

See entries for "Drama(s)," "Theater(s)," and names of playwrights.

Rudin, Alexander, and Rudin, Baerbel.

See Dahlmann, Friedrich Christoph, above.

Sherman, Robert L. DRAMA CYCLOPEDIA; A BIBLIOGRAPHY OF PLAYS AND

PLAYERS. Chicago: The Author, 1944. 612 p.

Alphabetical title list of plays professionally produced in the
United States from 1750 to 1940, showing year of first performance
and naming author and principal actor. Inaccurate in some details.

No locations given for library copies. No editions described.

Sibley, Gertrude Marian. THE LOST PLAYS AND MASQUES, 1500-1642.
Cornell Studies in English, no. 19. Ithaca, N.Y.: Cornell University Press,
1933. 205 p. Reprint. New York: Russell and Russell, 1971.

Title list, showing first performance and/or contemporary references
in British advertisements, literary works, or the STATIONERS'
REGISTER. Scholarly opinion also cited. Index of playwrights.

Cf. Bentley, Gerald Eades; and Harbage, Alfred, in Part IV-A,
as well as Bergeron, David Moore, above, and Steele, Mary Susan,
below.

Society for Theatre Research. THE THEATRE OF THE BRITISH ISLES.

See Loewenberg, Alfred, above.

Sper, Felix. THE PERIODICAL PRESS OF LONDON, THEATRICAL AND
LITERARY (EXCLUDING THE DAILY NEWSPAPER), 1800-1830. Boston: F.W.
Faxon, 1937. 58 p.

A finding list for weeklies and other journals owned by a few
scholarly libraries in Great Britain and the United States. Some
of these sources may also be available in various microform series.

See also Stratman, Carl J. BRITAIN'S THEATRICAL PERIODICALS,
in Part I-H, and TERCENTENARY HANDLIST, below, and Arnott,
James Fullerton, above.

Steele, Mary Susan. PLAYS AND MASQUES AT COURT DURING THE REIGNS
OF ELIZABETH, JAMES, AND CHARLES. Cornell Studies in English, no. 10.
New Haven: Yale University Press, 1926. 300 p. Reprint. New York:
Russell and Russell, 1968.

Chronological entries from 1558 to 1642, with notes and references
to historical sources and to criticism. Author and title indexes.

See also Bentley, Gerald Eades; Greg, Walter W.; and Harbage,
Alfred, in Part IV-A, and Bergeron, David Moore; and Sibley,
Gertrude Marian, above.

Stratman, Carl J. BIBLIOGRAPHY OF MEDIEVAL DRAMA.

See Part IV-A.

_____. A BIBLIOGRAPHY OF THE AMERICAN THEATRE, EXCLUDING NEW

YORK CITY. Chicago: Loyola University Press, 1965. 397 p.

> Limited to regional theater and classified geographically; annotations are given for articles, books, dissertations, and theses. Omitted are play reviews and references to motion pictures, radio, and television. Some library locations shown. Indexes.

> See also Gohdes, Clarence, above.

_____. BRITAIN'S THEATRICAL PERIODICALS.

> See Part I-H.

Stratman, Carl J., et al. RESTORATION AND EIGHTEENTH CENTURY THEATRE RESEARCH; A BIBLIOGRAPHICAL GUIDE, 1900-1968. Carbondale: Southern Illinois University Press, 1971. 811 p.

> Classified under subjects are more than 6,000 books, articles, theses, and dissertations completed between 1900 and 1968. Most items are annotated. Index of authors, subjects, and titles interfiled.

TERCENTENARY HANDLIST OF ENGLISH AND WELSH NEWSPAPERS, MAGAZINES, AND REVIEWS. 1920. Reprint. London: Dawsons, 1966. 324 p.

> Chronological list spanning 1620 to 1920, showing varying titles and dates of publication for each periodical. Shows library holdings of these periodicals in the Bodleian Library, the British Museum, and other British collections. Section I: London and Suburbs. Section II: The Provincial Press. Title index for each.

> See also Stratman, Carl J. BRITAIN'S THEATRICAL PERIODICALS in Part I-H, and Sper, Felix, above.

White, Beatrice. AN INDEX, COMP. BY BEATRICE WHITE TO 'THE ELIZABETHAN STAGE' AND 'WILLIAM SHAKESPEARE: A STUDY OF FACTS AND PROBLEMS,' BY SIR EDMUND CHAMBERS. Oxford: Clarendon Press, 1934. Reprint. New York: B. Blom Reprint, 1964. 161 p.

> Alphabetical list of persons, places, subjects, and titles, intended as a guide to these works of Edmund K. Chambers. Based on his indexes but amplified with players' names.

> See also Chambers, Edmund K., in Part IV-A.

Wicks, Charles Beaumont. THE PARISIAN STAGE: ALPHABETICAL INDEXES OF PLAYS AND AUTHORS. University of Alabama Studies, nos. 6, 8, 14, 17. 4 vols. Tuscaloosa: University of Alabama Press, 1950-67.

> Contents: Part 1, 1800-15; Part 2, 1816-30; Part 3, 1831-50; Part 4, 1851-75.

> Part 3 by Charles Beaumont Wicks and Jerome W. Schweitzer.

Theatrical productions in Paris are listed with title, author, theater, and date of premiere, etc. Short bibliographies.

Wilson, Sheila. THEATRE OF THE FIFTIES. Library Association Special Subject List, no. 40. London: Library Association, 1963. 64 p.

A basic list of reference works, journals, and annuals is followed by a classified, briefly annotated bibliography, with references to books and journal articles, predominantly in English, on world theater of the 1950s, with some British emphasis. Name index.

3. Music in the Theater

African Bibliographic Center. THE BEAT GOES ON and PHASE 2 OF THE BEAT GOES ON.

See Part VI-A2.

ANNALS OF OPERA, 1597–1940.

See Loewenberg, Alfred, below.

ANNOTATED BIBLIOGRAPHY OF NEW PUBLICATIONS IN THE PERFORMING ARTS.

A few items relate to music.

For full annotation, see Part VI-A1.

Bergeron, David Moore. TWENTIETH CENTURY CRITICISM OF ENGLISH MASQUES, PAGEANTS, AND ENTERTAINMENTS.

See Part VI-A2.

BIBLIOGRAPHIE DES MUSIKSCHRIFTTUMS. Published under auspices of the Institut fuer Musikforschung, Berlin. Frankfurt-am-Main: F. Hofmeister, 1937- . Annual.

Publication was suspended in 1940-49. After 1961 the bibliography was published by B. Schott, Mainz.

Edited after 1950 by Wolfgang Schmieder and usually associated with his name, this foremost German-language bibliography has unannotated entries for books and articles in scholarly musicological journals and other periodicals. Citations are in various languages; the headings are in German. Broad subject classification. Relates mainly to classical music. There is a short selective list of references on ballet, film music, musical comedy and other theater music, opera and operetta. See "Geschichte" (History); subdivision "Formen und Gattungen" (Forms and Genres). There are name and keyword indexes.

See also MUSIC INDEX, below.

Blume, Friedrich. DIE MUSIK IN GESCHICHTE UND GEGENWART.

Has notable scholarly bibliographies.

See Part II-B for full citation.

Boston Public Library. DICTIONARY CATALOG OF THE MUSIC COLLECTION. 20 vols. Boston: G.K. Hall, 1972.

Originated in a four-volume catalog of holdings of the Allen A. Brown bequest. The new catalog interfiles subject, author, and title entries representing four hundred years of music and music literature and is especially rich in nineteenth-century materials. Omitted are the library's sheet music and phonograph recordings as well as the Koussevitsky Archives.

Boustead, Alan, comp. MUSIC TO SHAKESPEARE, A PRACTICAL CATALOGUE OF CURRENT INCIDENTAL MUSIC, SONG SETTINGS, AND OTHER RELATED MUSIC. London: Novello; New York: Oxford University Press, 1964. 40 p.

Intended not as a complete catalog, but as a record of in-print or readily obtainable music. Has three divisions: "Plays," "Sonnets and Other Poems," and "Music of General Interest." Under play titles are listed song titles, with their variants; names of publishers are supplied. (Settings of adaptations of Shakespeare are not included.) Under the category "Other Music" are found the overtures, suites, and symphonic poems, etc., which have an association with each play. The section "Music of General Interest," p. 32, lists musical compositions with titles including mention of Shakespeare, e.g., R.W. Wood. SHAKESPEARE DANCES.

See also Long, John H., below.

British Broadcasting Corporation. Central Music Library. MUSIC LIBRARY CATALOGUES: CHORAL AND OPERA CATALOGUE. 2 vols. London: B.B.C., 1967.

An extensive catalog. Volume I: Composers; Volume II: Titles. Has 57,000 entries. Appendix 4: Libretti.

BRITISH UNION-CATALOGUE OF EARLY MUSIC PRINTED BEFORE THE YEAR 1801: A RECORD OF THE HOLDINGS OF OVER ONE HUNDRED LIBRARIES THROUGHOUT THE BRITISH ISLES. Edited by Edith B. Schnapper. 2 vols. London: Butterworth, 1957. xx, 1,178 p.

Entries under composer, anonymous title, and some keywords, e.g., "Shepherds" or "Shall" (as in "Shall Britain's sons disgrace their sires?") Periodicals shown under "Periodical Publications." Index of titles includes songs.

Library locations are shown.

Brown, Howard Myer. MUSIC IN THE FRENCH SECULAR THEATER, 1400–1550.
Cambridge, Mass.: Harvard University Press, 1963. 338 p.

> Treatise followed by a "Catalogue of Theatrical Chansons," with
> sources, pp. 181–282, and a bibliography, pp. 283–369, which
> concerns these songs but also relates to general study of the French
> secular theater from 1400 to 1550.

Brown University Library. Harris Collection. DICTIONARY CATALOG.

> Lists songsters, musical scores, and librettos, among other materials.

> See Part VI–B.

Caselli, Aldo. CATALOGO DELLE OPERE LIRICHE PUBBLICATE IN ITALIA.
Historiae Musicae Cultores Biblioteca, 27. Florence: Olschki, 1969. 894 p.

> Assembled alphabetically under composers' names are titles of
> operas which had their first performances in Italy, from the origin
> of opera to the present. Many entries, marked with asterisk, are
> based on Sonneck's catalog of librettos (pre-1800) housed in the
> Library of Congress. (See Sonneck, Oscar George Theodore, be-
> low.) Other sources used are acknowledged on p. 893.

> Entries show composer, title, librettist, city and theater where
> premiere took place, date, and a reference number to identify
> the entry.

> A list of cities repeats names of theaters and gives exact perfor-
> mance dates, if known. Alphabetical lists of titles and of libret-
> tists follow, each with reference numbers.

Clement, Felix, and Larousse, Pierre. DICTIONNAIRE DES OPERAS. Revised
by Arthur Pougin. Paris: Librairie Larousse, 1897. Reprint of 1905 revised
edition. 2 vols. New York: Da Capo, 1969.

> First published in 1869 as DICTIONNAIRE LYRIQUE; updated and
> revised in 1897 by Pougin under the title DICTIONNAIRE DES
> OPERAS, and again revised in 1905 (Paris: Librairie Larousse,
> 1,203 p.). Alphabetized by title are operas and comic operas
> performed in several countries from earliest times to 1905. Entry
> shows composer, librettist, number of acts, place and date of
> premiere and of some revivals. There are critical plot summaries.

> See also Towers, John; and Loewenberg, Alfred, below.

Davies, J.H. MUSICALIA: SOURCES OF INFORMATION IN MUSIC.

> Somewhat British in focus but full of good suggestions.

> See Part I–D.

Day, Cyrus Lawrence, and Murrie, Eleanore Boswell. ENGLISH SONGBOOKS,

1651-1702; A BIBLIOGRAPHY WITH A FIRST-LINE INDEX OF SONGS. London: Printed for the Bibliographical Society at the University Press, Oxford, 1940 [1937]. 439 p. Illustrated. Reprint. St. Clair Shores, Mich.: Scholarly Press, 1970. 439 p.

> Describes songbooks of England and Scotland containing two or more secular songs with both words and music. The listing is chronological. There are indexes of first lines, authors, composers, tunes, song collections, singers, and actors.

DIRECTORY OF AMERICAN CONTEMPORARY OPERAS. Central Opera Service Bulletin, vol. 10, no. 2. New York: Central Opera Service, 1967. 70 p.

> Lists more than 1,000 operas with information on casting, orchestration, libretto, premiere, and publisher.
>
> Limited to composers whose works were premiered after January 1, 1930.
>
> See also Drummond, Andrew H., below.

DIRECTORY OF ENGLISH OPERA TRANSLATIONS. Edited by Maria F. Rich. Central Opera Service Bulletin, vol. 16, no. 21. New York: Central Opera Service, 1974. 48 p.

> This is a revision of ENGLISH TRANSLATION OF FOREIGN LANGUAGE OPERAS (see below). This enlarged edition shows more than 500 operas in 1,245 translations.

DIRECTORY OF FOREIGN CONTEMPORARY OPERAS. Central Opera Service Bulletin, vol. 12, no. 2. New York: Central Opera Service, 1969. 66 p.

> Limited to composers whose works were premiered after January 1, 1950. Composers whose operatic premieres after 1950 were posthumous are not included.
>
> The DIRECTORY was issued as the "Annual Survey Issue" of the COS BULLETIN.
>
> Alphabetized under composers, the directory supplies nationality, date of completion for each work, librettist's name, literary or other source, length, place and date of premiere, North American premiere, college or other workshop production, and sources for scores. Appendix A gives addresses of publishers and other sources. Index of titles.

DISSERTATIONS, MUSICAL.

> See Part VI-C.

Drummond, Andrew H. AMERICAN OPERA LIBRETTOS. Metuchen, N.J.: Scarecrow Press, 1973. 277 p.

Discusses opera librettos by American composers from late nineteenth century to 1948, especially as used at the New York City
Opera, with a critical appraisal. Selected bibliography, pp. 147–
62.

Appendix A: Complete repertoire of the New York City Opera,
1948–71. Appendix B: Synopses. Index of authors, theaters,
newspapers, and subjects.

See also DIRECTORY OF AMERICAN CONTEMPORARY OPERAS,
above, and Johnson, Harold Earle, below.

Duckles, Vincent. "The Music for the Lyrics in Early Seventeenth Century
English Drama: a Bibliography of Primary Sources."

See Long, John H., below.

_____. MUSIC REFERENCE AND RESEARCH MATERIALS.

See Part I-D.

Eaton, Quaintance. OPERA PRODUCTION, A HANDBOOK. 2 vols. Minneapolis: University of Minnesota Press, 1961–74.

Information on production of contemporary operas and older works
in standard repertoire. More than 500 works are discussed in
Volume I, grouped in a main and a supplementary list. Entries
give synopsis, casting requirements, duration, sources for scores,
etc. Volume II adds a greater number of titles, old and new, all
in one list, under title.

ENCICLOPEDIA DELLO SPETTACOLO and AGGIORNAMENTO, 1955–1965.

See Part II-A.

ENGLISH TRANSLATION OF FOREIGN LANGUAGE OPERAS. New York:
Central Opera Service, 1966. For a new edition, see DIRECTORY OF EN-
GLISH OPERA TRANSLATIONS, above.

Fiske, Roger. ENGLISH THEATRE MUSIC IN THE EIGHTEENTH CENTURY,
London and New York: Oxford University Press, 1973. xv, 684 p. Illustrated.

A history of the period from 1695 to 1796. Appendix A: "Operas
That Survive Orchestrally"; Appendix B: "Theatre Overtures and
Ayres Published in Parts, 1698–1708"; Appendix C: "Theatre
Overtures Published in Parts, 1740–1800"; Appendix D: "Ballad
Operas Published with Their Airs, 1728–1736"; Appendix E; "Bor-
rowings, 1760–1800"; Appendix F: "Arne's 'The Fairy Prince'";
Appendix G: "The Singers." (Appendix G consists of biographi-
cal sketches.)

Bibliography, pp. 641–45. There are two indexes: "English Music

and Its Composers" (an alphabetical list of composers and titles);
general index.

Ford, Wyn Kelson. MUSIC IN ENGLAND BEFORE 1800: A SELECT BIBLIOG-
RAPHY. Library Association Bibliography, no. 7. London: Library Association, 1967. xiv, 128 p.

 Annotations for books and articles in English, French, or German,
 together with some unpublished dissertations, mainly those listed
 in Aslib's INDEX TO THESES (British). See Part VI-C.

 Ford's concern is music and its environment, beginning with the
 Middle Ages. Part I, "Music and its Environment," describes
 general works, some relating to musical instruments, e.g., the
 lute. There are also subsections on church music, social condi-
 tions of musicians, and royal music. These are followed by period
 subdivisions, with various topics, including "Music and Drama,"
 "Music and Shakespeare," and "Court Entertainments."

 Part II is a list of composers, with bibliographies.

Green, Stanley. THE WORLD OF MUSICAL COMEDY; THE STORY OF THE
AMERICAN MUSICAL STAGE AS TOLD THROUGH THE CAREERS OF ITS FORE-
MOST COMPOSERS AND LYRICISTS. New York: A.S. Barnes, 1968. 541 p.
Illustrated. 3d ed., rev. and enl., in prep. 1973. 556 p.

 Composers' careers and musical productions are discussed, as are
 those of the lyricists. An appendix lists productions by title,
 noting cast, opening date, length of run, credits for book and
 lyric, etc. Both Broadway and Off-Broadway musicals are shown.

Grout, Donald Jay. A SHORT HISTORY OF OPERA.

 Has a valuable and extensive bibliography.

 See Part I-D.

Grove, Sir George, ed. DICTIONARY OF MUSIC AND MUSICIANS.

 Has bibliographies.

 See Part II-B.

GUIDE TO THE MUSICAL ARTS.

 See Part V.

GUIDE TO THE PERFORMING ARTS.

 See Part IV-A.

Hatch, James Vernon. THE BLACK IMAGE ON THE AMERICAN STAGE.

Has some material on musical shows.

For full annotation, see Part VI-A2.

Haywood, Charles. A BIBLIOGRAPHY OF NORTH AMERICAN FOLKLORE AND FOLKSONG. New York: Greenberg, 1951. 2d rev. ed. New York: Dover, 1961.

> The Dover edition is an unabridged, corrected republication in two volumes of the first edition, to which has been added a new index supplement. Classified arrangement. Volume I: "The American people north of Mexico"; Volume II: "The American Indians north of Mexico, including the Eskimos."

> Printed music and recordings are among matters discussed. Indexes include song titles, authors, subjects, composers, arrangers, and performers; the last three groups found in an "Index Supplement" new in the Dover edition. See "Dance Music," "Dances," "Drama," and "Theater" in subject index.

> See also Lawless, Ray McKinley; and Lomax, Alan, and Cowell, Sidney Robertson, below.

Huerta, Jorge A. A BIBLIOGRAPHY OF CHICANO AND MEXICAN DANCE, DRAMA, AND MUSIC.

> See Part VI-A2.

Johnson, Harold Earle. OPERAS ON AMERICAN SUBJECTS. New York: Coleman-Ross Co., 1964. 125 p.

> Lists alphabetically the composers of various nationalities whose operas were based on Latin American or North American subjects. Provides some information on sources, performances, and published scores and librettos. Indexes of topics, locales, titles, as well as a general index.

> Cf. Drummond, Andrew H., above, and Sonneck, Oscar George Theodore. CATALOGUE OF OPERA LIBRETTOS PRINTED BEFORE 1800, in Part IV-A.

Kosch, Wilhelm. DEUTSCHES THEATER-LEXIKON.

> Has bibliographies on German theater, inclusive of its musical activities.

> See Part II-A.

Lawless, Ray McKinley. FOLKSINGERS AND FOLKSONGS IN AMERICA; A HANDBOOK OF BIOGRAPHY, BIBLIOGRAPHY, AND DISCOGRAPHY. Rev. ed. New York: Duell, Sloan, and Pearce, 1965. xviii, 750 p. Illustrations.

Lives of composers; miscellaneous material, on instruments, etc.;
discography; annotated list of published folksong collections. Indexes of names, titles, subjects.

See also Haywood, Charles, above, and Lomax, Alan, and Cowell,
Sidney Robertson, below.

Lewine, Richard, and Simon, Alfred. SONGS OF THE AMERICAN THEATER.

See Part II-B.

Limbacher, James L. FILM MUSIC: FROM VIOLIN TO VIDEO. Metuchen,
N.J.: Scarecrow Press, 1974. 835 p.

Includes 189 pages of essays by film composers, critics, and others.
List of film titles, with dates, pp. 195-305. Chronology of films
and their composers, pp. 530-687. Discography, pp. 688-828.
The period covered is 1908-72.

Loewenberg, Alfred. ANNALS OF OPERA, 1597-1940, COMPILED FROM THE
ORIGINAL SOURCES. Introduction by Edward J. Dent. 2d ed. Revised and
corrected by Frank Walter. 2 vols. Geneva: Societas Bibliographica, 1955.
Reprint. Totowa, N.J.: Rowman and Littlefield, 1970.

Volume I: text; Volume II: indexes of composers, librettists,
operas; general index.

Basically a chronology of first performances for nearly 4,000 operas.
Also gives composers' birth and death dates and information on
translations and title changes.

See also Clement, Felix, and Larousse, Pierre, above.

Lomax, Alan, and Cowell, Sidney Robertson. AMERICAN FOLK SONG AND
FOLK LORE, A REGIONAL BIBLIOGRAPHY. Progressive Education Association
Service Center Pamphlet, no. 8. New York: Progressive Education Associa-
tion, 1942. 59 p. Reprint. New York: Scholarly Reprints, 1973.

Annotates books and articles. Geographical arrangement, with
subdivision for dance, work, and worship songs.

Long, John H., comp. MUSIC IN ENGLISH RENAISSANCE DRAMA. Lexington: University of Kentucky Press, 1968. xvi, 184 p.

Essays on the use of music in English dramatic and semidramatic
works composed and presented between 1550 and 1650; together
with "The Music for the Lyrics in Early Seventeenth-Century English Drama: a Bibliography of the Primary Sources" by Vincent
Duckles, pp. 117-60, which identifies manuscripts and library locations but also notes modern editions. General manuscript collections are followed by separate entries for playwrights, 1603-42,
naming one or more songs associated with each play, e.g.: Shake-

speare, William. AS YOU LIKE IT. "It was a lover and his lass."

See also Boustead, Alan, above.

McCarty, Clifford. FILM COMPOSERS IN AMERICA; A CHECKLIST OF THEIR WORK. Da Capo Press Music Reprint Series. 1953. Reprint. New York: Da Capo Press, 1972. xx, 193 p.

> An alphabetical listing of 163 composers, with credits for American-made motion pictures to which they contributed musical composi-tions or other work such as arranging, orchestrating, etc. Song writers and arrangers are excluded.

> Shows Academy Award winners (musical) from 1934 through 1971, pp. 142–44. Indexes of film titles and of orchestrators.

> See also Limbacher, James L., above.

Marks, Jeannette. ENGLISH PASTORAL DRAMA.

> See Part VI-B.

Mattfeld, Julius. A HANDBOOK OF AMERICAN OPERATIC PREMIERES, 1731-1962. Detroit Studies in Music Bibliography, no. 5. Detroit: Informa-tion Service, 1963. 142 p. Reprint. St. Clair Shores, Mich.: Scholarly Press, 1973. 142 p.

> Title list of approximately 2,000 operas, with composer index.

Merriam, Alan P., with Brenford, Robert J. A BIBLIOGRAPHY OF JAZZ. Publications of the American Folklore Society. Bibliographical Series, vol. 4. Philadelphia: American Folklore Society, 1954. 145 p. Reprint. New York: Da Capo, 1970.

> A listing of 3,324 items under authors. Subject index. Periodicals list.

METROPOLITAN OPERA ANNALS.

> See Seltsam, William H., below.

Modern Language Association of America. General Topics IX. Bibliography Committee. A BIBLIOGRAPHY ON THE RELATIONS OF LITERATURE AND THE OTHER ARTS.

> Under "Music and Literature" occur references to masques and operas.

> See Part VI-B.

MUSIC INDEX.

> See Part V.

Music Library Association. A CHECKLIST OF MUSIC BIBLIOGRAPHIES AND INDEXES IN PROGRESS AND UNPUBLISHED. MLA Index Series, no. 3. 3d ed., Compiled by Linda Solow. Ann Arbor, Mich.: MLA, 1973.

> Entries include work in progress ranging from new editions of published works to library indexes on cards. Most items pertain to concert music, but there are entries for dance, dance music, film music, musical comedy, opera, and Shakespeare. A short description of each work is accompanied by a statement of availability for reference, loan, or purchase of photocopy.

New York Public Library. DICTIONARY CATALOG OF THE DANCE COLLECTION.

> See Part VI-A1.

_____. DICTIONARY CATALOG OF THE MUSIC COLLECTION. 33 vols. Boston: G.K. Hall, 1964.

SUPPLEMENT 1. Boston: 1966. 811 p.

> Interfiles entries for title, author, and subject, representing music and books on music in a large research collection especially strong in American music. Periodicals, programs, and manuscripts are also shown. There are extensive analytics for journal articles.

> The SUPPLEMENT shows added holdings to August 31, 1965.

Rapee, Erno. ENCYCLOPEDIA OF MUSIC FOR PICTURES. The Literature of Cinema. New York: Belwin, 1925. 510 p. Reprint. New York: Arno Press and the New York Times, 1970.

> Of interest for students of popular culture is this subjective selection of "mood music," which was originally addressed to musical directors and theater organists. Larger theaters sometimes employed singers and even symphony orchestras to enhance their programs, but more often it was the mighty Wurlitzer organ which thundered through the canyon as the cowboys swept silently by.

> Titles in this list are arranged by mood, i.e., under topical headings from "Agitato" to "Zoo." Note suggestions for comic opera, minstrel music, etc. Composers and publishers are identified.

> See also Limbacher, James L.; and McCarty, Clifford, above.

RECORDINGS, MUSICAL; AND REVIEWS OF RECORDINGS.

> See Part VII-F.

Schmieder, Wolfgang, ed.

> See BIBLIOGRAPHIE DES MUSIKSCHRIFTTUMS, above.

Seltsam, William H. METROPOLITAN OPERA ANNALS; A CHRONICLE OF ARTISTS AND PERFORMANCES. New York: Wilson, 1947. 751 p. Illustrated.

SUPPLEMENT I: (1947–57), 1957. 115 p.

SUPPLEMENT II: (1957–66), 1968. 126 p.

> Chronology of seasons at the Metropolitan Opera, New York, from 1833–84 through 1946–47 found in the basic volume. Supplements carry the record onward.

> Very well illustrated, with many portraits of singers in their roles. Press reviews are quoted, especially for openings and debuts.

> Index of reviews, artists, performances, and portraits.

Sibley, Gertrude Marian. THE LOST PLAYS AND MASQUES.

> See Part VI–A2.

SONG INDEXES.

> For indexes to collections of songs or of songs available on recordings, see also Part VII–F.

Sonneck, Oscar George Theodore. BIBLIOGRAPHY OF EARLY SECULAR AMERICAN MUSIC, 18TH CENTURY. Revised and enlarged by William Treat Upton. Washington, D.C.: Library of Congress Music Division, 1945. 616 p. Illustrated. Reprint. Preface by Irving Lowens. New York: Da Capo, 1964. 616 p.

> Alphabetical title list, intended as a complete record of published and manuscript music, together with books, pamphlets, and essays relating to American secular music to 1800. Sonneck's 1905 work was revised and more than tripled by Upton. Several indexes were added.

> Entries indicate whether the materials include songs from opera or other theater entertainments. Notes may show performers, composers, etc.

> Library locations are given. Some items are in private collections.

> Richard J. Wolfe has published a three-volume continuation of this record. See annotation below.

_____. CATALOGUE OF OPERA LIBRETTOS PRINTED BEFORE 1800.

> See Part IV–A.

_____. DRAMATIC MUSIC.

> See U.S. Library of Congress. Music Division. DRAMATIC MUSIC, below.

TANZBIBLIOGRAPHIE.

>This German-language bibliography has material on music relating to dance.

>See Part VI-A1.

Towers, John. DICTIONARY CATALOGUE OF OPERAS AND OPERETTAS. Morgantown, W. Va.: Acme Publishing Co., 1910. 1,045 p. Reprint. 2 vols. New York: Da Capo, 1967.

>Volume I shows 28,000 opera titles, with variants, and gives composers' names, dates, and nationalities. Volume II contains Part II, an index of composers, with works; it also identifies librettos and tells the number of times they have been set to music for the stage.

>See also Clement, Felix; and Caselli, Aldo, above.

U.S. Copyright Office. CATALOG OF COPYRIGHT ENTRIES. DRAMAS AND WORKS PREPARED FOR ORAL DELIVERY.

>Includes "books" (librettos) for musicals.

>For annotation, see Part IV-A.

_____. CATALOG OF COPYRIGHT ENTRIES . . . PT. 3: MUSICAL COMPOSITIONS. Washington, D.C.: Government Printing Office, 1906-   .

>Described by Constance M. Winchell's GUIDE TO REFERENCE BOOKS (8th ed. Chicago: ALA, 1967) as "the most comprehensive bibliography of music available." Frequency, arrangement, and subtitle have varied. [The reader is referred to Winchell (BH37) for details of these changes.]

>A list of music, domestic and foreign, deposited for U.S. copyright registration. Arranged under titles. A name index includes authors, composers, arrangers, and compilers as shown in the title entry.

U.S. Library of Congress. LIBRARY OF CONGRESS CATALOG. MUSIC AND PHONORECORDS; A CUMULATIVE LIST OF WORKS REPRESENTED BY LIBRARY OF CONGRESS PRINTED CARDS. Washington, D.C.: Library of Congress, 1953-   . Semiannual, with annual quinquennial cumulations. (Title varies.)

>Entries for music scores and phonograph records, musical or nonmusical. These represent holdings both at the Library of Congress and in other U.S. libraries. Prior to 1972, only those works were listed for which Library of Congress cards were made. Name and subject index.

>See also U.S. Copyright Office. CATALOG OF COPYRIGHT ENTRIES. . . PT 3: MUSICAL COMPOSITIONS, above.

U.S. Library of Congress. Music Division. DRAMATIC MUSIC: CATALOGUE OF FULL SCORES IN THE COLLECTION OF THE LIBRARY OF CONGRESS. Compiled by Oscar George Theodore Sonneck. Washington, D.C.: Government Printing Office, 1908. Reprint. New York: Da Capo, 1969. 170 p.

> Shows the library's holdings acquired by December 1907. Opera is most heavily represented, although incidental music for dramas, melodramas, ballets, and pantomimes is also recorded.

> Arrangement is under composers. For each work, manuscript copy or published edition is described. For operas, date and place of premiere are given.

> See also U.S. Library of Congress. LIBRARY OF CONGRESS CATALOG. MUSIC AND PHONORECORDS, above.

Upton, William Treat.

> See Sonneck, Oscar George Theodore. BIBLIOGRAPHY OF EARLY SECULAR AMERICAN MUSIC, above.

Weichlein, William Jessel. CHECKLIST OF AMERICAN MUSIC PERIODICALS, 1850-1900. Detroit Studies in Music Bibliography, no. 16. Detroit: Information Coordinators, Inc., 1970. 103 p.

> Selective checklist of periodicals, some of which were devoted to music, drama, literature, and/or society. Brief statement of editorship, frequency, duration, and title changes. Library holdings shown. The main title list is followed by a chronology, a geographical distribution chart, and a list of editors and publishers.

Wolfe, Richard J. SECULAR MUSIC IN AMERICA, 1801-1825; A BIBLIOGRAPHY. Introduction by Carleton Sprague Smith. 3 vols. New York: New York Public Library, 1964.

> Continues the work of Oscar George Theodore Sonneck. BIBLIOGRAPHY OF EARLY SECULAR AMERICAN MUSIC. (See above.)

> Listed by composer or anonymous title are 10,000 editions or single titles of music published in America, 1801-25. Detailed bibliographic information and some biographical notes. Several indexes.

> Locates copies.

4. Design for the Theater: Architecture, Costume, Stagecraft

American Educational Theatre Association. Stage Design and Technical Developments Project. INDUSTRIAL AND TECHNICAL PUBLICATIONS: A BIBLIOGRAPHY OF INTEREST TO THEATRE WORKERS. Compiled by Robert C. Burroughs. Washington, D.C.: A.E.T.A., 1960? 43 p.

Information on manufacturers' booklets, pamphlets, and catalogs, mostly free, which were available at time of publication. Items of possible interest for lighting, painting, and set design, stagecraft, sound, makeup, and stage properties. Index of companies, pp. 40–43.

American Theatre Planning Board. THEATRE CHECK LIST: A GUIDE TO THE PLANNING AND CONSTRUCTION OF PROSCENIUM AND OPEN STAGE THEATRES. Middletown, Conn.: Wesleyan University Press, 1969. 71 p.

Items deal with physical layout of theaters from plan to finish. Indexed.

See also Silverman, Maxwell, below.

Anthony, Pegaret, and Arnold, Janet. COSTUME; A GENERAL BIBLIOGRAPHY. London: Victoria and Albert Museum in Association with the Costume Society, 1966. 49 p. Rev. ed. Costume Society Bibliographies, no. 1. London: Costume Society, 1974.

Annotated classified references to books, articles, exhibition catalogs, etc., chiefly in French and English.

APPLIED SCIENCE AND TECHNOLOGY INDEX. New York: H.W. Wilson, 1913– . Quarterly.

Formerly INDUSTRIAL ARTS INDEX (1913–57), this subject index carries on the volume numbering of its predecessor and appears monthly and in quarterly and annual cumulations. References are to articles in English-language technical journals, especially those published in the United States. There are subject headings for "Auditoriums," "Stage Lighting," "Textiles," "Theaters," and, in some volumes, "Stage Machinery."

See also BRITISH TECHNOLOGY INDEX and ENGINEERING INDEX, below.

ARCHITECTURAL INDEX. Norman, Okla., 1950– . Annual.

Indexes a few American journals of architecture and interior design. Its focus is on new building, public and domestic. A few subject entries appear under "Acoustics," "Stage," and "Theater," as well as name entries grouped under "Architects and Designers."

See also Royal Institute of British Architects. ARCHITECTURAL PERIODICALS INDEX, below.

ARCHITECTURAL PERIODICALS INDEX.

See Royal Institute of British Architects. ARCHITECTURAL PERIODICALS INDEX, below.

ART INDEX.

See Part V.

BRITISH TECHNOLOGY INDEX: A CURRENT SUBJECT-GUIDE TO ARTICLES IN BRITISH TECHNICAL JOURNALS. London: The Library Association, 1962-   . Monthly, with cumulation in twelfth month.

Indexes, under subjects, the contents of 360 British technical journals. Includes subjects such as "Stage" and "Theatre" as well as specific technical topics.

See also APPLIED SCIENCE AND TECHNOLOGY INDEX, above, and ENGINEERING INDEX, below.

Chicago Art Institute. Ryerson Library. INDEX TO ART PERIODICALS. 11 vols. Boston: G.K. Hall, 1962.

FIRST SUPPLEMENT in preparation. Boston: G.K. Hall, 1974.

Based on a card file begun in 1907 in a major art library, this subject index is useful for the years before ART INDEX began and later as well since the journals cited are not those scanned by ART INDEX. See headings such as "Costume," "Costume, Theater," "Stage Settings and Scenery," and also artists' names.

See also Columbia University Libraries. Avery Architectural Library. AVERY INDEX TO ARCHITECTURAL PERIODICALS, below, and ART INDEX, in Part V.

Colas, Rene. BIBLIOGRAPHIE GENERALE DU COSTUME ET DE LA MODE. Paris: R. Colas, 1933. Reprint. 2 vols. New York: Hacker Art Books, 1963.

Colas records works on costume and accessories and also materials found in major serials and sets. Volume I is an author list; Volume II consists of title and subject indexes.

The Hilers' basic bibliography of costume makes frequent reference to Colas for detail. See Hiler, Hilaire, and Hiler, Meyer, in Part I-C.

Columbia University Libraries. Avery Architectural Library. AVERY INDEX TO ARCHITECTURAL PERIODICALS. 2d ed., rev. and enl. 15 vols. Boston: G.K. Hall, 1973. To be supplemented.

This edition incorporates the entire original INDEX and the seven supplements published since 1963. Corrections have been made.

Periodicals have been added to the titles scanned, and much back-indexing has been done.

Although architecture predominates, there are many references for archaeology, urban planning, design, and the decorative arts.

Entries for subjects, titles, and authors are interfiled. Many references occur under "Theaters" and under names of architects and designers of all periods.

See also Chicago Art Institute. Ryerson Library, above, and ART INDEX in Part V.

_____. CATALOG OF THE AVERY MEMORIAL ARCHITECTURAL LIBRARY. 2d ed. 19 vols. Boston: G.K. Hall, 1968.

SUPPLEMENT, FIRST (1968-72). 4 vols. Boston: G.K. Hall, 1972.

Catalog of a great architectural library. This edition adds 18,000 titles to those listed in the 1958 catalog. Includes books and manuscripts on the fine and decorative arts, archaeology, design, urban planning, and, chiefly, architecture. Subject, author, and selected title entries are interfiled. There are many entries under "Theater" and "Theaters" as well as under names of architects and designers, either as subject or author. Under the heading "Architectural Drawings" are entered 10,000 original drawings owned by the library.

COSTUME.

In addition to the bibliographies shown here, consult the encyclopedias of costume introduced in Part II-D. Several of these have up-to-date bibliographies.

Dameron, Louise, comp. BIBLIOGRAPHY OF STAGE SETTINGS, TO WHICH IS ATTACHED AN INDEX TO ILLUSTRATIONS OF STAGE SETTINGS. Baltimore, Md.: Enoch Pratt Free Library, 1936. 48 l. Mimeographed.

Comprises two lists: (1) Annotations for practical and theoretical studies in books published in the United States or abroad through 1934, pp. 1-11; (2) Separately paged title list of plays, operas, and ballets, with references to illustrations in books, pp. 1-48.

See also New York Public Library, below.

Doelle, Leslie L. ACOUSTICS IN ARCHITECTURAL DESIGN; AN ANNOTATED BIBLIOGRAPHY ON ARCHITECTURAL ACOUSTICS. Bibliography no. 29. Ottawa: National Research Council of Canada, Division of Building Research, 1965. 543 p.

Not limited to Canada, this treatise contains bibliographical notes on design of auditoriums and studios and also a brief history of architectural accoustics.

ENCYCLOPEDIA OF WORLD ART.

> The long articles, "Costume" and "Scenography," have scholarly but unannotated bibliographies.
>
> For full annotation, see Part II-E.

THE ENGINEERING INDEX, 1884-91-   . New York: Engineering Magazine Co., 1892-   . (Title and frequency have varied.)

> Indexes, under subject, journal articles, society publications, conference papers, documents, and selected books. Materials cited are in more than twenty languages. The annual volume has an author index.
>
> There are some references to theaters and theater lighting. See also APPLIED SCIENCE AND TECHNOLOGY INDEX, and BRITISH TECHNOLOGY INDEX, above.

Harvard University. Graduate School of Design Library. CATALOGUE OF THE LIBRARY OF THE GRADUATE SCHOOL OF DESIGN. 44 vols. Boston: G.K. Hall, 1968.

FIRST SUPPLEMENT. 2 vols. Boston: G.K. Hall, 1970.

> See subject entries for "Theaters," "Theaters--Stage Settings," "Theaters, Garden," "Theaters, Outdoor, Civic," etc. Both books and articles are entered.

Hiler, Hilaire, and Hiler, Meyer, comps. BIBLIOGRAPHY OF COSTUME.

> See Part I-C.

INDUSTRIAL ARTS INDEX.

> See APPLIED SCIENCE AND TECHNOLOGY INDEX, above.

Lasch, Hanna. ARCHITEKTEN-BIBLIOGRAPHIE: DEUTSCHSPRACHIGE VEROEFFENTLICHUNGEN, 1920-1960. Leipzig: E.A. Seeman Verlag, 1962. 215 p.

> Bibliography of German-language dissertations, periodical articles, and books published between 1920 and 1960. Unannotated entries arranged under names of architects from all periods and lands, including designers of theater buildings and stage sets.

Library Association. County Libraries Group. READER'S GUIDE TO BOOKS ON STAGECRAFT AND THE THEATRE. New series, no. 85. 2d ed. London: Library Association, 1965. 30 p.

> Approximately 400 books are classified by subject, without annotation. Emphasis is British.

Lipperheide, Franz Joseph, Freiherr von. KATALOG DER LIPPERHEIDESCHEN KOSTUEMBIBLIOTHEK. 2 vols. 2d ed., rev. and enl. Edited by Eva Nienholdt and Gretel Wagner-Neumann. Berlin: Gebr. Mann, 1965. Illustrated.

The first edition of this monumental bibliography was published in two volumes under the title KATALOG DER FREIHERRLICH VON LIPPERHEIDE'SCHEN KOSTUEMBIBLIOTHEK (Berlin: F. Lipperheide, 1896-1905). It represented the holdings of a famous collection of books and serials pertaining to costume. Since 1905, this major library, which is administered by the Kunstbibliothek, Berlin, has grown by more than a third, necessitating a new edition of the catalog. In 1965 the collection included 12,000 volumes, as well as 30,000 prints, costume plates, and other single-sheet items.

The revised catalog, like the first edition, does not list the pictorial materials but does cover the book and serial holdings. The last-named are mainly almanacs and fashion magazines. A table correlates the old and new numbers assigned to all items in the collection.

Many of the references pertain to social background and to such matters as the esthetics, hygiene, law, and manufacture of costume. Also of interest are references to daily life, social classes, and caricature of costumes. Annotations are brief.

New York Public Library. THE DEVELOPMENT OF SCENIC ART AND STAGE MACHINERY: A LIST OF REFERENCES IN THE NEW YORK PUBLIC LIBRARY. Compiled by William Burt Gamble. New York: New York Public Library, 1920. 128 p. (From the BULLETIN OF THE N.Y. PUBLIC LIBRARY. June-November 1919).

This publication includes 2,471 references to settings, machinery, lighting, and staging. Books, articles, and some newspaper items, classified by subject. Special mention made of useful pictures.

See also Dameron, Louise; and ENCYCLOPEDIA OF WORLD ART, above.

Rave, Paul Ortwin. KUNSTGESCHICHTE IN FESTSCHRIFTEN; ALLGEMEINE BIBLIOGRAPHIE KUNSTWISSENSCHAFTLICHER ABHANDLUNGEN IN DEN BIS 1960 ERSCHIENENEN FESTSCHRIFTEN. Berlin: Gebr. Mann, 1962. 314 p.

International list of essays on art and related studies published in Festschriften through 1960. See the subject entries "Tanz, Theater" (theatrical dance), p. 269, and "Trachtenkunde" (costume studies), pp. 244-45. See also the index of artists, which includes some architects and painters connected with the theater, pp. 298-305.

Royal Institute of British Architects. ARCHITECTURAL PERIODICALS INDEX. London: RIBA Pub., Ltd., 1973- . (Replaces RIBA ANNUAL REVIEW.)

Volume 1, number 1 covers August–December 1972, listing articles in a variety of journals, mainly architectural. Emphasizes current design and building. Frequent entries under "Theatres."

See also ARCHITECTURAL INDEX, above.

Royal Institute of British Architects. Sir Banister Fletcher Library. CATALOGUE OF THE DRAWINGS COLLECTION OF THE ROYAL INSTITUTE OF BRITISH ARCHITECTS. Farnborough, Eng.: Gregg, 1968– . Illustrated.

The main series will be published in twenty volumes, alphabetized by architects' names. The last volume will be a cumulative index of places (architectural sites) and of donors or patrons. For each architect there is a brief biography with bibliography and a detailed catalog of his drawings found in the library. These are illustrated by plates, of which there are about one hundred per volume.

A special series will be devoted to separate collections, e.g., a volume of the designs of Inigo Jones and John Webb. (Five of the Jones drawings are associated with the court masque and several others with the Banqueting House at Whitehall.)

Other separate volumes will deal with architects extensively represented in this collection of 300,000 drawings. Of theatrical interest is the representation of the Galli-Bibiena and the Wyatt families, as well as Palladio and others. Also notable is a collection donated by Sir John Drummond-Stewart, consisting of a sequence of seventeenth and early eighteenth-century Italian theater designs.

This library, which is open to scholars and students from any part of the globe, represents especially well the full range of English architectural design from the late Gothic to the contemporary period. Excellence has determined the selection.

Silverman, Maxwell. CONTEMPORARY THEATRE ARCHITECTURE; AN ILLUSTRATED SURVEY. A CHECKLIST OF PUBLICATIONS, 1946-1964, BY NED A. BOWMAN. New York: New York Public Library, 1965. 80 p.

Brief notes on representative theaters and auditoriums in various countries. There are photographs, plans, and a subject index. Added is a 1,700-item checklist of books and articles, classified geographically.

See also American Theatre Planning Board, above.

THEATRE DESIGN AND TECHNOLOGY (journal). Pittsburgh: U.S. Institute for Theatre Technology. Quarterly.

See its feature "Recent Publications on Theatre Architecture," a continuing bibliography. Cites journal articles worldwide, also pamphlets, exhibition catalogs, etc., and annotates briefly.

5. Motion Pictures and Broadcasting

American Film Institute. THE AMERICAN FILM INSTITUTE CATALOG OF MOTION PICTURES PRODUCED IN THE UNITED STATES.

See Part II-A.

BIBLIOGRAPHIE INTERNATIONALE DU CINEMA ET DE LA TELEVISION. Paris: Institut des Hautes Etudes Cinematographiques, 1966- .

This partially annotated international bibliography of cinema and television will consist of ten or more parts, each covering publication in one country. Only books (some being screenplays) and a few outstanding journal articles are cited. Classified arrangement. Author indexes.

See also INTERNATIONALE FILMBIBLIOGRAPHIE; and Vincent, Carl, below.

British Broadcasting Corporation. BRITISH BROADCASTING, 1922-1972: A SELECT BIBLIOGRAPHY. London: B.B.C., 1972. 49 p.

Briefly annotated items in classified order. References are to books and periodical articles, mainly those recently published in Great Britain. The editors have attempted a bibliographic survey of the art and technique of British broadcasting, its makers, and its impact on society. Index of names, subjects, and some titles.

BRITISH FILM CATALOGUE, 1895-1970.

See Gifford, Denis, below.

British Film Institute. MONTHLY FILM BULLETIN.

See Part V.

BRITISH NATIONAL FILM CATALOGUE. London: British Film Institute, 1963- . Bimonthly; annual cumulation.

Prior to December 1, 1972, the catalog was published by the British Industrial and Scientific Film Association. A list of English and foreign films available for sale, loan, or rental in Great Britain. From 1969 on, newsreels and features were omitted, the latter being listed by the British Film Institute's MONTHLY FILM BULLETIN.

Films are in fiction and nonfiction categories. A "Production Index" names sponsors, artists, distributors, and others. There are title and subject indexes, the latter with many references to ballet, drama, opera, puppets, and theater.

Typical entries show date, duration, dimension, color, distributor, and credits. A synopsis is given.

See also Gifford, Denis, below.

Bukalski, Peter J., comp. FILM RESEARCH; A CRITICAL BIBLIOGRAPHY WITH ANNOTATIONS AND ESSAY. Boston: G.K. Hall, 1972. 215 p.

An essay on film research is followed by annotations, for "essential works," pp. 28–38. Remarks are critical and helpful. Film rental is discussed, pp. 39–40, and distributors' addresses in the United States (one in Canada) are given. "Film Purchase," pp. 47–50, recommends agencies and also shows a brief selection of available films. "Film Periodicals," pp. 51–65, lists titles in various languages.

The main bibliography, pp. 66–215, is classified and has unannotated entries for books and some documents. All aspects of film are represented. Category 7, "Film Scripts," shows publications as late as 1971. Category 14 is a choice of books in foreign languages.

See also Gottesman, Ronald, in Part I-A; Manchel, Frank; and Rehrauer, George, below.

Buxton, Frank, and Owen, Bill. THE BIG BROADCAST, 1920–1950. A NEW, REVISED AND GREATLY EXPANDED EDITION OF 'RADIO'S GOLDEN AGE, THE COMPLETE REFERENCE WORK.' Introduction by Henry Morgan. New York: Viking Press, 1972. xv, 301 p. Illustrated.

Radio shows on the national networks through 1950 are listed under title, e.g., "The Abbott and Costello Program." There are the usual cast and production credits and a short description of the typical show. There are a few subject entries in the same alphabet, e.g., "Soap Operas," "Sound-Effects Men," "Singers," etc.

Bibliography, pp. 266–70. Index.

California. University of. Los Angeles. Library. MOTION PICTURES: A CATALOG OF BOOKS, PERIODICALS, SCREENPLAYS.

See Part IV-A.

Cinematheque royale de Belgique. WORLD DIRECTORY OF STOCKSHOT AND FILM PRODUCTION LIBRARIES.

See Part III.

Enser, A.G.S. FILMED BOOKS AND PLAYS FROM WHICH FILMS HAVE BEEN MADE.

See Part II-A.

FEATURE FILMS ON 8mm and 16mm; A DIRECTORY OF FEATURE FILMS AVAIL-

ABLE FOR RENTAL, LEASE, OR SALE IN THE UNITED STATES. Edited by James L. Limbacher. New York: Educational Film Library Association, 1967-   . Annual.

> Films are listed by title. Information given includes distributor, dimension, duration, sound, color, and subtitling.

> Monthly supplements appear in the periodical SIGHTLINES.

FILM INDEX.

> See Writers' Program (New York), FILM INDEX, below.

FILM LITERATURE INDEX; A QUARTERLY AUTHOR-SUBJECT PERIODICAL INDEX TO THE INTERNATIONAL LITERATURE OF FILM. Albany, N.Y.: Filmdex, Inc., April 1973-   .

> The unannotated references are based on examination of more than 300 film and general periodicals worldwide. Subject entries include persons, institutions, organizations, festivals, awards, distribution (films), editing (films), television, and many technical matters.

> See also INTERNATIONAL INDEX TO FILM PERIODICALS, below.

FILM RESEARCH.

> See Bukalski, Peter J., above.

GENERAL BIBLIOGRAPHY OF MOTION PICTURES.

> See Vincent, Carl, ed., below.

Gifford, Denis. BRITISH FILM CATALOGUE, 1895-1970; A GUIDE TO ENTER-TAINMENT FILMS. Newton Abbot: David and Charles, 1973. 967 p.

> Lists British films since the invention of cinematography, except for documentary, propaganda, educational, travel, and most animation films. Some films named are by American companies in Great Britain or British companies working with European studios.

> The arrangement is chronological. The following information is shown: title changes, if any; date of first showing; footage or running time; producer, director, and distributor; authors of original story and of screenplay; cast; type of drama; and a one-sentence summary. Awards and reissues also shown. Title index.

> See also BRITISH NATIONAL FILM CATALOGUE, above.

Gottesman, Ronald. GUIDEBOOK TO FILM.

> See Part I-A.

AN INDEX TO 'FILMS IN REVIEW,' 1950-1959 and 1960-1964.

See Part V.

INTERNATIONAL INDEX TO FILM PERIODICALS. Edited by Karen Jones. New York: R.R. Bowker, 1972- . Annual.

Sponsored by the International Federation of Film Archives, this first volume classifies and annotates briefly, in English, approximately 7,000 articles, reviews, essays, interviews, and filmographies published during 1972 in fifty-nine film periodicals in twenty-one countries. Index of subject headings.

The journal list is to be expanded, and books may eventually be listed also.

See also FILM LITERATURE INDEX, above.

INTERNATIONALE FILMBIBLIOGRAPHIE, 1952-1962. Schriftenreihe der Schweizerischen Gesellschaft fuer Filmwissenschaft und Filmrecht, Bd. I. Edited by H.P. Manz. Zurich: H. Rohr, 1963. 262 p.

Classified entries, many with annotations in German. Listed are books and annuals concerning motion pictures worldwide. Section VI in each current volume is a list of screenplays, and Section XII is a selection of periodicals. Name index.

From 1964 on, annual supplements have appeared: NACHTRAG 1, (1963) Zurich, 1964- .

See also Vincent, Carl, below, and BIBLIOGRAPHIE INTERNATIONALE DU CINEMA ET DE LA TELEVISION, above.

Lee, Walt, comp., assisted by Warren, Bill. REFERENCE GUIDE TO FANTASTIC FILMS; SCIENCE FICTION, FANTASY, AND HORROR. 3 vols. Los Angeles: Chelsea-Lee Books, 1972-73. Illustrated.

Volume I (A-F); Volume II (G-O); Volume III (P-Z) comprise an alphabetical title list of the films in all three categories named. Entries give the usual credits, a thumbnail summary, and a few references to books and articles. Each volume has two supplementary lists (1) films for which insufficient information was found; (2) likely-sounding films that were excluded as not fitting the compilers' definition of "fantastic."

Limbacher, James L. FILM MUSIC: FROM VIOLIN TO VIDEO.

See Part VI-A3.

_____, ed.

See FEATURE FILMS ON 8mm AND 16mm, above.

McCarty, Clifford. PUBLISHED SCREENPLAYS; A CHECKLIST. Serif Series, no. 18. Kent, Ohio: Kent State University Press, 1971. 127 p.

Shows book or periodical publication of screenplays in English, whether complete or excerpted. Some are translations. Included are feature films, shorts, documentaries, and experimental films. Entries tell director, author, producing company, and date.

See also California. University of. Los Angeles. Library; New York Public Library. CATALOG OF THE THEATRE AND DRAMA COLLECTIONS; and U.S. Copyright Office. DRAMAS, all in Part IV-A.

Manchel, Frank. FILM STUDY; A RESOURCE GUIDE. Rutherford, N.J.: Fairleigh Dickinson University Press, 1973. 422 p.

Annotations for books and films are classified under such subjects as technique and film genres. There is a selection of film dissertations, pp. 356-62. Appendices name periodicals, film distributors, etc.

See also Bukalski, Peter J., above, and Gottesman, Ronald, in Part I-A.

New York Public Library. CATALOG OF THE THEATRE AND DRAMA COLLECTIONS.

Scripts for motion pictures, radio, and television are among the materials cataloged. For full annotation, see Part IV-A.

Niver, Kemp R. MOTION PICTURES FROM THE LIBRARY OF CONGRESS PAPER PRINT COLLECTION, 1894-1912. Edited by Bebe Bergsien. Berkeley: University of California Press, 1967. 402 p.

A classified catalog of 3,000 items. (Not a complete list of films from 1894 to 1912, as some companies did not copyright films.) Entry tells producing company, copyright number and date, length in feet, film condition, film category (e.g., comedy), and gives a synopsis. Prints of films are available for purchase from the Library of Congress.

An index of subjects includes "Directors," with a list of films for each, and "Serials and Series," listing such films. There is an alphabetical title index.

See also U.S. Copyright Office. MOTION PICTURES 1894-1912, below.

Pickard, R.A.E. DICTIONARY OF 1,000 BEST FILMS. New York: Association Press, 1971. 496 p. Illustrated.

Films appear alphabetically by title, each with a brief critical summary. Screen credits are given and awards mentioned. The scope is international.

This avowedly personal selection includes both art films and entertainment films, the former group predominating.

Rehrauer, George. CINEMA BOOKLIST. Metuchen, N.J.: Scarecrow Press, 1972. 473 p.

SUPPLEMENT I. Metuchen, N.J.: Scarecrow Press, 1974. 405 p.

Evaluative notes on approximately 1,500 books of interest to the general reader. Includes short lists of classic screenplays and of moving picture periodicals. Author and subject indexes.

See also Bukalski, Peter J., above.

Schuster, Mel. MOTION PICTURE DIRECTORS: A BIBLIOGRAPHY OF MAGA-ZINE AND PERIODICAL ARTICLES, 1900-1972. Metuchen, N.J.: Scarecrow Press, 1973. 418 p.

There are entries for directors, filmmakers, and animators. Material is biographical and critical; reviews per se are excluded. All items are in English.

Note also a separate list of directors for whom no material was found, pp. xiii-xxii. List of journals, pp. 413-17.

_____. MOTION PICTURE PERFORMERS: A BIBLIOGRAPHY OF MAGAZINE AND PERIODICAL ARTICLES, 1900-1969. Metuchen, N.J.: Scarecrow Press, 1971. 702 p.

(First SUPPLEMENT in preparation, 1973.)

Items arranged chronologically under names of actors. Emphasis is on biography. Few reviews of performances are included.

U.S. Copyright Office. CATALOG OF COPYRIGHT ENTRIES. DRAMAS AND WORKS PREPARED FOR ORAL DELIVERY.

Includes scripts for films, radio, stage, and television. See annotation in Part IV-A.

_____. MOTION PICTURES 1894-1912 IDENTIFIED FROM THE RECORDS OF THE UNITED STATES COPYRIGHT OFFICE BY HOWARD LAMARR WALLS. Washington, D.C.: Copyright Office, Library of Congress, 1953. 92 p.

A list of about 6,000 motion pictures registered for copyright and of about 2,500 other films. Title entry.

_____. MOTION PICTURES 1912-1939 (1951); 1940-1949 (1953); 1950-1959 (1960); 1960-1969 (1971). Catalog of Copyright Entries. Cumulative Series. Washington, D.C.: Copyright Office, Library of Congress, 1951- .

In each catalog a title list gives information on copyrighted items, as follows: production date, company, credits, number of reels, source of story. There is a name index in each volume.

For the years 1894-1912, see also Niver, Kemp R., above.

U.S. Library of Congress. LIBRARY OF CONGRESS CATALOG. MOTION PICTURES AND FILMSTRIPS. Washington, D.C., 1953-   .

As stated in its introduction, this catalog is "[a] cumulative list of works represented by Library of Congress printed cards....Includes entries for all motion pictures and filmstrips...currently cataloged or recataloged on L.C. printed cards....Attempts to cover all educational motion pictures and filmstrips released in the United States and Canada."

Formerly included in the Library of Congress AUTHOR CATALOG and the SUBJECT CATALOG. Published as Volume 28 of the NATIONAL UNION CATALOG, 1953-1957 and Volumes 53-54 of the AUTHOR CATALOG, 1958-62.

Entries show dimension, duration, color, sound, and summarize briefly. In the subject index see "Theatrical Motion Pictures" for a list of films, giving release date and name of producer and distributor. See also "Western Films" and similar headings.

_____. MOTION PICTURES FROM THE LIBRARY OF CONGRESS PAPER PRINT COLLECTION.

See Niver, Kemp R., above.

_____. NATIONAL UNION CATALOG: FILMS AND OTHER MATERIALS FOR PROJECTION, 1973-   .

Continues the U.S. Library of Congress, CATALOG: MOTION PICTURES AND FILMSTRIPS. The first issue with new title appeared in 1973 and included items catalogued from October 1972 through June 1973. The title reflects inclusion of new media, namely, sets of slides and other transparencies. Microform materials are not included.

Vincent, Carl, ed. BIBLIOGRAFIA GENERALE DEL CINEMA. GENERAL BIBLIOGRAPHY OF MOTION PICTURES. Rome: Ateneo, 1953. Reprint. New York: Arno, 1972. 251 p.

Classified entries for books and articles on motion pictures from their origin to 1952, compiled by members of the Cinematographic Centre, University of Padua. Preface is in English, French, and Italian; a few items have abstracts in the language of the entry. Chapter X lists screenplays. Name index.

See also INTERNATIONALE FILMBIBLIOGRAPHIE, 1952-1962, and BIBLIOGRAPHIE INTERNATIONALE DU CINEMA ET DE LA TELE-VISION, above.

_____. GENERAL BIBLIOGRAPHY OF MOTION PICTURES.

See Vincent, Carl, ed. BIBLIOGRAFIA GENERALE DEL CINEMA, above.

WORLD LIST OF FILM PERIODICALS (1960).

See United Nations Educational, Scientific, and Cultural Organization. Belgian National Commission. REPERTOIRE MONDIAL DES PERIODIQUES CINEMATOGRAPHIQUES, in Part 1-H.

Writers' Program (New York). FILM INDEX.

See Part V.

B. LITERATURE

JOURNAL ARTICLES

Bibliographic control has been much firmer for current literary scholarship than for similar work on the performing arts. Such major bibliographies and surveys as the YEARBOOK OF COMPARATIVE AND GENERAL LITERATURE; the YEAR'S WORK IN MODERN LANGUAGE STUDIES (Modern Humanities Research Association); the ANNUAL BIBLIOGRAPHY OF ENGLISH LANGUAGE AND LITERATURE of the same association; the MLA INTERNATIONAL BIBLIOGRAPHY (Modern Language Association of America), and various publications of MLA committees provide a relatively detailed and dependable approach to criticism and research in a very broad field. Other works listed below are useful, although of lesser breadth.

FESTSCHRIFTEN

Two of the annuals noted above also undertake to analyze contents of notable literary Festschriften, some of which concern theater and drama. These homage studies or melanges are compilations of essays, usually honoring a scholar. Essays published in this manner are traced under subject (e.g., American drama or the name of some literary author) in both the MLA INTERNATIONAL BIBLIOGRAPHY and the ANNUAL BIBLIOGRAPHY OF ENGLISH LANGUAGE AND LITERATURE, in both cases with reference to a list of Festschriften at the front of the annual volume. Other specialized bibliographies of Festschriften are also annotated in Parts VI-A and VI-B of this guide.

BIBLIOGRAPHIES

Two major bibliographies of bibliographies are discussed in the headnote of Part VI-A, above.

NEW BOOKS AND BOOK REVIEWS

For general remarks on this subject, see the headnote of Part VI-A, above.

SCREENPLAYS, ETC. See VI-A5. LIBRETTOS. See VI-A 3.

ABSTRACTS OF ENGLISH STUDIES: AN OFFICIAL PUBLICATION OF THE NATIONAL COUNCIL OF TEACHERS OF ENGLISH. Boulder, Colo.: 1958- . Monthly, September through June.

> Summaries of articles on the literature of all periods in English-speaking lands. Broad subject classification. Arrangement has varied, with earlier volumes grouping items under title of periodical.

> Subject index in each issue, cumulating annually.

> Especially helpful for its up-to-date coverage and inclusion of criticism of many newer authors.

AMERICAN LITERARY SCHOLARSHIP, 1963- . Durham, N.C.: Duke University Press, 1964- . Annual.

> Edited by James Woodress and other scholars, this survey evaluates books and articles on American literature, grouping entries as follows: (1) Under major authors, singly or in pairs; (2) under period and genre, involving many authors, major and minor. There is a name index.

AMERICAN LITERATURE; A JOURNAL OF LITERARY HISTORY, CRITICISM, AND BIBLIOGRAPHY. Durham, N.C.: Duke University Press, March 1929- . Quarterly.

> Journal issued in cooperation with the American Literature Group of the Modern Language Association of America. Each issue carries a bibliography of current journal articles and a list of "Research in Progress," which includes dissertations and other scholarly work in preparation.

ANNUAL BIBLIOGRAPHY OF ENGLISH LANGUAGE AND LITERATURE.

> See Modern Humanities Research Association, below.

Arnold, Robert Franz. ALLGEMEINE BUECHERKUNDE ZUR NEUEREN DEUTSCHEN LITERATURGESCHICHTE. 4th ed. Revised by Herbert Jacob. Berlin: De Gruyter, 1966. 395 p.

> A standard bibliography of the "new" German literature (seventeenth century through 1965) and related subjects. Excellent coverage, with reliable comments, mainly found in brief chapter

headings. Author and subject indexes.

The section "Theatergeschichte," pp. 315-17, names important studies in all branches of German theater research, some of which are by German scholars. Some materials for motion pictures and radio.

See also Koerner, Josef, in Part I-E4.

Bailey, Richard W., and Burton, Dolores M. ENGLISH STYLISTICS: A BIBLIOGRAPHY. Cambridge, Mass.: M.I.T. Press, 1968. 198 p.

Partly annotated references to linguistic studies of literary texts, found in books or journals. Some references to the rhetoric of drama.

Bailey, Robert B. GUIDE TO CHINESE POETRY AND DRAMA. The Asian Literature Bibliography Series. Boston: G.K. Hall, 1973. 100 p.

Annotated guide intended for the nonspecialist. Drama coverage is slight, pp. 76-95. An interpretive essay on Chinese drama is followed by fifteen or more summaries and evaluations of dramas of various periods in English translation. These texts are said to be readily available in libraries or from dealers. Index of titles, authors, editors, and translators.

See also Columbia University. A GUIDE TO ORIENTAL CLASSICS, and Davidson, Martha, both in Part IV-A.

Baldensperger, Fernand, and Friederich, Werner P. BIBLIOGRAPHY OF COMPARATIVE LITERATURE.

See Part I-E4.

Bate, John. HOW TO FIND OUT ABOUT SHAKESPEARE. Oxford and New York: Pergamon Press, 1968. 161 p.

A discursive, evaluative bibliography, helpful for both graduate and undergraduate students. Bate outlines approaches to many areas of Shakespearean study; he relates research problems to general library resources as well as to more specialized materials.

Chapter 10 describes great library collections of Shakespearean interest. Appendix 1 briefly notes phonograph recordings, while Appendix 2 is a general list of literary periodicals. Author index.

See also Berman, Ronald, in Part I-A, and Payne, Waveney R.N., below.

Bindoff, Stanley Thomas. RESEARCH IN PROGRESS IN ENGLISH AND HISTORICAL STUDIES IN THE UNIVERSITIES OF THE BRITISH ISLES. London: St. James Press, 1971. 109 p.

Ongoing research by faculty members is listed briefly under sub-ject. There are separate sections for English and American litera-ture, subdivided by period and genre. Index of scholars, with addresses.

British Children's Theatre Association. SELECTED BIBLIOGRAPHY OF PLAYS RECOMMENDED FOR [PERFORMANCE TO] CHILD AUDIENCES. 2d ed. Children's Theatre Press, 1965. 16 p. Reprint. Bromley, Eng.: Stacey Publications, 1973.

Not examined.

See also American Library Association. SUBJECT INDEX TO CHILDREN'S PLAYS, in Part IV-A.

Brown University Library. Harris Collection. DICTIONARY CATALOG OF THE HARRIS COLLECTION OF AMERICAN POETRY AND PLAYS. 13 vols. Providence, R.I.: Brown University Library; Boston: G.K. Hall, 1972.

Authors, titles, and subjects are interfiled, representing the 150,000 books and pamphlets by American and Canadian authors held in this library. (Not listed are the library's 25,000 manu-scripts, 20,000 broadsides, or the 127,000 pieces of American sheet music.) The catalog shows original editions of most of the plays recorded in Frank Pierce Hill's AMERICAN PLAYS PRINTED, 1714-1830 (see Part IV-A).

The play collection has grown with the times and includes off-Off-Broadway specimens. The catalog is rich in musical scores, librettos, dramatic readings, songsters, and pageant and pantomime materials. Numerous entries are found under "Theater," "Minstrels," "Negro Minstrels," "Monologs," etc.

The representation of literary periodicals is also good, including many "little magazines."

Cabeen, David Clark, ed. A CRITICAL BIBLIOGRAPHY OF FRENCH LITERA-TURE. Syracuse, N.Y.: Syracuse University Press, 1947-   .

A selective bibliographic guide, organized under periods, with evaluations in English of books, articles, and dissertations. Re-views are also noted.

This work will extend from the Middle Ages to the twentieth cen-tury, with well known scholars contributing in their specialties. Useful for background as well as for literary studies.

Some volumes have supplements.

Caldwell, Harry B., and Middleton, David L., comps. ENGLISH TRAGEDY, 1370-1600: FIFTY YEARS OF CRITICISM. Checklists in the Humanities and Education. San Antonio, Tex.: Trinity University Press, 1971. 89 p.

Cites primary and secondary materials, omitting all references to

Marlowe and Shakespeare. Lists, without annotation, books, articles, dissertations, and some passages in books. An appendix suggests works in need of further research. Index includes both primary and secondary authors.

CAMBRIDGE BIBLIOGRAPHY OF ENGLISH LITERATURE.

See Part I-E2.

Dobree, Bonamy, ed.

See OXFORD HISTORY OF ENGLISH LITERATURE, below.

ELIZABETHAN BIBLIOGRAPHIES.

See Tannenbaum, Samuel Aaron, and Tannenbaum, Dorothy.

See also ELIZABETHAN BIBLIOGRAPHIES SUPPLEMENTS, below.

ELIZABETHAN BIBLIOGRAPHIES SUPPLEMENTS. London: Nether Press, 1967- .

No. 1 (1967) issued as a supplement to ELIZABETHAN BIBLIOG-RAPHIES (see Tannenbaum, Samuel Aaron, and Tannenbaum, Dorothy, below).

The SUPPLEMENTS provide bibliographies for authors not in the original series. Most volumes arrange items chronologically by date of criticism. There is an index of critics.

English Association. THE YEAR'S WORK IN ENGLISH STUDIES. London: Oxford University Press, 1919-20- . Annual.

Evaluative survey of books and articles on English and American literature published in Great Britain, Europe, and the United States during the year past. Less comprehensive than the annual bibliography of the Modern Humanities Research Association. (See below.) See also Modern Language Association of America. MLA INTERNATIONAL BIBLIOGRAPHY, below.

ENGLISH LITERARY PERIODICALS. Ann Arbor, Mich.: University Microfilms, 1951- .

This microfilm series reproduces contents of English literary periodicals of the seventeenth through nineteenth centuries. A booklet, ENGLISH LITERARY PERIODICALS, SEVENTEENTH, EIGHTEENTH, AND NINETEENTH CENTURIES; A GUIDE TO THE CONTENTS, relates microfilm reel numbers to periodical volume numbers. There is no index of contents. Individual articles must be located by using various period or author bibliographies.

ENGLISH LITERATURE, 1660-1800: A BIBLIOGRAPHY OF MODERN STUDIES,

COMPILED FOR THE 'PHILOLOGICAL QUARTERLY'. Compiled by Ronald S. Crane et al. 4 vols. London: Oxford University Press; Princeton, N.J.: Princeton University Press, 1950–62.

> The annual bibliographies from the PHILOLOGICAL QUARTERLY have been assembled, with indexes in Volumes 2 and 4. There are critical annotations for both books and articles. The record is continued in the annual volumes of the journal.

Folger Shakespeare Library. CATALOG OF MANUSCRIPTS.

> See Part IV–A.

———. CATALOG OF PRINTED BOOKS.

> See Part IV–A.

French, Frances-Jane. THE ABBEY THEATRE SERIES OF PLAYS; A BIBLIOGRAPHY. Abbey Theatre Series no. 25. Dublin, Ireland: Dolmen Press, 1969. 53 p. Illustrated.

> Describes first editions in the first and second series issued for the famous Irish theater, including works of Lady Gregory, Lennox Robinson, William Butler Yeats, and others.

Golden, Herbert Hershel, and Simches, Seymour O. MODERN FRENCH LITERATURE AND LANGUAGE; A BIBLIOGRAPHY OF HOMAGE STUDIES. Cambridge: Harvard University Press, 1953. Reprint. New York: Kraus, 1971. 158 p.

> An index to selected homage studies, Festschriften or melanges, treating French literature and language from the sixteenth into the twentieth century.
>
> A list of homage volumes, pp. 1–23, is followed by entries classified under "French Literature" (Section II), "Literary and Intellectual Relations between France and Other Countries" (Section III), and "French Language" (Section IV). Section II is subdivided by period, under which are grouped general matters, genre studies, and individual authors. Section III has geographical arrangement. Index of names, titles, and subjects.

———. MODERN IBERIAN LANGUAGE AND LITERATURE; A BIBLIOGRAPHY OF HOMAGE STUDIES. Cambridge, Mass.: Harvard University Press, 1958. 184 p.

> Similar to the other Golden and Simches works, above and below. Items concern Catalan, Portuguese, and Spanish literature and language from the sixteenth century through 1956, with some material on Spanish America and Brazil.

———. MODERN ITALIAN LANGUAGE AND LITERATURE; A BIBLIOGRAPHY

OF HOMAGE STUDIES. Cambridge, Mass.: Harvard University Press, 1959.
Reprint. New York: Kraus, 1971. 207 p.

> A classified index to nearly 2,000 <u>Festschriften</u> on Italian literature
> and language from the Renaissance into the twentieth century. In-
> cluded are both books and "homage numbers" (or volumes) of
> journals through 1957.

> Section III is concerned with Italian literature, and Section IV
> with Italian literature and authors in relation to the United States.
> There is an index of names, subjects, and titles.

GOLDENTREE BIBLIOGRAPHIES.

> See Long, Eugene Hudson, and Ribner, Irving, both below.

Grismer, Raymond L. BIBLIOGRAPHY OF THE DRAMA OF SPAIN AND SPAN-
ISH AMERICA. 2 vols. in 1. Minneapolis: Burgess-Beckwith, [1968?].

> Volumes I (A-L) and II (M-Z) have separate pagination. Grismer
> lists, without annotation, journals and articles as well as critical
> editions. Entries are under critics' names, except the editions,
> which are under primary author.

> See also Hebblethwaite, Frank P., in Part IV-A.

Guttman, Selma. THE FOREIGN SOURCES OF SHAKESPEARE'S WORKS; AN
ANNOTATED BIBLIOGRAPHY OF THE COMMENTARY WRITTEN ON THIS
SUBJECT BETWEEN 1904 AND 1940, TOGETHER WITH LISTS OF CERTAIN
TRANSLATIONS AVAILABLE TO SHAKESPEARE. New York: King's Crown
Press, 1947. Reprint. New York: Octagon, 1968. xxi, 168 p.

> Around 570 references to books and articles in English, French, or
> German. The annotated entries appear in chapters on the major
> European literatures, listed under authors thought to have influenced
> Shakespeare. Short lists of translations are added to these entries.
> An index includes both primary authors and critics.

> Guttman's bibliography will inevitably be examined with reference
> to Geoffrey Bullough's major collection, THE NARRATIVE AND
> DRAMATIC SOURCES OF SHAKESPEARE (8 vols. London: Rout-
> ledge & Paul; New York: Columbia University Press, 1957-75).

> See also Baldensperger, Fernand, and Friederich, Werner P., above,
> and Velz, John W., below, as well as the Shakespeare items in
> Part I-E3.

Hill, Claude, and Ley, Ralph. THE DRAMA OF GERMAN EXPRESSIONISM:
A GERMAN-ENGLISH BIBLIOGRAPHY. University of North Carolina Studies
in the Germanic Languages and Literatures, no. 28. Chapel Hill, N.C.:
University of North Carolina, 1960. 211 p.

> Unannotated list of books, articles, and dissertations through 1957-
> 58. Part I: "General"; Part II: "Individual Dramatists." Primary

texts, some unpublished, appear first, followed by separate lists of German and of English reviews and articles. Indexes of titles and of authors.

Houle, Peter J. THE ENGLISH MORALITY AND RELATED DRAMA; A BIB-LIOGRAPHICAL SURVEY. Hamden, Conn.: Archon Books, 1972. 195 p.

Fifty-nine morality plays are named, with references to principal editions or collections where the plays can be found. Also supplied are the dramatis personae, a plot summary, brief comment, and a list of critical studies. Appendices I-V explore themes in the moralities. Also appended are two bibliographies and a character index.

See also Stratman, Carl J. BIBLIOGRAPHY OF MEDIEVAL DRAMA, in Part IV-A.

Howard-Hill, Trevor Howard. BIBLIOGRAPHY OF BRITISH LITERARY BIBLIOG-RAPHIES. Index to British Literary Bibliography, no. 1. London: Oxford University Press, 1969. 570 p.

First of a three-volume series, the second of which is devoted entirely to Shakespeare (see Part I, "Guides"). A third volume will cover textual criticism.

Brief notes on bibliographies published as books or in books and serials since 1890 in England, the Commonwealth, and the United States. Five thousand items are classified under subjects. There are references to dramas, pamphlets and playbills, and to many playwrights. Index of editors, publishers, and authors.

INDEX TO AMERICAN LITTLE MAGAZINES.

See INDEX TO LITTLE MAGAZINES, below.

INDEX TO LITTLE MAGAZINES. Denver: A. Swallow, 1920-   . Annual.

The index began with a 1948 volume (Denver, 1949), compiled by Avalon Smith et al. Thirty-one "little magazines" were scanned. Some volumes have entries for "Drama," "Theater," and names of playwrights, especially those of the avant garde. No play reviews are cited, but there are review articles.

Retrospective volumes were issued, as follows:

INDEX TO AMERICAN LITTLE MAGAZINES, 1920-1939. By Stephen H. Goode. Troy, N.Y.: Whitston Publishing Co., 1969. 346 p.

INDEX TO AMERICAN LITTLE MAGAZINES, 1940-1942. By Stephen H. Goode. New York: Johnson Reprint Corp., 1967. (Not a reprint; an original edition.)

In 1974 Whitston will publish Goode's INDEX TO AMERICAN LITTLE MAGAZINES, 1900-1919, in three volumes.

See also INDEX TO COMMONWEALTH LITTLE MAGAZINES, 1964–65, in Part V.

Jacob, Herbert.

See Arnold, Robert F., above.

Johnson, Albert. BEST CHURCH PLAYS; A BIBLIOGRAPHY OF RELIGIOUS DRAMA. Philadelphia: Pilgrim Press, 1968. 180 p.

Alphabetical list of play titles, noting author, publisher, price, royalty, cast, sets, and playing time, together with capsule comment. A subject index, pp. 159–80, groups Biblical plays, Easter drama, etc. Publishers' addresses, pp. 150–57.

See also Coleman, Edward D. THE BIBLE IN ENGLISH DRAMA, in Part IV-A, and Houle, Peter J., above, and National Council of the Churches of Christ, below.

Koehmstedt, Carol L.

See PLOT SUMMARY INDEX, below.

Ley, Ralph.

See Hill, Claude, above.

LITERARY HISTORY OF THE UNITED STATES.

See Part I-E2.

LITERATURE AND SOCIETY.

See Modern Language Association of America, General Topics VI, below.

Logan, Terence P., and Smith, Denzell S., eds. THE PREDECESSORS OF SHAKESPEARE; A SURVEY AND BIBLIOGRAPHY OF RECENT STUDIES IN ENGLISH RENAISSANCE DRAMA. Lincoln: University of Nebraska Press, 1973. xiv, 348 p.

Evaluates new editions and critical studies, mainly from 1923 through 1968. Authors considered are Greene, Kyd, Lodge, Lyly, Marlowe, Nashe, and Peele. Classification proceeds, under each author, from general to particular, ending with unannotated lists of additional studies. These chapters are by various specialists.

"Anonymous Plays," pp. 161–310, is edited by Anne Lancashire and Jill Levenson. "Other Dramatists," pp. 312–22, is by Logan and Smith.

There are indexes of contributors, of names, and of plays.

See also Tannenbaum, Samuel Aaron, and Tannenbaum, Dorothy, below.

Long, Eugene Hudson, comp. AMERICAN DRAMA FROM ITS BEGINNINGS TO THE PRESENT. Goldentree Bibliographies in Language and Literature. New York: Appleton-Century-Crofts, 1970. 78 p.

Helpful for students, this list evaluates basic books and articles. General topics are followed by studies of individual playwrights.

See also Ryan, Pat N., below.

Marks, Jeannette. ENGLISH PASTORAL DRAMA FROM THE RESTORATION TO THE DATE OF THE PUBLICATION OF THE 'LYRICAL BALLADS' (1660-1798). London: Methuen, 1908. Reprint. New York: Blom, 1972. 228 p.

A treatise on English, Italian, and Spanish plays and operas with pastoral setting and theme. A bibliography, pp. 214-19, lists criticism. The play list, pp. 135-212, does not locate copies.

Marshall, Thomas F.

See Modern Language Association of America, General Topics VI, below.

Mikhail, E.H. COMEDY AND TRAGEDY; A BIBLIOGRAPHY OF CRITICAL STUDIES. Troy, N.Y.: Whitston Publishing Co., 1972. 54 p.

Unannotated checklists for "Comedy," pp. 3-29, and "Tragedy," pp. 33-54. Under these two headings are found separate lists of references to books and to periodical articles published through 1970.

Modern Humanities Research Association. ANNUAL BIBLIOGRAPHY OF ENGLISH LANGUAGE AND LITERATURE. Cambridge, Eng.: Bowes and Bowes, 1920- . Annual. (Title varies. Some volumes cover more than one year.)

Comprehensive bibliography for English and American literature as well as the English language. General and linguistic bibliography precedes "Literature, General," a section devoted to the literary genres. The main list, which follows, has period subdivision, with authors appearing alphabetically.

References are to books, periodical articles, book reviews, new critical editions, some dissertations, and essays published in Festschriften. Materials are in various languages. A section entitled "Academies, Learned Societies, Miscellanies" reveals the publication of new volumes in important monographic series. There are indexes.

See also English Association. YEAR'S WORK IN ENGLISH STUDIES, above, and Modern Language Association of America. MLA INTERNATIONAL BIBLIOGRAPHY, below.

_____. YEAR'S WORK IN MODERN LANGUAGE STUDIES. London: Oxford University Press, H. Milford, 1931- . Annual. (Publisher varies.)

This scholarly survey evaluates journal articles and books, including new scholarly editions, published in the year covered. References are to modern European languages and literatures, including medieval and neo-Latin and, in recent volumes, the Slavonic languages. Materials cited are in various languages.

See "Drama" entries under periods, within each language group.

See also Modern Language Association of America. MLA INTERNATIONAL BIBLIOGRAPHY, below.

Modern Language Association of America. MLA INTERNATIONAL BIBLIOGRAPHY OF BOOKS AND ARTICLES ON THE MODERN LANGUAGES AND LITERATURES. New York: MLA, 1921- . Annual. (Title varies.)

From 1921 to 1955 this was known as AMERICAN BIBLIOGRAPHY and was limited to the work of American scholars on various national literatures. From 1956 on, references are to material in various languages. Books, articles, and some dissertations are included; Festchriften and other compilations are analyzed.

From 1969 on, each annual contains four "volumes," as follows: I: "General Literature, English and American, Medieval and Neo-Latin, and Celtic Literatures"; II: "European, Asian, African, and Latin-American Literatures"; III: "Linguistics"; IV: "Pedagogy of Foreign Languages." Each has its own index of MLA authors.

In the literary volumes, arrangement is under the various national literatures, subdivided chronologically. General topics within each period (genre studies, etc.) are followed by items concerning individual authors.

See also Modern Humanities Research Association. YEAR'S WORK IN MODERN LANGUAGE STUDIES, above.

Modern Language Association of America. General Topics VI. LITERATURE AND SOCIETY, 1950-1955; A SELECTIVE BIBLIOGRAPHY. Edited by Thomas F. Marshall, with the assistance of George K. Smart and Louis J. Budd. Publications in English and American Literature, no. 2. Coral Gables, Fla.: University of Miami Press, 1956. 57 p.

_____. LITERATURE AND SOCIETY, 1956-1960; A SELECTIVE BIBLIOGRAPHY. Edited by Thomas F. Marshall and George K. Smart. Publications in English and American Literature, no. 4. Coral Gables, Fla.: University of Miami Press, 1962. 71 p.

_____. LITERATURE AND SOCIETY, 1961-65; A SELECTIVE BIBLIOGRAPHY. Edited by Paul J. Carter and George K. Smart. Publications in English and American Literature, no. 9. Coral Gables, Fla.: University of Miami Press, 1967. 160 p.

Organization throughout this series is uniform, but later volumes contain a greater number of references, including some for earlier years.

Books and articles relating literature to society are annotated in separate lists, each alphabetized by author. Most journals cited are in English, with a few in French or German. There is a subject index with headings such as "Comedy," "Depression Plays," "Drama," "Heroes," "Theater," as well as names of authors and some play titles.

Modern Language Association of America. General Topics IX. Bibliography Committee. A BIBLIOGRAPHY ON THE RELATIONS OF LITERATURE AND THE OTHER ARTS, 1952-1967. New York: AMS Press, 1968. (various pagings).

Consists of a reprint of the committee's LITERATURE AND THE OTHER ARTS, A SELECTIVE BIBLIOGRAPHY, 1952-1958 (1959) and annual bibliographies for 1959-67. The basic list, pp. 7-37, and the annual lists are arranged under the headings "Theory and General," "Music and Literature," and "Visual Arts and Literature," with period subdivision. Many references to plays, masques, and operas occur. Notes are sparse. The books and articles cited are in various languages.

The annual lists contain some references which were omitted from the basic list. Only that list has an index of scholars and critics.

Nairn, John Arbuthnot. CLASSICAL HANDLIST.

See Part IV-A.

National Book League. DRAMA IN EDUCATION. Selected by Gerald Slevin. London: National Book League, 1971. 29 p.

Not examined.

National Council of the Churches of Christ in the U.S.A. Department of Worship and the Arts. PLAYS FOR THE CHURCH. A LIST COMPILED BY A COMMITTEE OF THE COMMISSION ON DRAMA. New York: The Council, c. 1957. 40 p.

Annotated list. (Not examined.)

See also Johnson, Albert. BEST CHURCH PLAYS, above.

NEW CAMBRIDGE BIBLIOGRAPHY OF ENGLISH LITERATURE.

See Part I-E2.

New York Public Library. Berg Collection. DICTIONARY CATALOG OF THE HENRY W. AND ALBERT A. BERG COLLECTION OF ENGLISH AND AMERICAN LITERATURE. 5 vols. Boston: G.K. Hall, 1969.

Subject, author, and title entries are interfiled for the holdings
of an important research collection which includes manuscripts,
first editions, other rare books, and autograph letters. The alphabet runs on into the fourth volume, which also contains a file of
"Correspondents, A-G"; that file is concluded in Volume V.

All periods of English and American literature are represented by
20,000 printed items and 50,000 manuscripts. Theater students
will find much of interest under entries for the Abbey Theatre,
Dublin, as well as under many noted playwrights, e.g., Lady
Gregory, Sean O'Casey, Eugene O'Neill, George Bernard Shaw,
and William Butler Yeats.

OXFORD HISTORY OF ENGLISH LITERATURE. Edited by F.P. Wilson and
Bonamy Dobree. Oxford: Clarendon Press, 1945-   . [Appears in irregular
numbering.]

Planned as twelve volumes in fourteen. Will cover all periods of
English literature into the early twentieth century. Texts by re-
nowned scholars are followed, in each volume, by excellent selective and critically annotated bibliographies. For the earlier volumes these are still basic lists, by now a little dated. There are
also chronological tables of events and literary works.

For the medieval period, see Edmund K. Chambers. ENGLISH
LITERATURE AT THE CLOSE OF THE MIDDLE AGES, 1945, 247 p.
(Drama Bibliography, pp. 207-18). Note also F.P. Wilson. THE
ENGLISH DRAMA, 1485-1585, 1969, 244 p. Part 2 of this
volume, when issued, will cover the drama from 1585-1642. See
also Sutherland, James. ENGLISH LITERATURE OF THE LATE
SEVENTEENTH CENTURY, 1969, 589 p.

Payne, Waveney R.N. A SHAKESPEARE BIBLIOGRAPHY. London: Library
Association, 1969. 93 p.

Intended as a guide for the general reader and the advanced student. Lists books only, for the most part those in print or readily
available in libraries. There are concise evaluations for modern
editions of Shakespeare's works, single or collected. Most of the
bibliography concerns criticism of the plays and poems and historical studies, including stage history of the plays.

See also Berman, Ronald, in Part I-A, and Bate, John, above.

PLOT SUMMARY INDEX. Compiled by Carol L. Koehmstedt. Metuchen,
N.J.: Scarecrow Press, 1973. 312 p.

Indexes all volumes of Frank Magill's MASTERPLOTS and ten other
compilations of summaries, including Sprinchorn's TWENTIETH-
CENTURY PLAYS IN SYNOPSIS. Separate lists for titles and
authors refer to collections indexed.

Pronko, Leonard C. GUIDE TO JAPANESE DRAMA. The Asian Literature Bibliography Series. Boston: G.K. Hall, 1973.

> Fully annotated bibliography listing English-language translations of Japanese works from all periods. Historical introduction, chronology, and supplementary reading list. Index of titles, authors, editors, and translators.

> See also Columbia University. A GUIDE TO ORIENTAL CLASSICS; and Nihon Pen Kurabu, in Part IV-A.

Quinn, Edward G., et al. THE MAJOR SHAKESPEAREAN TRAGEDIES; A CRITICAL BIBLIOGRAPHY. New York: Free Press, 1973. 293 p.

> Treats HAMLET, OTHELLO, KING LEAR, and MACBETH. Major critical studies of each play are examined in detail. Other references concern editions, sources, staging, and general works containing Shakespearean studies.

> Index of critics, pp. 3-4.

Rela, Walter. GUIA BIBLIOGRAFICA DE LA LITERATURA HISPANOAMERICANA, DESDE EL SIGLO XIX HASTA 1970. Buenos Aires: Casa Pardo, 1971. 613 p.

> More than 6,000 unannotated entries for books on Latin American literature. Classified arrangement, with name index.

> See also Simon Diaz, Jose, in Part I-E4.

RESEARCH OPPORTUNITIES IN RENAISSANCE DRAMA. Evanston, Ill.: Northwestern University Press, 1955- . (Title has varied.)

> Each issue of this journal has a report, "Current Projects," which mentions both dissertations and other research in progress.

> See also SHAKESPEAREAN RESEARCH AND OPPORTUNITIES, below.

Ribner, Irving. TUDOR AND STUART DRAMA. Goldentree Bibliographies in Language and Literature. New York: Appleton-Century-Crofts, 1966. 72 p.

> Classified, unannotated list of basic books, articles, and dissertations on theater and drama. Not comprehensive, but handy and inexpensive for student use.

Ryan, Pat N. AMERICAN DRAMA BIBLIOGRAPHY; A CHECKLIST OF PUBLICATIONS IN ENGLISH. Fort Wayne, Ind.: Public Library, 1969. 240 p.

> Lists books, articles, and pamphlets on American drama of all periods but excludes material on motion pictures, radio, television, and pageants.

> Entries for playwrights emphasize biography and criticism, seldom reviews.

See also Long, Eugene Hudson, above.

SHAKESPEAREAN RESEARCH AND OPPORTUNITIES. Riverside: Department of English, University of California, 1965-   . Annual. (Title varies.)

> In 1965-67, numbers 1-3 were issued as SHAKESPEAREAN RESEARCH OPPORTUNITIES. Prints the annual report of the Modern Language Association of America Conference, "Opportunities for Research in Shakespearean Studies," along with various annotated checklists. A feature is "Work in Progress," which records ongoing research in more than twenty nations. Dissertations are listed as well as articles and books in preparation. Subject index.

> See also RESEARCH OPPORTUNITIES IN RENAISSANCE DRAMA, above.

"Shakespearean Work in Progress."

> See SHAKESPEAREAN RESEARCH AND OPPORTUNITIES, above. .

Simches, Seymour O.

> See Golden, Herbert Hershel, above.

SOCIAL SCIENCES AND HUMANITIES INDEX.

> Of special interest to literary students because of its indexing of PMLA, among other journals.

> See annotation in Part V.

Stratman, Carl J. BIBLIOGRAPHY OF ENGLISH PRINTED TRAGEDY.

> See Part IV-A.

Tannenbaum, Samuel Aaron, and Tannenbaum, Dorothy. ELIZABETHAN BIBLI-OGRAPHIES. 41 vols. New York: the Authors, 1937-50. Reprint. 10 vols. New York: Kennikat Press, 1967.

> The separate bibliographies concern various literary matters but chiefly individual authors. Items are unannotated and are grouped under broad headings for primary and secondary material. Contents vary with the authorship, for example, the Beaumont and Fletcher, Philip Massinger, George Chapman volume (no. 3) has a section for "Songs and Music" which identifies traditional music related to the plays and names modern editions.

> Continued by ELIZABETHAN BIBLIOGRAPHIES SUPPLEMENTS. See above.

> See also Logan, Terence P., and Smith, Denzell S., above.

Trewin, John Courtenay. VERSE DRAMA SINCE 1800. National Book League.

READER'S GUIDES, 2d ser., no. 8. Cambridge, Eng.: Published for the National Book League by the University Press, 1956. 27 p.

> An essay, pp. 5-17, surveys English-language verse drama since the Elizabethan Age. A classified reading list of primary and secondary materials has some critical and historical annotation, especially for nineteenth and twentieth-century plays through 1955.

Velz, John W. SHAKESPEARE AND THE CLASSICAL TRADITION; A CRITICAL GUIDE TO COMMENTARY, 1660-1960. Minneapolis: University of Minnesota Press, 1968. 459 p.

> Extensively annotated critical bibliography of books, articles, and some dissertations (after the mid 1930s in English, French, or German). Classified arrangement. An index interfiles critics, primary authors, subjects, and titles.

> See also Guttman, Selma, above, and Baldensperger, Fernand, and Friederich, Werner P., in Part I-E4.

Wells, Stanley W., ed. SHAKESPEARE: SELECT BIBLIOGRAPHICAL GUIDES. London: Oxford University Press, 1973. 312 p.

> Consists of revealing bibliographic essays by noted scholars, each with a list of references to books and articles, mainly in English. Recommended for graduate and undergraduate students.

Wilson, F.P.

> See OXFORD HISTORY OF ENGLISH LITERATURE, above.

Woodress, James.

> See AMERICAN LITERARY SCHOLARSHIP, above.

> See also Woodress, James, in Part VI-C.

YEARBOOK OF COMPARATIVE AND GENERAL LITERATURE. (Places of publication have varied; originally published in Chapel Hill, N.C.) 1952- . Annual.

> Published in collaboration with the Comparative Literature Committee of the National Council of Teachers of English, the American Comparative Literature Association, and the Comparative Literature Section of the Modern Language Association of America.

> Among the contents of each volume there is a "Bibliography of Comparative Literature," consisting of unannotated references to books and articles of the preceding year or earlier. Items are classified under "Literary Genres," "Literary Themes," and names of literary authors. From 1960 on there is a separate list of English-language translations published in the United States.

See also Modern Humanities Research Association. YEAR'S WORK IN MODERN LANGUAGE STUDIES, above. See also Baldensperger, Fernand, and Friederich, Werner P., in Part I-E4.

YEAR'S WORK IN ENGLISH STUDIES.

See English Association. YEAR'S WORK IN ENGLISH STUDIES, above.

YEAR'S WORK IN MODERN LANGUAGE STUDIES.

See Modern Humanities Research Association, above.

C. DISSERTATIONS AND THESES

Access to a good proportion of American dissertations and theses on all subjects is possible through DISSERTATION ABSTRACTS and MASTERS' ABSTRACTS. However, as author and subject citations in the DA may appear years ahead of the abstracts and, as some dissertations are never abstracted, a search through successive volumes is time-consuming and sometimes fruitless. The COMPREHEN-SIVE DISSERTATION INDEX, 1861-1972 is, therefore, a very welcome aid. The thirty-seven volumes comprise a master index to virtually all dissertations presented in the U.S.* There will be annual supplements. These may pick up older items previously omitted.

Theodore Besterman's important WORLD BIBLIOGRAPHY OF BIBLIOGRAPHIES, (see Part VI-A), shows bibliographies of dissertations under the heading "Academic Writings." In addition, for currently published bibliographies the reader should consult quarterly issues or annual volumes of BIBLIOGRAPHIC INDEX under the heading "Dissertations, Academic." (Note also the subheading "Research in Progress.") Both of these major reference works are international in coverage.

A reader who may find it convenient to own or consult a list limited to disserta-tions on drama and theater should examine the bibliography by Fredric M. Litto, bearing in mind its restriction to U.S. dissertations. In the field of English and American literature, both McNamee, Lawrence F., and Woodress, James, give access to dissertations produced abroad and in this country. Other compilers have reviewed dissertations produced abroad and relevant to one or another national literature or sometimes only to its drama and theater. (See Knudsen, Hans; Magner, Thomas F.; and others, below.)

Adkins, Cecil, ed. DOCTORAL DISSERTATIONS IN MUSICOLOGY. 5th ed.

---

* Some institutions have reported dissertations only in recent years; others have reported selectively. The editors of COMPREHENSIVE DISSERTATION INDEX have queried many institutions and have added dissertations hitherto unreported.

Philadelphia: American Musicological Society, 1971. 203 p.

> The first four editions were compiled by Helen Hewitt. The first
> (1952) had relatively more coverage of ancillary matters, e.g.,
> acoustics. The second through the fourth editions were limited to
> musicological research. The fifth is again broader in concept.
> There are entries under "Ballet," "Dances," "Drama and Music,"
> "Theaters," etc.

> In this edition a chronological-topical format is used, and there is
> an extensive index of subjects. There are references to DISSERTA-
> TION ABSTRACTS and to RILM ABSTRACTS.

> See also De Lerma, Dominique Rene, below.

American Association for Health, Physical Education, and Recreation. Dance
Division. RESEARCH IN DANCE I. Washington, D.C.: The Association,
1968. 45 p.

> Supplement to DANCE RESEARCH, 1901-1964. (See American
> Association for Health, Physical Education, and Recreation, Na-
> tional Section, below.) Includes research in progress.

> To be updated at five-year intervals.

American Association for Health, Physical Education, and Recreation. National
Section on Dance. DANCE RESEARCH, 1901-1964. Edited by Esther E. Pease.
Washington, D.C.: The Association, 1964. 52 p.

> Lists graduate research completed in the United States from 1901 to
> 1964. Author entries give title of thesis or project, date and name
> of institution.

> This work has been supplemented. See above.

AMERICAN LITERATURE; A JOURNAL.

> See Part VI-B, above.

L'ANNEE PHILOLOGIQUE.

> See Part VI-A2.

Association of Special Libraries. [ASLIB]. INDEX TO THESES ACCEPTED FOR
HIGHER DEGREES IN THE UNIVERSITIES OF GREAT BRITAIN AND IRELAND.
London: 1950-51-   . Annual.

> Classified list of M.A. and Ph.D. theses and dissertations. Subject
> headings include "Music," "Art and Architecture," and "Language
> and Literature." Author and subject indexes.

Besterman, Theodore. A WORLD BIBLIOGRAPHY OF BIBLIOGRAPHIES.

> See Part VI-A1.

BIBLIOGRAPHIC INDEX.

See Part VI-A1.

Black, Dorothy M., comp. GUIDE TO LISTS OF MASTER'S THESES. Chicago: American Library Association, 1965. 114 p.

Black classifies and annotates U.S. and Canadian theses presented for degrees through 1964. "Special Fields" are listed, pp. 12–86, as well as "Specific Institutions," pp. 87–144. There are references for dance, drama, music, and theater.

See also MASTERS' ABSTRACTS; and Howard, Patsy C., below.

Caldwell, Harry B., and Middleton, David L. ENGLISH TRAGEDY, 1370–1600: FIFTY YEARS OF CRITICISM.

See Part VI-B, above.

Canadian Bibliographic Centre. CANADIAN GRADUATE THESES.

See Social Science Research Council of Canada, below.

Chatham, James R., and Ruiz-Fornells, Enrique. DISSERTATIONS IN HISPANIC LANGUAGES AND LITERATURES; AN INDEX OF DISSERTATIONS COMPLETED IN THE UNITED STATES AND CANADA, 1876–1966. Lexington: University Press of Kentucky, 1970. 120 p.

Unannotated classified list treating of Spain, Spanish America, Portugal, and Brazil. Index includes authors, subjects, and titles.

COMPREHENSIVE DISSERTATION INDEX, 1861–1972. 37 vols. Ann Arbor, Mich.: Xerox University Microfilms, 1973. To be supplemented annually.

Computer-generated index to DISSERTATION ABSTRACTS INTERNATIONAL; AMERICAN DOCTORAL DISSERTATIONS; U.S. Library of Congress, LIST OF AMERICAN DOCTORAL DISSERTATIONS, and to other dissertations not previously reported by American universities. Records virtually all dissertations from universities with doctoral programs. The annual supplements planned may pick up some older items omitted in the basic set.

This is an index of keywords selected from the dissertation titles and arranged alphabetically under broad subjects.

Volumes 29–30 cover "Language and Literature," with numerous entries for playwrights and for plays. Volume 31, "Communication and the Arts," covers the fine arts, pp. 23–125; music and dance, pp. 269–589; and "Speech and Theater," pp. 591–961.

For more specific detail on the various dissertation indexes mentioned in the first paragraph, above, see Winchell, Constance M. GUIDE TO REFERENCE BOOKS, as well as the brief annotations, below.

Dahlmann, Friedrich Christoph.

See Part VI-A2.

De Lerma, Dominique Rene. A SELECTIVE LIST OF MASTERS' THESES IN MUSICOLOGY; COMPILED FOR THE AMERICAN MUSICOLOGICAL SOCIETY. Bloomington, Ind.: Denia Press, 1970. 42 p.

Fifty-five American universities were asked to submit data on outstanding theses. The list shows 257 titles, with a statement regarding availability on microfilm or through inter-library loan. Most of the theses concern concert music, but an index also discloses dance music, masques with music, liturgical drama, and operas among topics treated.

See also Adkins, Cecil, above.

Direction des Bibliotheques de France. CATALOGUE DES THESES DE DOCTORAT SOUTENUES DEVANT LES UNIVERSITES FRANCAISES, 1884-   . Paris: Cercle de la Librairie, 1885-   . Issued annually, five annuals forming a volume. (Title varies.)

The official French record of doctoral dissertations presented for degrees. Under names of universities, theses are gouped by faculties. There are indexes of persons and subjects.

DISSERTATION ABSTRACTS.

See DISSERTATION ABSTRACTS INTERNATIONAL, below.

DISSERTATION ABSTRACTS INTERNATIONAL. Ann Arbor, Mich.: University Microfilms, 1956-   . Monthly.

Issued from 1935-51 as MICROFILM ABSTRACTS, Vols. 1-11; 1952-55, as DISSERTATION ABSTRACTS. (Coverage has varied.)

Institutions have contributed information selectively. The author and subject indexes, which cumulate annually, include only the dissertations abstracted (not all dissertations which appeared in INDEX TO AMERICAN DOCTORAL DISSERTATIONS).

While use of current issues may be necessary, for retrospective research it is better to use COMPREHENSIVE DISSERTATION INDEX, 1861-1972 and its annual supplements. (See above.)

DOCTORAL DISSERTATIONS ACCEPTED BY AMERICAN UNIVERSITIES, 1933/34-1954/55. Compiled for the Association of Research Libraries. New York: H.W. Wilson, 1934-56. (Has ceased publication.)

See COMPREHENSIVE DISSERTATION INDEX, 1861-1972, above.

"Doctoral Projects in Progress in Theatre Arts."

See EDUCATIONAL THEATRE JOURNAL, below.

EDUCATIONAL THEATRE JOURNAL. "Doctoral Projects in Progress in Theatre Arts."

> This special section of the journal has appeared in the May issues and has been edited by Albert E. Johnson. With the October 1974 issue the section was retitled "Scholarly Work in Progress" and is to be edited by William C. Young in each March issue.

> The section has listed U.S. dissertations in classified arrangement (geographical, subdivided by period), showing candidate, institution, and proposed date of completion.

Gesellschaft fuer Theatergeschichte, Berlin. SCHRIFTEN.

> See Rojek, Hans Juergen, and Schwanbeck, Gisela, both below.

Gottesman, Ronald. GUIDEBOOK TO FILM.

> See Part I-A.

Hewitt, Helen. DOCTORAL DISSERTATIONS IN MUSICOLOGY.

> See Adkins, Cecil, above.

Howard, Patsy C., comp. THESES IN AMERICAN LITERATURE, 1896-1971. Ann Arbor, Mich.: Pierian Press, 1973. 307 p.

> References to unpublished baccalaureate and masters' theses presented in the United States and Canada are arranged alphabetically by names of literary authors treated. There is an index of thesis authors.

> See also Black, Dorothy M., above, and MASTERS' ABSTRACTS, below.

INDEX TO AMERICAN DOCTORAL DISSERTATIONS, 1955/56. Compiled for the Association of Research Libraries. Ann Arbor, Mich.: University Microfilms, 1957- . Annual.

> The index has appeared as no. 13 of DISSERTATION ABSTRACTS. Lists doctorates conferred in the United States and Canada during the past academic year. Has subject arrangement and author index. Includes information on the lending of dissertations and availability of microfilm copy.

> Current issues may be needed, but for retrospective research, it is better to consult COMPREHENSIVE DISSERTATION INDEX, 1861-1972 and its annual supplements. (See above.)

JAHRESVERZEICHNIS DER DEUTSCHEN HOCHSCHULSCHRIFTEN, 1885- .
Compiled by the Deutsche Buecherei. Leipzig: VEB Verlag, 1887- . (Publisher and title have varied.)

> Official list for all German universities and a few other German
> institutions of higher learning. Entries are grouped under institu-
> tions. Indexes of authors and subjects.

Johnson, Albert E.

> See EDUCATIONAL THEATRE JOURNAL. "Doctoral Projects in
> Progress in Theatre Arts," above.

Knudsen, Hans, ed. THEATER-WISSENSCHAFT IN BERLIN. BESCHREIBENDE
BIBLIOGRAPHIE DER AM THEATER-WISSENSCHAFTLICHEN INSTITUT UNTER
HANS KNUDSEN ENTSTANDENDEN DISSERTATIONEN. Friedrich-Wilhelms
Universitaet, 1945, and Freie Universitaet, Berlin, 1949-66. Berlin: Collo-
quium Verlag, 1966. 141 p.

> Detailed description of seventy-seven dissertations on German the-
> ater, arranged chronologically. Name and subject indexes.

> See also Rojek, Hans Juergen; and Schwanbeck, Gisela, below.

Lasch, Hanna. ARCHITEKTEN-BIBLIOGRAPHIE.

> See Part VI-A4.

Litto, Fredric M. AMERICAN DISSERTATIONS ON THE DRAMA AND THE
THEATRE; A BIBLIOGRAPHY. Kent, Ohio: Kent State University Press, 1969.
544 p.

> The dissertations cited are all American in origin. Subject matter
> is international and treats theater broadly including dance, motion
> pictures, radio, television, vaudeville, musical theater, legitimate
> theater, and related literary and social studies.

> Arrangement is somewhat complex. A "reference code" index
> (planned as basis for a data bank) is followed by conventional in-
> dexes of dissertation authors, keywords in context, and subjects.
> The subject index has geographical arrangement with chronological
> and subject divisions.

> See also McNamee, Lawrence F.; and Woodress, James, below.

McDowell, John, and McGaw, Charles J.

> See American Educational Theatre Association, in Part VI-A1.

McNamee, Lawrence F. DISSERTATIONS IN ENGLISH AND AMERICAN
LITERATURE; THESES ACCEPTED BY AMERICAN, BRITISH, AND GERMAN

UNIVERSITIES, 1865-1964. New York: R.R. Bowker, 1968. 1,124 p.

Unannotated list with entries classified under the headings "Shake-speare," "Renaissance," etc. For "Drama and Theatre," see pp. 462-544 (English) and pp. 813-23 (American).

_____. SUPPLEMENT I, 1964-68. New York: R.R. Bowker, 1969. 450 p.

SUPPLEMENT II, 1969-73. New York: Bowker, in preparation, 1974.

See also Woodress, James, below, and Litto, Fredric M., above.

Magner, Thomas F. SOVIET DISSERTATIONS FOR ADVANCED DEGREES IN RUSSIAN LITERATURE AND SLAVIC LINGUISTICS, 1934-1962. University Park: Department of Slavic Languages, Pennsylvania State University, 1966. 100 p.

About forty pages are devoted to dissertations. Arrangement is by period and thereunder by author. Index.

Manchel, Frank. FILM STUDY.

See Part VI-A5.

MASTERS' ABSTRACTS: ABSTRACTS OF SELECTED MASTERS THESES ON MICROFILM. Ann Arbor, Mich.: University Microfilms, 1962-   . Quarterly. (Frequency has varied.)

Selective classified list of theses from U.S. universities, with information on available microfilm or other copy. Cumulative author and subject indexes.

MICROFILM ABSTRACTS.

See DISSERTATION ABSTRACTS INTERNATIONAL, above.

Mikhail, E.H. DISSERTATIONS ON ANGLO-IRISH DRAMA: A BIBLIOGRA-PHY OF STUDIES, 1870-1970. London: Macmillan, 1973. 73 p.

Shows more than 500 dissertations completed in Great Britain, Ireland, France, Germany, Canada, and the United States. Has indexes of dissertation authors and of institutions.

Naaman, Antoine Youssef. GUIDE BIBLIOGRAPHIQUE DES THESES LITTERAIRES CANADIENNES DE 1921 A 1969. Paris: Nizet; Montreal: Editions Cosmos, 1970. 342 p.

Entries obtained from printed sources and from questionnaires sent to faculties of arts and letters. Threefold arrangement: theses in French or English on Canadian literature; on the literature of other French-speaking areas; on foreign and ancient literature. Material on drama and theater can be found in each section under play-wright's name and under genre. In addition to an index of thesis authors, there is an analytical subject index.

See also National Library of Canada, and Social Science Research Council of Canada, below.

National Library of Canada. CANADIAN THESES, A LIST OF THESES ACCEPTED BY CANADIAN UNIVERSITIES. THESES CANADIENNES, 1960-61- . Ottawa: 1962- . Annual.

Classified list. A few drama items found under "Literature."

See also Naaman, Antoine Youssef, above, and Social Science Research Council of Canada, below.

Pease, Esther E.

See American Association for Health, Physical Education, and Recreation. National Section on Dance, above.

RESEARCH OPPORTUNITIES IN RENAISSANCE DRAMA (current projects).

See Part VI-B, above.

Rojek, Hans Juergen. BIBLIOGRAPHIE DER DEUTSCHSPRACHIGEN HOCH-SCHULSCHRIFTEN ZUR THEATER-WISSENSCHAFT, 1953-1960. Schriften der Gesellschaft fuer Theatergeschichte, Band 61. Berlin: Gesellschaft fuer Theatergeschichte, 1962.

Continues the work of Schwanbeck, Gisela, below.

See also Knudsen, Hans, above.

Ruiz-Fornells, Enrique.

See Chatham, James R., above.

Schaal, Richard. VERZEICHNIS DEUTSCHSPRACHIGER MUSIKWISSENSCHAFT-LICHER DISSERTATIONEN, 1861-1960. Musikwissenschaftliche Arbeiten, no. 19. Kassel and New York: Baerenreiter, 1963. 167 p. To be supplemented.

Lists alphabetically by author some 2,800 German-language disserta-tions on music and allied topics, presented for degrees at German, Austrian, and Swiss universities. Entries give name of dissertation author, institution, date, re-publication, if any, and pagination.

Subject index has entries for opera, libretto, and ballet, etc.

Schwanbeck, Gisela. BIBLIOGRAPHIE DER DEUTSCHSPRACHIGEN HOCHSCHUL-SCHRIFTEN ZUR THEATERWISSENSCHAFT VON 1885 BIS 1952. Schriften der Gesellschaft fuer Theatergeschichte, Band 58. Berlin: Gesellschaft fuer The-atergeschichte, 1956. 563 p.

Classified list of dissertations on theater presented for degrees between 1885 and 1952 in the German-language area of Europe. Name and subject indexes.

Continued by Rojek, Hans Juergen, above. See also Knudsen, Hans, above.

SHAKESPEAREAN RESEARCH AND OPPORTUNITIES.

See Part VI-B, above.

"Shakespearean Work in Progress."

See SHAKESPEAREAN RESEARCH AND OPPORTUNITIES in Part VI-B, above.

Social Science Research Council of Canada. CANADIAN GRADUATE THESES IN THE HUMANITIES AND SOCIAL SCIENCES, 1921-1946. Ottawa: E. Cloutier, Printer to the King, 1951. 194 p.

Prepared at the Canadian Bibliographic Centre, Ottawa. Lists more than 3,000 theses in classified arrangement, subdivided by institution. Author index. French and English subject indexes.

See also Naaman, Antoine Youssef; and National Library of Canada, above.

Stratman, Carl J. A BIBLIOGRAPHY OF MEDIEVAL DRAMA.

See Part IV-A.

_____. A BIBLIOGRAPHY OF THE AMERICAN THEATRE EXCLUDING NEW YORK CITY.

See Part VI-A2.

Stratman, Carl J., et al. RESTORATION AND EIGHTEENTH-CENTURY THEATRE RESEARCH.

See Part VI-A2.

Thompson, Lawrence S. BIBLIOGRAPHY OF AMERICAN DOCTORAL DISSERTATIONS IN CLASSICAL STUDIES AND RELATED FIELDS. Hamden, Conn.: Shoe String Press, 1968. 250 p.

Coverage goes through 1963. Unannotated list of dissertation authors, with an index of subjects, titles, and places. Many entries for theater, theater temples, Latin drama, Greek drama, and playwrights.

See also L'ANNEE PHILOLOGIQUE, in Part VI-A2.

U.S. Library of Congress. Catalog Division. LIST OF AMERICAN DOCTORAL DISSERTATIONS PRINTED IN 1912-38. 26 vols. Washington, D.C.: Government Printing Office, 1913-40. (Has ceased publication.)

See COMPREHENSIVE DISSERTATION INDEX, 1861-1972, above.

Velz, John W. SHAKESPEARE AND THE CLASSICAL TRADITION.

See Part VI-B, above.

Woodress, James. DISSERTATIONS IN AMERICAN LITERATURE, 1891-1966. Rev. ed. Durham, N.C.: Duke University Press, 1968. 185 p.

Classified unannotated list of nearly 4,700 dissertations produced from 1891 through 1966 in the United States and abroad. Drama entries, numbered 2926-3281, include some pertaining to theater history. Note also headings such as "Literary History," "Negro," and "Periodicals and Journalism."

See also McNamee, Lawrence F.; and Litto, Fredric M., above.

Young, William C.

See EDUCATIONAL THEATRE JOURNAL. "Scholarly Work in Progress," above.

Part VII

ILLUSTRATIVE AND AUDIOVISUAL SOURCES
FOR THE PERFORMING ARTS

In the history of the performing arts the visual element is vital. Granted that a play text, filmscript, or other adaptation is the usual source from which a theatrical work is created and that even an insipid libretto seems necessary to opera, yet the literary element by itself lacks the quality which strongly distinguishes theater--its visual rendering. The exception is the radio play, really an individual genre. Mime, motion pictures, and the dance all attest to the predominance of the visual in theatrical creation. Even opera depends greatly on spectacle.

Therefore, the visual record is of prime importance for research. The ephemera such as posters and playbills, the more enduring photographs and portraits, as well as architects' drawings and scene and costume designers' sketches, make up a good proportion of the primary materials needed by scholars in search of the performing arts as they were experienced.

Interest in such sources is not, however, limited to the scholar seeking authenticity. The curious student and, increasingly, the amateur of popular culture are becoming aware of lively possibilities in these media of historical communication. Teachers are using this treasure to elucidate the past and illustrate the contemporary performing arts.

Public collecting of theatrical artifacts is relatively new; but many informed amateurs have amassed splendid hoards, some of which are now in public institutions. These resources are scattered and little-known.

It was left to the twentieth century to make commercial recordings and tapes of famous voices in their prime, great scenes in opera, and entire dramatic performances. Also, taking advantage of new techniques, historians, librarians, and curators have instituted oral history programs as a way of preserving the recollections of those who helped to make the theatrical events of the past. Many archives are now enriched by field recordings of this nature.

For some decades the motion pictures have united sight and sound, bringing complete musical and dramatic performances to life, either as original productions or as adaptations.

Thus, no other period has been more favorable for examination of the performing arts as they must be examined in leisurely and repeated study of the infinite detail which makes up their achievement. True, there may still be supreme moments in performances never trapped on tape. This alone should make us more grateful for what has been retrieved.

The bibliographic record, in the shape of catalogs of collected ephemera, films, and recordings, certainly limps behind. Yet, in regard to the ephemera alone, it must be said that the difficulties of identifying, organizing, and preserving these illustrative materials make it remarkable that there is as much bibliographic access as we already have. More hands and funds are needed.

At the present there are some good descriptive bibliographies for all of these types of materials, of which the selected entries below are typical. For those collections which lack catalogs, it is possible to gain a general description by consulting several of the works discussed in Part III, "Directories." Cross-references to these appear in Part VII. In particular, attention is called to the International Federation of Library Associations' PERFORMING ARTS LIBRARIES AND MUSEUMS and to William C. Young's AMERICAN THEATRICAL ARTS: A GUIDE TO MANUSCRIPTS AND SPECIAL COLLECTIONS IN THE UNITED STATES AND CANADA. A serial publication of the Theatre Library Association, PERFORMING ARTS RESOURCES, scheduled to appear in 1975 (New York: Drama Book Specialists), will provide a partial record of new acquisitions as well as historical articles on theater libraries and their collections.

In addition to the primary materials existing in collections there are numerous illustrations buried in reference works, to some of which Part VII makes brief reference. Access to enough visual material on art and architecture is important for designers, not so much for historical accuracy as for a source of fresh ideas. To students, the need of a sufficient acquaintance with period styles that have influenced the theater should be apparent. Therefore a number of the reference works listed in this part relate to art, architecture, and the decorative arts. (Acquaintance with many more illustrated books on these arts is possible through use of the guides in Part I. Some encyclopedias in Part II are themselves good sources of illustrations.) Part VII is subdivided as follows:

   (A) Performing Arts and General Illustration.

   (B) Posters, Playbills, Programs, Advertisements.

   (C) Portrait Catalogs and Indexes.

   (D) Architectural Illustration.

   (E) Art and Design Illustration.

   (F) Songs and Recordings (Sources and Reviews).

(G) Films for Study of the Performing Arts.

(H) Audiovisual Catalogs, Equipment, Services.

A. PERFORMING ARTS AND GENERAL ILLUSTRATION

Ash, Lee, comp. SUBJECT COLLECTIONS.

> Leads to pictorial and other sources on theater and related studies, as well as other subjects.
>
> For full annotation, see Part III.

THE BALLET ANNUAL: A RECORD AND YEAR-BOOK OF THE BALLET. 18 vols. London: A and C. Black, 1947–63. Illustrated. (Title has varied; has ceased publication.)

> The editor, first through eighteenth volumes, was A.L. Haskell; excepting Volume 17, edited by Haskell with Mary Clarke. After Volume 18, this publication was absorbed into the monthly DANCING TIMES.
>
> Summarized outstanding events of the year and discussed seasons in several U.S. and European cities. Obituaries. Index.
>
> Many full-page photographs, especially of ballerinas.

Besseler, Heinrich, ed., with Schneider, Max. MUSIKGESCHICHTE IN BILDERN. Leipzig: VEB Deutscher Verlag fuer Musik. Band I. 1961– . Illustrated.

> Finely illustrated, scholarly record of musical history throughout the world. Some volumes are anthropologically oriented and will interest dancers, Volume I, for example, which is illustrated with photographs taken in the field. Volume IV: MUSIK DER NEUZEIT. Part 1 is concerned with opera scenes and settings from 1600 to 1900 and is edited by Hellmuth Christian Wolff. Reproduces many handsome illustrations from contemporary sources. Notes are in German. Bibliography, pp. 199–201, is in various languages. Index of illustrations, listed under geographical and topical headings, e.g., "Buehnenmaschinerie" (Stage machinery). Index of names and subjects.

Bettmann, Otto, ed. BETTMANN PORTABLE ARCHIVE: A GRAPHIC HISTORY OF ALMOST EVERYTHING, PRESENTED BY WAY OF 3669 ILLUSTRATIONS CULLED FROM THE FILES OF THE BETTMANN ARCHIVE AND TOPICALLY ARRANGED AND CROSS-REFERENCED TO SERVE AS AN IDEA STIMULATOR AND IMAGE FINDER. New York: Picture House Press, 1966. 229 p. Illustrated.

> This book consists of 3,669 reproductions of illustrations in various media and on many subjects. Most illustrations are small. Well indexed.

Only a sampling of the great number of illustrations of which copies can be bought from The Bettmann Archive in full-sized reproduction.

Bibliotheque Nationale. Departement des Estampes. CATALOGUE DES DESSINS RELATIFS A L'HISTOIRE DU THEATRE CONSERVES AU DEPARTEMENT DES ESTAMPES..., AVEC LA DESCRIPTION D'ESTAMPES RARES ACQUIRES DE M. DESTAILLEUR. Compiled by Henri Bouchot. Paris: Bibliotheque Nationale, 1896. 82 p. (Extracted from the REVUE DES BIBLIOTHEQUES, Oct. 1895-March 1896.)

Catalog of drawings relating to the history of theater, as acquired by M. Destailleur and held in the Print Department of the Bibliotheque Nationale.

Blume, Friedrich. DIE MUSIK IN GESCHICHTE UND GEGENWART. Source for fine illustrations of musical history.

For full annotation, see Part II-B.

Boussinot, Roger. ENCYCLOPEDIE DU CINEMA.

Volume II contains 3,000 photographs.

For full annotation see Part II-A.

DANCE INDEX. New York: Ballet Caravan, January 1942 to July-August 1948. (Has ceased publication.) Reprint. 7 vols. New York: Arno Press, 1970.

Not an index; rather, a distinguished monthly periodical (sometimes issued irregularly). Source for rare illustrations of ballet and modern dance, along with significant articles.

DANCE WORLD. Edited by John Willis. New York: Crown Publishers, 1966- . Annual. Illustrated.

Chronological record of performances arranged under names of theaters in New York, followed by summer festivals and regional companies (these arranged alphabetically by name of company). Repertoire, cast, and production credits for the past season. Many small photographs. Biographies of dancers and choreographers. Obituaries. General index.

DANIEL BLUM'S OPERA WORLD: SEASONS 1952-53, 1953-54. New York: Putnam, 1955. 192 p. Illustrated.

Survey of the season at the New York Metropolitan Opera, New York City Center Opera, and the San Francisco Opera. Also highlights of the European scene, including summer festivals. For the U.S. companies there are chronologies of openings, with casts. List of outstanding recordings. Obituaries.

Many photographs of scenes and singers in costume.

DANIEL BLUM'S SCREEN WORLD.

See SCREEN WORLD, below.

DANIEL BLUM'S THEATRE WORLD.

See THEATRE WORLD, below.

DICTIONARY OF MODERN BALLET.

Many illustrations, some in color.

For full annotation, see Part II-C.

Ellis, Jessie. INDEX TO ILLUSTRATIONS. Boston: F.W. Faxon, 1966, c. 1967. 682 p.

References to picture materials in all fields except nature. (Natural forms do appear in symbolic form, e.g., rosette in architecture.) Based on a short list of books and periodicals likely to be found in libraries. Many entries for the decorative arts, for places, and theater-related entries, e.g., actor, Japanese (in HOLIDAY).

See also ILLUSTRATION INDEX, below.

ENCICLOPEDIA DELLO SPETTACOLO.

Major encyclopedia for all of the performing arts. Profusely illustrated. Some colored plates.

For full annotation, see Part II-A.

ENCYCLOPEDIA OF THE ARTS.

Imaginatively selected illustrations of small scale pertaining to all of the arts.

For full annotation see Part II-E.

Evans, Hilary, and Evans, Mary. SOURCES OF ILLUSTRATIONS, 1500-1900. Bath: Adams and Dart, 1971. 162 p. Illustrated.

An essay on visual documentation of historical studies also sketches in the development of graphic media, pp. 1-22. This is followed by a miscellany of reproduced woodcuts, engravings, and lithographs in chronological order, illustrating the graphic styles from 1500 to 1900, pp. 23-153. Lacks an index. Suggestions for purchase of pictures from various sources, with a list of addresses in Great Britain, Europe, and the United States, pp. 155-61.

Folger Shakespeare Library. THE FOLGER SHAKESPEARE LIBRARY PRINTS.

See Part VII-C, below.

Forrester, Felicitee Sheila. BALLET IN ENGLAND.

    See Part VI-A2.

Greer, Roger C.

    See ILLUSTRATION INDEX, below.

GUIDE TO DANCE PERIODICALS.

    From Volume V on, this index listed illustrations in periodical articles. Ceased publication in 1962 with Volume X.

    For full annotation see Part V.

GUIDE TO THE MUSICAL ARTS.

    Over one-third of this work (Part II) is an unpaged index to illustrations in "the world's leading journals" dealing with music, opera, dance, and the theater. The timespan is 1953 through 1956, with some back-indexing to 1949. Continued by GUIDE TO THE PERFORMING ARTS, below.

    For full annotation, see Part V.

GUIDE TO THE PERFORMING ARTS.

    Refers, under subject, to illustrations in periodicals. Portraits indicated under personal names.

    For full annotation, see Part IV-A.

ILLUSTRATION INDEX. By Roger C. Greer. 3d ed. Metuchen, N.J.: Scarecrow Press, 1973. 164 p.

    Earlier editions were by Lucile E. Vance (New York: Scarecrow Press, 1957. 192 p.) and Lucile E. Vance and Esther M. Tracey (2d ed. New York: Scarecrow Press, 1966. 527 p.)

    Companion to the 1963 edition, which covered 1950-63, indexing illustrations on most subjects, as found in a short list of general magazines available in many public libraries. The present volume continues from 1963 through 1971, with the same method and scope. Excluded in both volumes are such subjects as furniture, nature, paintings, and individuals, unless these illustrate costume, historical events, or other topics of general interest.

    The Preface states, "[s]pecial emphasis has been given...to costumes; fashion designs; theatrical stage settings."

    Most of the illustrations referred to are photographs. Others are identified as "drawing," etc.

    See also Ellis, Jessie, above.

AN INDEX TO 'FILMS IN REVIEW', 1950-1959 and 1960-1964.

> Separately published indexes, with some lists of illustrations occurring in the monthly FILMS IN REVIEW.
>
> For full annotation, see Part V.

International Federation of Library Associations. PERFORMING ARTS LIBRARIES AND MUSEUMS.

> In the main index, see entries for places, names of persons and of libraries. There is also a selective subject index, pp. 799-801, with entries such as "Promptbooks." Many collections described are especially noteworthy for their primary materials including posters, photographs, etc.
>
> For full annotation, see Part III.

Kinsky, Georg. HISTORY OF MUSIC IN PICTURES. Edited with the cooperation of Robert Haas et al. Introduction by Eric Blom. New York: Dover, c. 1951. xiv, 363 p. Illustrated.

> Originally issued in Germany as GESCHICHTE DER MUSIK IN BILDERN (Leipzig: Breitkopf, 1930; English edition: London: Dent, 1930).
>
> The introduction tells the difficulties of iconographic research. There follows a chronological arrangement of pictures of many sorts relating to music, instruments, and composers; a few show opera settings and theater interiors. Note especially the seventeenth and eighteenth-century material.
>
> See also Besseler, Heinrich, above.

Lewanski, Richard Casimir. SUBJECT COLLECTIONS IN EUROPEAN LIBRARIES.

> See national listings under "Theater" section. Has statistics for holdings of musical scores, photographs, prints, etc. No details.
>
> For full annotation, see Part III.

New York Public Library. DICTIONARY CATALOG OF THE DANCE COLLECTION.

> Lists audiovisual material in several forms. For annotation, see Part VI-A1.

NINETEENTH CENTURY READERS' GUIDE.

> Illustrations in periodicals are referred to under personal names, e.g., Bernhardt, Sarah, and under subjects such as "Theater."
>
> For full annotation, see Part IV-A.

Nunn, George Walter Arthur, ed. BRITISH SOURCES OF PHOTOGRAPHS AND

PICTURES. London: Cassell, 1952. 220 p.

> (Not examined.)
>
> Comprises several lists: photographers and agencies, with addresses and notes on their collections; institutions, including libraries, museums, and societies; journals and yearbooks. Subject index.
>
> Includes some continental but mainly British sources.

OXFORD COMPANION TO MUSIC.

> Has illustrations for dance and music.
>
> See Part II-B.

OXFORD COMPANION TO THE THEATRE. 3d ed.

> Has an illustrated supplement of 176 pages, preceded by notes.
>
> For full annotation, see Part II-A.

PERFORMING ARTS RESOURCES.

> See headnote, Part VII, above.

Ploetz, Gerhard. BILDQUELLEN-HANDBUCH; DER WEGWEISER FUER BILD-SUCHENDE. 1. Ausg., Wiesbaden: Chmielorz, 1961. 611 p. Plates.

> Part 1 has indexes of subjects, places, artists, and other persons, relating each to a collection or collections in which photographs are found. Parts 2-5 comprise a list of twenty categories of archives and other collections, grouped geographically. Part 7 is an index of frequently sought subjects.

Rasi, Luigi. I COMICI ITALIANI; BIOGRAFIA, BIBLIOGRAFIA, ICONO-GRAFIA. 2 vols. in 3. Florence: Bocca, 1897-1905. Illustrated.

> Volume III was published by Francesco Lumachi.
>
> Basic source for study of Italian theater in the lives of its actors from mid-sixteenth through nineteenth century. Articles alphabetized by actors' names. Illustrated with portraits, facsimiles, engravings of stage sets, commedia dell'arte scenes, etc. (some in color).

THE READERS' GUIDE TO PERIODICAL LITERATURE.

> Many subject entries call attention to illustrations in articles.
>
> For full annotation, see Part IV-A.

Sadoul, Georges. DICTIONNAIRE DES CINEASTES.

> Many illustrations. These are lacking in the English-language edition of this motion picture reference work.
>
> For full annotation, see Part II-A.

SCREEN WORLD. New York. 1949-   . Annual. Illustrated. (Publisher varied.)

> Now John Willis's SCREEN WORLD (New York: Crown Publishers), this illustrated survey was founded, edited, and published for many years by Daniel C. Blum.
>
> Gives cast, credits, and month of release for new films. Has many small photographs, biographical data for actors, and obituaries. Index of names and film titles.

Speaight, Robert. SHAKESPEARE ON THE STAGE; AN ILLUSTRATED HISTORY OF SHAKESPEARIAN PERFORMANCES. Boston: Little, Brown; London: Collins, 1973. 304 p. Illustrated.

> Surveys 400 years of celebrated performance from Burbage to Olivier. Especially notable for its illustrations, some in color.

Special Libraries Association. Picture Division. PICTURE SOURCES. Edited by Ann Novotny. 3d ed. New York: Special Libraries Association, 1973.

> Earlier editions were the work of Helen Faye (1959) and Celestine G. Frankenberg (1964). A directory of library and other collections of pictures, some with very special emphasis. Entries describe scope of collections, and reveal the possibility of access, as well as availability of reproductions for sale, rental, or free. Bibliography. Index.
>
> See also Wasserman, Paul, below, and Clapp, Jane, ART REPRODUCTIONS, Part VII-E, below.

THEATRE WORLD. New York. 1944-45-   . Annual. Illustrated. (Publisher and title vary.)

> This survey of the New York season's musical and legitimate theater was founded and edited for many years by Daniel C. Blum. It is now issued by Crown Publishers as JOHN WILLIS' THEATRE WORLD.
>
> The main section is the "Broadway Calendar," a chronology of openings, followed by the "Off-Broadway Calendar," material on national touring companies, Shakespeare festivals, and various U.S. professional resident companies. This last section is not a chronology but lists company members, staff, and productions.

Basic entries in the New York list show opening date, cast, credits, and length of run.

Also lists of awards, biographies, and obituaries. Name and title index. Heavily illustrated.

THEATRE WORLD ANNUAL: A PICTORIAL REVIEW OF WEST END PRODUCTIONS WITH A RECORD OF PLAYS AND PLAYERS. London: Rockliff, 1949-50 to 1964-65. (Has ceased publication.)

Edited 1949-50 by Frances Stephens.

Well illustrated annual of the London stage. Includes "Personalities of the Year"; "Review of the Year" (rather laudatory); "Play casts" June 1 to May 31 of each year. The main section is organized around particular theater companies, with a generous selection of photographs for each. List of play runs. Ballet and opera section. Obituaries. Index.

Tracey, Esther M.

See ILLUSTRATION INDEX, above.

U.S. Library of Congress. Reference Department. GUIDE TO THE SPECIAL COLLECTIONS OF PRINTS AND PHOTOGRAPHS IN THE LIBRARY OF CONGRESS. Compiled by Paul Vanderbilt. Washington, D.C.: Library of Congress, 1955. 200 p.

Describes more than 800 collections in the library, not attempting to index individual pictures but describing contents in terms of media and general subject matter. Entries are alphabetized by names of collections. Some have short bibliographies. (The preface points to the need for further bibliographic work on these valuable collections.)

An index refers to numbered entries and includes such subjects as "Architecture (Theaters, European)," "Ballet," "Portraits (Actors and Actresses)," "Singers," "Posters," and "Theater." One notable collection concerns the Federal Theater Project.

U.S. National Historical Publications Commission. GUIDE TO ARCHIVES AND MANUSCRIPTS IN THE UNITED STATES.

See entries for "Theatrical Posters," names of persons, theaters, and other institutions.

For full annotation, see Part III.

Vance, Lucile E. ILLUSTRATION INDEX.

See ILLUSTRATION INDEX, above.

Wasserman, Paul, managing ed. MUSEUM MEDIA; A BIENNIAL DIRECTORY AND INDEX OF PUBLICATIONS AND AUDIOVISUALS AVAILABLE FROM UNITED STATES AND CANADIAN INSTITUTIONS. Esther Herman, associate ed. Detroit: Gale Research Co., 1973. 455 p.

> A listing of 732 museums, with addresses and with prices of in-print items and ordering information. Items include books, pamphlets, exhibition catalogs, documents, maps, slide assortments, photographs, prints, filmstrips, films, and tapes, for some of which more complete details are available on request. There are indexes of titles, keywords, locations, and subjects.

> See also Clapp, Jane. ART REPRODUCTIONS, in Part VII-E, below, and Special Libraries Association, above.

WORLD ENCYCLOPEDIA OF FILM. Illustrated.

> For full annotation, see Part II-A.

Young, William C. AMERICAN THEATRICAL ARTS; A GUIDE TO MANU-SCRIPTS AND SPECIAL COLLECTIONS IN THE UNITED STATES AND CANADA.

> Many subjects cited in Young's index will lead to special collections rich in visual materials, e.g., posters. See "Actors and Actresses," "Authors," "Composers," "Variety Performers," "Vaudeville," and, especially, "Theaters."

> For full annotation, see Part III.

B. POSTERS, PLAYBILLS, PROGRAMS, ADVERTISEMENTS

Ash, Lee, comp. SUBJECT COLLECTIONS.

> Note entries for "Posters" and "Theater."

> For full annotation, see Part III.

Bibliotheque Nationale. Departement de la Musique. LE CIRQUE, ICONOGRAPHIE. Catalogues de la Bibliotheque de l'Opera. Paris: Bibliotheque Nationale, 1969. 166 p.

> Catalog of special library collections devoted to the circus in France. Materials, which are briefly described, include mainly lithographic posters, featuring circus scenes and performers of many nationalities. A few excellent posters are reproduced.

> Bibliography, pp. 151-52. General index.

BIOGRAPH BULLETINS, 1908-1912. Edited, with an Introduction, by Eileen Bowser. New York: Octagon, 1973. 471 p. Illustrated.

> Continues the record in Kemp R. Niver's BIOGRAPH BULLETINS, 1896-1908. (See below.) Similar material and illustrations. Title index.

Neither compilation gives film credits. Original materials, preserved in the Archives of the Museum of Modern Art, New York, also lack this information.

Book Club of California. PIONEER WESTERN PLAYBILLS. Keepsake Series, no. 14. Edited by Frank L. Fenton. San Francisco: Book Club of California, 1951. Illustrated.

Facsimiles of twelve important early Western play programs, with notes by various writers, concerned with such events as the appearance of Lola Montez at the American Theater in San Francisco in 1853 and Laura Keene at the Sacramento Theater, Sacramento, California in 1854.

Boston Public Library. Allen A. Brown Collection. A CATALOGUE OF THE ALLEN A. BROWN COLLECTION OF BOOKS RELATING TO THE STAGE IN THE PUBLIC LIBRARY OF THE CITY OF BOSTON.

Despite its title, this catalog also lists some playbills, programs, and collections of newspaper clippings found in the library. See names of theaters under place names, e.g., "London. Theatres. His Majesty's Theatre."

For full annotation, see Part IV-A.

British Museum. Department of Printed Books. REGISTER OF PLAYBILLS, PROGRAMMES, AND THEATRE CUTTINGS. London: 1950. 54 l. This list was "reproduced from typewriting."

(Not examined.)

A single reel of microfilm was also made, reproducing the typescript. London: British Museum Photographic Service, 1967.

Brown, James H. CATALOGUE OF THE VALUABLE COLLECTION OF PLAYBILLS, PORTRAITS, PHOTOGRAPHS, ETC. Boston: C.F. Libbie and Company, Auctioneers and Appraisers, 1898. 102 p.

Sale catalog of a private collection which included about 3,000 books concerning the stage, 2,500 autograph letters, and 80,000 playbills, as well as framed programs, photographs, lithographs, paintings, and memorabilia.

Playbills are listed under place. There are very brief notes, some with information on actors and roles.

CIRCUS AND ALLIED ARTS.

Has many references to illustrations in books (e.g., "Cover by J. Cheret") and to collections of photographs, etc. Each volume closes with a selection of reproductions, including some posters.

For full annotation, see Part I-A.

Edwards, Francis. PLAYBILLS; A COLLECTION AND SOME COMMENTS.
London: F. Edwards, Bookseller, 1893. 37 p.

> (Not examined.)
>
> Concerns nineteenth-century British playbills.

Evans, Charles. AMERICAN BIBLIOGRAPHY.

> In this major catalog of books, pamphlets, and periodicals pub-
> lished in America from 1639 through 1800, there are also entries
> for theatrical ephemera such as playbills and broadsides. See the
> index volume under names of theaters, plays, etc. In the index
> to the supplement, see similar entries, e.g., "Boston Theatre.
> (broadside). Positively the last appearance of ...."
>
> For full annotation, see Part IV-A. Also in Part IV-A, see Shaw,
> Ralph R., and Shoemaker, Richard H., AMERICAN BIBLIOGRAPHY,
> which continues Evans. (Note entries under "Theatre.")

DAS FRUEHE PLAKAT IN EUROPA UND DEN USA; EIN BESTANDS-KATALOG.
Forschungsunternehmen 19 Jahr. der Fritz Thyssen Stiftung. Edited by Lise
Lotte Moeller et al., for Kunstbibliothek Staatliche Museen Preussischer Kul-
turbesitz, Berlin [and] Museum fuer Kunst und Gewerbe, Hamburg. Berlin:
Gebr. Mann, c. 1973- . Illustrated.

> Part of a series in nineteenth-century research sponsored by the
> Fritz Thyssen Foundation, this fine scholarly catalog of early post-
> ers represents the holdings of this popular art form in public collec-
> tions within the Federal Republic of Germany and West Berlin.
> The collections are international (Europe and the United States)
> and extend from the beginning of the modern poster to 1914.
>
> Published to date are Volumes I (England and the United States)
> and II (France and Belgium). Volume I alone has 686 black and
> white reproductions and twenty-four colored plates. There are two
> sections, the English and the American, each alphabetized by
> artists' names. Notes and brief bibliographies pertain to posters
> on the facing page. Many relate to theater and opera productions.
>
> There are biographies of artists, a list of sources, and a general
> index, which reveals names of theaters, theatrical companies, and
> play titles.
>
> Introductory essays by Heinz Spielmann and Ruth Malhotra, summa-
> rized in English, sketch the historical and esthetic outlines for a
> study of early posters. A chronology of cultural and political
> events, pp. lvii-lxxiii, makes occasional reference to the poster
> catalog.

Gottesman, Ronald. GUIDEBOOK TO FILM.

> Note "Stills and Posters", p. 147.
>
> For full annotation, see Part I-A.

Howard, Diana. LONDON THEATRES AND MUSIC HALLS, 1850-1950.

> Includes references to collections of playbills, programs, etc.

> For full annotation, see Part III.

Howard-Hill, Trevor Howard. BIBLIOGRAPHY OF BRITISH LITERARY BIBLIOG-RAPHIES.

> Some references to playbills. For full annotation, see Part VI-B.

International Federation of Library Associations. PERFORMING ARTS LIBRARIES AND MUSEUMS.

> See Part VII-A.

Kobal, John, comp. FIFTY YEARS OF MOVIE POSTERS. London: Hamlyn; New York: Bounty Books, Crown Publishers, 1973. 175 p. Illustrated.

> Spiral-bound picture book, with historical introduction. Posters reproduced were used between 1911 and 1955.

Ledger Job Printing Establishment, Philadelphia. SPECIMENS OF SHOW PRINTING, BEING FACSIMILES IN MINIATURE OF POSTERS, COMPRISING COLORED AND PLAIN DESIGNS. Philadelphia: 1869, 1872. Reprint. Hollywood, Calif.: Cherokee Book, [1966]. 519 p. Illustrated.

> Cover title "Early American Theatrical Posters."

> Facsimile reprint of a printer's specification book for theatrical posters available for use in the United States during the 1860s and 1870s. These miniatures occupy a half or full page (27 cm) and are in black and white. Captions show title, price, and avail-ability in color. More than 500 specimens are shown, preceded by a title index. Some cuts are of a general purpose variety (e.g., black-face minstrels, knife jugglers, trapeze artists) and are un-titled.

Lewis, John Noel C. PRINTED EPHEMERA; THE CHANGING USES OF TYPE AND LETTERFORMS IN ENGLISH AND AMERICAN PRINTING. Ipswich, Suffolk: W.S. Cowell; London: Faber and Faber, 1962. 288 p. Illustrated.

> Chiefly fine typographic specimens for many kinds of materials. See entries under "Entertainment Posters and Playbills," pp. 100-115, and "Entertainment Tickets," p. 148. Also see index for names of theaters.

> See also Martin, Gordon, below, and LEDGER JOB PRINTING ESTABLISH-MENT, above.

Loewenberg, Alfred, comp. THE THEATRE OF THE BRITISH ISLES, EXCLUDING LONDON.

Mentions collections which include playbills, etc. For full annotation, see Part VI-A2.

THE LONDON STAGE, 1660-1800. 11 vols.

Consult indexes of many volumes for references to playbills. See also pp. lxxv-lxxviii for a discussion of theatrical advertising in the Restoration period. For full annotation, see Part VI-A2.

Martin, Gordon. THE PLAYBILL; THE DEVELOPMENT OF ITS TYPOGRAPHIC STYLE. Chicago: Institute of Design of the Illinois Institute of Technology, 1963. 58 p. Illustrated.

American and English playbills of late eighteenth and nineteenth centuries are shown in facsimile, slightly reduced.

See also Lewis, John Noel C. PRINTED EPHEMERA, above.

New York Public Library. DICTIONARY CATALOG OF THE DANCE COLLECTION.

Includes entries for playbills, programs, and other ephemera. For full annotation, see Part VI-A1.

New York Public Library. Reference Department. DICTIONARY CATALOG OF THE MUSIC COLLECTION.

Lists printed programs, among other materials held by the library.

Niver, Kemp R., comp. BIOGRAPH BULLETINS, 1896-1908. Compiled with an introduction and notes by Kemp R. Niver. Edited by Bebe Bergsten. Los Angeles: Locare Research Group, 1971. 464 p. Illustrated.

The historical introduction, pp. 3-10, relates the Biograph Company to the early development of motion pictures. From 1896 on, the company made Mutoscope flip cards and viewers for home entertainment; its films and projector were used for vaudeville bookings. On pp. 11-51 are reproduced press clippings from the United States and England which review these entertainments.

The bulk of this volume reproduces the BULLETINS, numbers 1-200 (with a few gaps), pp. 76-416. These were issued from 1902-8 as advertising handbills. Each film is advertised with a synopsis and a captioned still photograph, e.g., FALSELY ACCUSED. "Go, you contemptible villain, go!"

General index. List of film titles, with dates.

Continued by BIOGRAPH BULLETINS, 1908-1912, above.

THE OXFORD COMPANION TO THE THEATRE.

> There are excellent articles on "Playbill, Programme" and "Posters, Theatrical."

> For full annotation, see Part II-A.

Rigdon, Walter, ed. THE BIOGRAPHICAL ENCYCLOPEDIA AND WHO'S WHO OF THE AMERICAN THEATRE.

> Reproduces the playbills (casts and credits) of various American repertory groups and of theaters in New York City, 1959-64. Not illustrated.

> For full annotation, see Part II-A.

U.S. Library of Congress. Reference Department. GUIDE TO THE SPECIAL COLLECTIONS OF PRINTS AND PHOTOGRAPHS.

> See Part VII-A, above.

U.S. National Historical Publications Commission. GUIDE TO ARCHIVES AND MANUSCRIPTS IN THE UNITED STATES.

> See Part VII-A, above.

Young, William C. AMERICAN THEATRICAL ARTS; A GUIDE TO MANU-SCRIPTS AND SPECIAL COLLECTIONS IN THE UNITED STATES AND CANADA.

> See Part VII-A, above.

C. PORTRAIT CATALOGS AND INDEXES

A L.A. PORTRAIT INDEX; INDEX TO PORTRAITS CONTAINED IN PRINTED BOOKS AND PERIODICALS. Edited by William Coolidge Lane and Nina E. Browne. Washington, D.C.: Government Printing Office, 1906. lxxiv, 1,600 p. Reprint. 3 vols. New York: Franklin, 1934.

> Indexes portraits in books, periodicals, and published collections (not original portraits). More than 6,200 books were examined, omitting, in general, local histories and genealogical works. See list of sources, pp. xi-lxxiv. This list also names periodicals which were indexed through 1904. Approximately 120,000 portraits are alphabetized by personal names of all nationalities, e.g., "Cushman, Charlotte, actress, 1816-74." Some of the portraits listed after her name are identified with roles, e.g., Romeo.

> Some sources cited will be found only in older and larger libraries.

Arrigoni, Paolo.

> See Civica Raccolta delle Stampe e dei Disegni, below.

Bertarelli, Achille.

> See Civica Raccolta delle Stampe e dei Disegni, below.

Bibliotheque Nationale. Departement des Estampes. CATALOGUE DE LA COLLECTION DES PORTRAITS FRANCAIS ET ETRANGERS CONSERVES AU DEPARTEMENT DES ESTAMPES. Edited by M.G. Duplessis et al. 7 vols. Paris, 1896-1911. (Stops with the letter "M.")

> Catalog edited by various scholars, of a collection of French and foreign portraits held in the Print Department of the Bibliotheque Nationale.

British Museum. Department of Prints and Drawings. CATALOGUE OF EN-GRAVED BRITISH PORTRAITS PRESERVED IN THE DEPARTMENT OF PRINTS AND DRAWINGS IN THE BRITISH MUSEUM. By Freeman O'Donoghue. 6 vols. London: Printed by order of the Trustees, 1908-25.

> Supplement and indexes by Henry M. Hake. Bibliographies included.
>
> Lists notable Britons in alphabetical order and shows location of reproduced portraits in books, pamphlets, and periodicals held by the British Museum. A typical entry for Sir Henry Irving (found in Volume VI: "Supplement") notes a group of illustrations of the actor-manager "in 37 of his characters"; indicates artist, engraver, and source. Date, size, art medium, and a short description are usually presented.
>
> More than 50,000 pieces (depicting more than 15,000 persons) were described in the original five volumes. Volume V is a catalog of group portraits, e.g., "Shakespearean Critics."
>
> Volume VI, compiled entirely by H.M. Hake, adds a new alphabetical series of 6,000 items and also includes indexes of painters and of engravers for all volumes. An appendix, pp. 721-38, is a brief listing of sources.

Celletti, Rodolfo., ed. LE GRANDI VOCI. DIZIONARIO CRITICO - BIO-GRAFICO DEI CANTANTI.

> Has numerous fine photographs of great opera singers in costume.
>
> For full annotation, see Part II-B.

Cirker, Hayward, and Cirker, Blanche, eds. DICTIONARY OF AMERICAN PORTRAITS: 4045 PICTURES OF IMPORTANT AMERICANS FROM EARLIEST TIMES TO THE BEGINNING OF THE TWENTIETH CENTURY. New York: Dover, 1967. xiv, 756 p. Illustrated.

This dictionary gives direct access, in one volume, to reproductions of 4,000 portraits of Americans through 1905, with the exception of a few categories which have been carried on nearly to the date of publication. These are major figures in government. Selected for inclusion were persons thought to have contributed significantly to American life and culture, although others who made some significant mark on history have been admitted, e.g., "John Wilkes Booth, 1838-65, actor, assassin of Abraham Lincoln."

Many of the original portraits were photographs, but work in other media has also been reproduced, in all cases with the intention of finding the best likeness.

See pp. 701-4 for a supplement; pp. 705-6, persons not included; pp. 707-11, sources of pictures; pp. 713-15, bibliography; pp. 717-21, index of variant names; pp. 723-24, table of contents to index; pp. 725-56, the index, which lists individuals under "Actors, Actresses," "Performers," "Singers," "Theater Figures: Directors, Impresarios, Managers, Producers," among other occupations.

Civica Raccolta delle Stampe e dei Disegni. Castello Sforsesco. RITRATTI DI MUSICISTI ED ARTISTI DI TEATRO CONSERVATI NELLA RACCOLTA DELLE STAMPE E DEI DISEGNI. CATALOGO DESCRITTIVO. Edited by Paolo Arrigoni and Achille Bertarelli. Milan: Tipografia del "Popolo d'Italia," 1934. 454 p.

At head of title: Comune di Milano, Istituto di storia e d'arte. Paolo Arrigoni e Achille Bertarelli.

Catalog of approximately 5,600 entries for portraits of actors, ballerinas, acrobats, magicians, musicians, singers, and others in European theater. Alphabetized by names of those portrayed. Indexes of theaters, authors, engravers, etc.

For Italian actors' portraits, see also Rasi, Luigi, in Part VII-A.

CUMULATED DRAMATIC INDEX, 1909-1949.

Many references to portraits and sketches in periodicals are entered under names of actors; scenes are under play title; costume pictures, under both actor and character portrayed.

For full annotation, see Part I-A.

Folger Shakespeare Library. THE FOLGER SHAKESPEARE LIBRARY PRINTS. Washington, D.C.: c. 1935.

Issued in portfolios. Contents: Volume 1--Portraits of Shakespeare;

Volume 2--Shakespeare's London; Volume 3--The Shakespearian Theatre.

Harvard University Library. Theatre Collection. CATALOGUE OF DRAMATIC PORTRAITS IN THE THEATRE COLLECTION OF THE HARVARD COLLEGE LIBRARY. By Lillian Arvilla Hall. 4 vols. Cambridge, Mass.: Harvard University Press, 1930-34.

> A descriptive index to the engraved dramatic portraits in the collections, arranged alphabetically by names. Entries indicate role (if shown), publisher, artist, and engraver. Around 40,000 prints are recorded. Persons included are critics, dramatists, composers, managers, and some scene painters and costumers, as well as actors.

> In the final volume there are indexes of engravers and artists and the corrigenda.

> Materials are not for loan but may be consulted; photocopies may be ordered.

Highfill, Philip H., Jr., et al. A BIOGRAPHICAL DICTIONARY OF ACTORS.

> In the twelve volumes planned, there will be reproductions of approximately 1,500 portraits of actors and others active in British theater from 1660-1800.

> For full annotation, see Part II-A.

Lee, Cuthbert, PORTRAIT REGISTER. Asheville, N.C.: Biltmore Press, 1968. 725 p.

> Volume I, the only one published thus far, is not limited to portraits of or by Americans. It lists around 8,000 portraits, mainly originals (but with the addition of some painted copies) owned in the United States. Three-quarters of these are in institutions. The preface suggests means of securing photographic copies from major sources.

> There are separate lists alphabetized by subjects and by artists, showing locations of works. A volume of corrections and additions is intended.

Lyonnet, Henry. DICTIONNAIRE DES COMEDIENS FRANCAIS.

> Does not provide reproductions but leads to sources for costumed portraits of French actors.

> For full annotation see Part II-A.

Odell, George Clinton Densmore. ANNALS OF THE NEW YORK STAGE. INDEX TO THE PORTRAITS IN ODELL'S 'ANNALS OF THE NEW YORK STAGE.' Transcribed from the file in the Theatre Collection at Princeton University. New York: American Society for Theatre Research, 1963. 179 p.

The index makes accessible the portraits in the fifteen volumes of the ANNALS, which report on the day-by-day stage life of New York from 1700 to 1894, its opera, ballet, vaudeville, circus, and concert activities as well as those of the legitimate theater.

Alphabetical list of personal names, interfiled with play titles. Costumed portraits shown by reference to the roles.

PORTRAIT INDEX.

See A.L.A. PORTRAIT INDEX, above.

Seltsam, William H. METROPOLITAN OPERA ANNALS.

Well illustrated with portraits and photographs.

For full annotation, see Part VI-A3.

Singer, Hans Wolfgang. ALLGEMEINER BILDNISKATALOG. 13 vols. and Index. Leipzig: Hiersemann, 1930-36. Reprint. 5 vols. in 2. Leipzig: Hiersemann, 1967.

Lists more than 100,000 portraits of 25,000 persons, depicted in graphic media and held by twenty German public collections. Volume 14 is an index of artists, together with an index of professions of the persons portrayed, "Register der Berufe." (See actor entries under "Schauspieler" and "Schauspielerin.") Persons depicted are of many nationalities.

See supplementary volumes, below.

_____. NEUER BILDNISKATALOG. 5 vols. Leipzig: Hiersemann, 1937-38. Reprint. 5 vols. in 2. Leipzig: Hiersemann, 1967.

Complements the Singer catalog of portraits described above. Has similar arrangement but lists painted and sculptured portraits in public and private collections worldwide, giving locations. Also lists early photographic portraits and more than 6,000 woodcuts in German journals.

Society for Theatre Research. London Group. CATALOGUE OF THEATRICAL PORTRAITS IN LONDON PUBLIC COLLECTIONS. Compiled by Mavis Bimson et al. Edited with an introduction by J.F. Kerslake. London: The Society, 1961. 63 p.

A handlist of portraits, many of which have never been reproduced. Omitted are portraits in schools of dramatic art and in theaters, as well as those already in other major catalogs (such as that of the Garrick Club, London). Portraits of professional performers are included, whether in ballet, opera, music hall, drama, or circus, British or foreign, from seventeenth to twentieth century. "Group Portraits," pp. 51-57 (under play titles). Indexes of artists and titles.

D. ARCHITECTURAL ILLUSTRATION

Aloi, Roberto. ARCHITETTURE PER LO SPETTACOLO. CON UN SAGGIO
DELL' ARCHITETTO AGNOLDOMENICO PICA. Esempi di Architettura di
Tutto il Mondo, no. 14. Milan: U. Hoepli, 1958. lxiv, 504 p. Illustrated.

> Theater sites and buildings from the classical era in Greece until
> the end of the nineteenth century throughout the world are illus-
> trated and briefly described. Captions are in English, French,
> German, and Italian. Excellent photographs of interiors and ex-
> teriors. Indexes of theaters, of photographers, and of architects,
> engineers, and artists.

> Continued by Aloi's TEATRI E AUDITORI (1972), below.

_____. TEATRI E AUDITORI. THEATRES AND AUDITORIUMS. Preface by
Agnoldomenico Pica. Milan: U. Hoepli, 1972. 453 p. Illustrated.

> Continues the author's ARCHITETTURE PER LO SPETTACOLO,
> above.

> The present volume is concerned with "the most recent theatrical
> architecture" worldwide. There are 421 illustrations, mainly good
> photographs, some in color, and 453 architectural drawings. Text
> and captions are in English and Italian.

Bentham, Frederick. NEW THEATRES IN BRITAIN (1970).

> Photographs, seating charts, plans.

> For full annotation, see Part III.

Briggs, Martin Shaw. EVERYMAN'S CONCISE ENCYCLOPEDIA OF ARCHITEC-
TURE. Everyman's Reference Library. London: Dent; New York: Dutton,
1966, c. 1959. 372 p. Illustrated.

> Definitions of terms and biographical entries are interfiled. Archi-
> tectural details are clarified by the many line drawings by the
> author. There are thirty-two pages of photographs.

Columbia University Libraries. Avery Architectural Library. AVERY INDEX
TO ARCHITECTURAL PERIODICALS.

> Many entries under "Theaters" include references to illustrations,
> plans, architectural details, etc.

> For full annotation, see Part VI-A4.

_____. CATALOG OF THE AVERY MEMORIAL ARCHITECTURAL LIBRARY.

> Contains some material on theater architecture and architects, as
> well as a notable list of architectural drawings held by the library,
> shown under the heading "Architectural Drawings."

> For full annotation, see Part VI-A4.

ENCICLOPEDIA DELL'ARTE ANTICA: CLASSICA E ORIENTALE. 7 vols.
Rome: Istituto della Enciclopedia Italiana, 1958–66. Illustrated.

SUPPLEMENT. 1970. Rome: Istituto della Enciclopedia Italiana, 1973. 951 p.

> Handsomely illustrated, detailed source of information on classical
> art and archaeology, inclusive of material on ancient theaters and
> their sites. (See "Teatro e Odeon." See also place names, shown
> in Italian.) There are also biographical entries. Developments
> to about 500 A.D. are covered.

> Text and bibliographies are in Italian. Volume 7 concludes the
> alphabet. The supplement adds information from A to Z. A final
> volume is planned as an index to articles and illustrations.

Fletcher, Sir Banister. A HISTORY OF ARCHITECTURE ON THE COMPARATIVE
METHOD [FOR STUDENTS, CRAFTSMEN, AND AMATEURS]. 17th ed. Revised by R.A. Cordingley. New York: Scribner's; London: Athlone Press,
1961. 1,366 p. Illustrated.

> The seventeenth edition of this standard work was considerably
> revised, with the aid of various specialists. An excellent source
> for the ground plans and other architectural drawings of famous
> buildings, e.g., The Banqueting House at Whitehall. Also has
> numerous photographs.

Henderson, Mary C. THE CITY AND THE THEATRE; NEW YORK PLAYHOUSES
FROM BOWLING GREEN TO TIMES SQUARE.

> Includes maps of New York and exterior views of theaters (some
> now demolished).

> For full annotation, see Part III.

Highfill, Philip H., Jr. A BIOGRAPHICAL DICTIONARY OF ACTORS.

> Has city maps and exterior and interior views of London theaters.

> For full annotation, see Part II-A.

Howard, Diana. LONDON THEATRES AND MUSIC HALLS, 1850-1950.

> Includes references to architects' plans and relevant documents.

> For full annotation, see Part III.

London Survey Committee. SURVEY OF LONDON. London: Athlone Press,
University of London, 1900-   . Illustrated.

> This multi-volume publication comprises an historical survey of the
> parishes in the County of London, with much detail on the notable
> buildings of each parish. Especially interesting for theater students
> are Volume XXII, "Bankside" ("Playhouses and Beargardens,"
> pp. 66-77 and plate 59) and Volume XXXV, "The Theatre Royal,

Drury Lane, and the Royal Opera House, Covent Garden." The latter volume has a full discussion of the sites, the buildings, and their management, along with many photographs and plans.

Mander, Raymond. THE LOST THEATRES OF LONDON.

Includes maps, plans, and illustrations.

For full annotation, see Part III.

_____. THE THEATRES OF LONDON.

Has an index of architects.

For full annotation, see Part III.

OXFORD COMPANION TO THE THEATRE. 3d ed.

Has an illustrated supplement of 176 pages pertaining to theater(s) from ancient times to 1957. Notes on the illustrations, (pp. 1075-88), precede the supplement.

For full annotation, see Part II-A.

Royal Institute of British Architects. CATALOGUE OF THE DRAWINGS COLLECTION.

See Part VI-A4.

Sachs, Edwin O., and Woodrow, Ernest A.E. MODERN OPERA HOUSES AND THEATRES. London, 1896-98. Reprint. 3 vols. New York: Blom, 1968. Illustrated.

A treatise on individual opera houses and theaters "recently erected" in Europe. It is regarded by its authors as a continuation of the atlas of theaters compiled by Clement Contant (Paris, 1842). Volume I has a selection of examples in Great Britain, Germany, Austria, Russia, Scandinavia, and the Netherlands. Volume II: France, Italy, and Spain. Five classes of theaters are described: court, national, municipal, subscription, and private. Each entry discusses the architect's conception and the history of construction, ending with a critique of the completed structure, comparing it with other theaters. Sachs also provides for each theater a table of dimensions (seating area, stage, etc.).

More than one-half of Volume I consists of architectural plans, interior and exterior.

Volume III consists of a treatise on theater planning and construction, pp. 1-122, illustrated with many small photographs and detail drawings. It also includes three supplements as follows--I: "Stage Construction"; II: "Theatre Fires"; III: "Protective Legislation." General index.

Although outdated as a construction manual, this is an important historical source.

Silverman, Maxwell. CONTEMPORARY THEATRE ARCHITECTURE; AN ILLUS-TRATED SURVEY.

See Part VI-A4.

STUBS; THE THEATRE GUIDE.

Shows stage dimensions, seating plans, etc., of New York theaters, studio theaters, and music halls.

For full annotation, see Part III.

Sturgis, Russell, ed. A DICTIONARY OF ARCHITECTURE AND BUILDING, BIOGRAPHICAL, HISTORICAL, AND DESCRIPTIVE. 3 vols. New York: Macmillan, 1901. Reprint. 3 vols. Detroit: Gale Research Co., 1966; New York: Gordon Press, 1972. Illustrated.

Never superseded as a standard reference work. Has brief defini-tions interfiled with longer signed articles. Biographical entries are included. Numerous short bibliographies, and in Volume 3, a list of sources, pp. 1141-1212.

Many illustrations of architectural details.

WASMUTHS LEXIKON DER BAUKUNST. 5 vols. Berlin: E. Wasmuth, 1929-37. Illustrated.

Authoritative German-language dictionary of architectural terms. Biographical articles are interfiled. Some bibliographies.

The many illustrations include photographs, plans, and numerous line drawings of architectural details. A few plates are in color.

E. ART AND DESIGN ILLUSTRATION

Anthony, Pegaret, and Arnold, Janet. COSTUME.

Includes references to illustrated exhibition catalogs. For full annotation, see Part VI-A4.

Arnold, Janet. A HANDBOOK OF COSTUME. London: Macmillan, 1973. 336 p. Illustrated.

An introduction discusses visual and documentary sources for the study of costume. Various chapters relate to the arts and crafts as they represent fashion trends; archival and literary sources; pattern books and other technical manuals; conservation of costumes; costume for the stage, pp. 206-16. A classified bibliography of costume follows, pp. 217-32.

Another section devoted to collections of costumes in the United Kingdom, pp. 233-336, completes this scholarly treatise. An index is lacking. Well illustrated with photographs and drawings.

Aronson, Joseph. THE NEW ENCYCLOPEDIA OF FURNITURE. 3d rev. ed. New York: Crown Publishers, 1967. 484 p. Illustrated.

First and second editions published as THE ENCYCLOPEDIA OF FURNITURE.

Definitions of terms, short discussions of period styles, and biographical entries are presented in one alphabet and copiously illustrated with photographs and drawings. Bibliography, pp. 476-79. Glossary of designers and craftsmen, pp. 480-84.

ART AND THE STAGE.

See Rischbieter, Henning, comp., below.

ART INDEX.

Entries for periodical articles mention illustrations of art works. These are shown under names of artists and designers. Sometimes the citations consist solely of works illustrated. This often occurs at the time of an exhibition.

For full annotation, see Part V.

Barton, Lucy. HISTORIC COSTUME FOR THE STAGE. Frontispiece and drawings by David Sarvis. London: Black; Boston: Walter H. Baker, c. 1961. 609 p. Illustrated.

New material has been added in the 1961 edition. Originally issued in 1935, this respected work has a detailed text well related to numerous line-drawings, and includes bibliographies.

Note a companion volume, PERIOD PATTERNS, below.

See also Prisk, Berneice; and Brooke, Iris, below.

Barton, Lucy, with Edson, Doris. PERIOD PATTERNS; A SUPPLEMENT TO 'HISTORIC COSTUME FOR THE STAGE.' Boston: Baker, 1942. 106 p. Illustrated.

Has scale drawings of costumes, photographs of garment construction, and historical charts.

See also Prisk, Berneice; and Tompkins, Julia, below.

Beaumont, Cyril W. FIVE CENTURIES OF BALLET DESIGN. London: The Studio, Ltd., 1939. 135 p. Illustrated.

Companion volume to Beaumont's DESIGN FOR THE BALLET (London: The Studio, Ltd., 1938) which discussed productions of the fifteen years past. The later volume traces the evolution of ballet pictorially, from the late sixteenth century to 1922, principally as seen in productions at the Paris Opera and in a few other European theaters. Scholarly notes accompany the fine illustrations, which reproduce the drawings of many designers, mainly French and Russian, for both costumes and sets. Historical introduction, pp. 5-24.

Brooke, Iris. WESTERN EUROPEAN COSTUME AND ITS RELATION TO THE THEATRE. 2 vols. 2d ed. New York: Theatre Arts Books, 1964, c. 1963-66. Illustrated.

Lacks the color plates of the first edition (Harrap, 1939-40), but is well illustrated, mainly with full-page line drawings, some of which are new in this edition.

Brooke's text is scholarly but attractive in style and unburdened by footnotes. Contents: Volume I: thirteenth to seventeenth century: Volume II: seventeenth to early nineteenth century. The index in Volume II lists details of costume discussed in both volumes.

Bruhn, Wolfgang, and Tilke, Max. A PICTORIAL HISTORY OF COSTUME; A SURVEY OF COSTUME OF ALL PERIODS AND PEOPLES FROM ANTIQUITY TO MODERN TIMES INCLUDING NATIONAL COSTUME IN EUROPE AND NON-EUROPEAN COUNTRIES. New York: Hastings House Publishers, 1973. 74 p. plus 200 p. of illustrations.

Translation of DAS KOSTUEMWERK. Both Bruhn's captions and Tilke's 200 plates are authoritative. The nearly 4,000 specimens of costume represent the most important garments of all times.

"Details of the Plates," pp. 7-72, reveal materials used in dress and accessories, reasons for usage, etc.

Plates are separately paged, pp. 2-200, with a few changes from the sequence in the German edition. "The color-plates are facsimiles from originals colored by Max Tilke. The monochrome plates have been produced partly from Tilke's drawings and partly from engravings and photographs in the Lipperheide Kostuembibliothek." (Preface.)

Burris-Meyer, Harold, and Cole, Edward C. SCENERY FOR THE THEATRE; THE ORGANIZATION, PROCESSES, MATERIALS, AND TECHNIQUES USED TO SET THE STAGE. Rev. ed. Boston: Little, Brown and Co., 1971. xix, 518 p. Illustrated.

Revision of a standard text, well illustrated with practical drawings. Bibliography, pp. 495-99.

_____. THEATRES AND AUDITORIUMS. 2d ed. New York: Reinhold Publishing Corp., 1964. 376 p. Illustrated.

Text discusses design and equipment of theaters and auditoriums as suited to the needs of audience, designers, directors, and performers. Has numerous photographs and drawings of backstage as well as public areas. Chapter 8 deals with backstage operation; 9, scenery; 10 and 11, stage machinery; 12, light; 13, sound and intercommunication; and 14, production services (paint shop, etc.)

Carrick, Neville. HOW TO FIND OUT ABOUT THE ARTS.

Helpful for both visual and performing arts.

For full annotation, see Part I-D.

Chamberlin, Mary W. GUIDE TO ART REFERENCE BOOKS.

Principal guide to the fine arts, including pictorial sources. Also has good basic coverage of decorative arts, excluding theater. (See "Applied Arts, Furniture.")

Note chapters on periodicals, major art libraries, and special collections and resources.

For full annotation, see Part I-D.

Clapp, Jane. ART IN 'LIFE.' New York: Scarecrow Press, 1959. 504 p.

Index to paintings and graphic art reproduced in the magazine LIFE and to selected portraits and photographs of architecture, decorative art, and sculpture in the same source, from 1936 through 1956.

_____. ART IN 'LIFE.' SUPPLEMENT: New York: Scarecrow Press, 1965. 379 p.

Covers 1957-63 in manner similar to that of the basic volume, above, but adds references to selected photographs of events, including theater.

_____. ART REPRODUCTIONS. New York: Scarecrow Press, 1961. 350 p.

Under names of various art media, Clapp groups references to reproductions obtainable from ninety-five U.S. and Canadian museums. An index includes some subjects, as well as names of artists and of persons depicted in portraits. A list of museums is added.

See also Wasserman, Paul; and Special Libraries Association, in Part VII-A, above.

Cook, Dorothy E.

See Monro, Isabel Stevenson. COSTUME INDEX, below.

COSTUME.

In addition to references in Part VII, see illustrated works described in Part II-D.

COSTUME INDEX.

See Monro, Isabel Stevenson, and Cook, Dorothy E., below.

Dameron, Louise, comp.   BIBLIOGRAPHY OF STAGE SETTINGS.

See Part VI-A4.

DENKMAELER DES THEATERS.   12 vols.   Portfolio; new series.   Munich: R. Piper, 1926-   .   Illustrated.

Publication suspended, 1931-53.   New series called MONUMENTA SCENICA, Volume 1:   English text, corrected, revised, and issued by Samuel J. Hume, Berkeley, Calif., 1954.   Illustrated.

Published by the Nationalbibliothek, Vienna, 1925-30; by the Gesellschaft der Freunde der Oesterreichischen Nationalbibliothek, 1954.

Twelve portfolios, each with a fascicle of text by Joseph Gregor, exhibit the treasures of theatrical design in the Austrian National Library, Vienna, which relate mainly to the Baroque and Rococo periods, from the designs of Burnacini, 1636-1707, to the "last great period of the Vienna stage," 1800-35.   Costume, stagecraft, garden theaters, festivals, fireworks, and even state funerals are depicted in these unique designs, shown here in excellent facsimile reproduction.

Dubech, Lucien, et al.   HISTOIRE GENERALE ILLUSTREE DU THEATRE.   5 vols. Paris: Librairie de France, 1931-34.   Illustrated.

History of European theater from ancient Greece to the twentieth century, inclusive of ballet, with a short treatment of the film as art (Volume V, chapter 8).   The text, in French, is developed along national lines under each period.   Well illustrated.   Volume V includes indexes of actors, authors, and titles, covering all volumes.

Edson, Doris.

See Barton, Lucy.   PERIOD PATTERNS.

ENCYCLOPEDIA OF WORLD ART.

Valuable source of illustrations, some in color, for art, architecture, decorative arts, costume, and scenography. Maps of cities, archaeological sites, etc.

For full annotation, see Part II-E.

Fueloep-Miller, Rene.

See Gregor, Joseph. DAS AMERIKANISCHE THEATER UND KINO, below.

Gascoigne, Bamber. WORLD THEATRE; AN ILLUSTRATED HISTORY. Boston: Little, Brown and Co., 1968. 335 p. Illustrated.

The 290 monochrome illustrations and thirty-one color plates are carefully selected to support the author's ideas concerning the difficulties in scholarly interpretation of visual artifacts relating to theater. Some have disputed his theories, but the pictures and text are of interest.

Bibliography, pp. 317-26.

Gregor, Joseph.

See DENKMAELER DES THEATERS, above.

Gregor, Joseph, and Fueloep-Miller, Rene. DAS AMERIKANISCHE THEATER UND KINO; ZWEI KULTURGESCHICHTLICHE ABHANDLUNGEN; MIT 47 BUNTEN, 459 EINFARBIGEN BILDERN UND EINER SPIELPLANTABELLE. Zurich (etc.): Amaltheaverlag, c. 1931. 111 p. Illustrated.

At head of title: Joseph Gregor/Rene Fueloep-Miller. Contents: "Das Amerikanische Theater" by Joseph Gregor; "Das Amerikanische Kino" by Rene Fueloep-Miller.

Text is in German. Consists of Gregor's scholarly survey of American theater and its scenic design from colonial times to the era of the "Little Theater" movement, pp. 9-56; and of Fueloep-Miller's survey of American motion pictures as art for the masses, from penny arcade to Mickey Mouse, pp. 59-97.

The bulk of the volume consists of illustrations, preceded by indexes. Included are reproduced scenic designs and photographs ranging from Indian masks to Norman Bel-Geddes models. For the motion pictures a separate group of illustrations includes good examples of art deco sets, of movie palace interiors, and a panorama of celebrities in character, e.g., Theda Bara, the first vamp. Emphasis throughout is on the development of themes and types.

Hainaux, Rene, comp., with Yves-Bonnat. STAGE DESIGN THROUGHOUT THE WORLD SINCE 1960. TEXT AND ILLUSTRATIONS COLLECTED BY THE NATIONAL CENTRES OF THE INTERNATIONAL THEATRE INSTITUTE. Foreword by Paul Louis Mignon. New York: Theatre Arts Books, 1973. 239 p. Illustrated.

Continuation of STAGE DESIGN THROUGHOUT THE WORLD SINCE 1950 (1964) and STAGE DESIGN THROUGHOUT THE WORLD SINCE 1935 (1954).

The compilers planned to emphasize developments in design which "in both dramatic and musical fields denote a break with the tradition in the treatment of the classic repertory and of the new forms of drama" (Preface). Yet some excellent traditional designs were included.

Arrangement in this volume is chronological by author; entries consist of illustrations (some in color), pp. 17-168, exemplifying recent stage treatment of these authors. All entries are captioned in original languages. (See index for titles given in English.) This section shows works produced under directors. The work of groups (theater collectives) is also shown, pp. 169-74; and opera and ballet, pp. 175-216.

Prefatory essays by Yves-Bonnat, pp. 9-15, relate to the work of collectives as well as directed productions. Additional material of interest: Design with projections, mirror, and puppets, pp. 219-22; working notes of designers, pp. 223-26.

Selective bibliography of works published since 1960 worldwide, pp. 227-30; illustrations listed by names of designers, pp. 231-32, and by names of composers and playwrights, pp. 233-38.

Earlier volumes of this series (not annotated here) were arranged geographically. The 1964 volume has a biographical "Dictionary of Scenic Designers."

Havlice, Patricia Pate. ART IN 'TIME.' Metuchen, N.J.: Scarecrow Press, 1970. 350 p.

Index to all the pictures in the art section of TIME magazine, 1923-69. Some references to designers of stage settings and costume, e.g., Berman, Eugene.

Hayward, Helena, ed. WORLD FURNITURE; AN ILLUSTRATED HISTORY. New York: McGraw-Hill, 1965. 320 p. Illustrated.

Introduction by Helena Hayward. Essays by various experts are arranged geographically and then by period styles. Final chapters deal with the Orient, the Middle East, design of furniture in the twentieth century, and a short treatment of primitive furniture. Glossary, pp. 308-11. Reading list, p. 312. General index.

Excellent illustrations, mainly photographs of museum pieces. Some plates are in color.

Huerlimann, Martin, ed. ATLANTISBUCH DES THEATERS.

Well illustrated. Has much material on stage design and production. Text in German.

For full annotation, see Part II-A.

Janson, Horst Woldemar. KEY MONUMENTS OF THE HISTORY OF ART: A VISUAL SURVEY. Edited by Horst W. Janson with Dora Jane Janson. New York: Abrams, 1959. 1,068 p. Illustrated.

A photographic history of art and architecture, extending from pre-historic times into the 1940s. There is no text, except for lists of illustrations. Index.

Kranich, Friedrich. BUEHNENTECHNIK DER GEGENWART. 2 vols. Munich and Berlin: R. Oldenbourg, 1929-33. Illustrated.

There are 442 text illustrations (mainly photographs) and sixteen plates. These reveal the backstage equipment and methods of im-portant theaters in the 1920s and early 1930s in explicit detail. Of considerable historical interest. The text is by the technical director of the Festspielhaus-Bayreuth and of the Staedtische Buehnen, Hanover. Illustrations are found in both volumes, along with the text.

Lackschewitz, Gertrud. INTERIOR DESIGN AND DECORATION; A BIBLIOG-RAPHY. New York: New York Public Library, 1961. 86 p.

Compiled for the American Institute of Decorators, this is a classi-fied, partly annotated selection of illustrated books on interior design in many lands and periods. Periodicals list, pp. 75-78. Author index.

LIFE (magazine). ART IN 'LIFE.'

See Clapp, Jane, above.

Lipperheide, Franz Joseph, Freiherr von. KATALOG DER KOSTUEMBIBLIOTHEK LIPPERHEIDESCHEN.

Many excellent illustrations for the history of costume.

For full annotation, see Part VI-A4.

Lucas, Edna Louise. ART BOOKS.

Principally helpful for its lists of standard biographies and critical works on artists of all periods. Also shown are the catalogues raisonnes for many artists. Works are in various languages.

For full annotation, see Part I-D.

MCGRAW-HILL DICTIONARY OF ART.

Five volumes with many illustrations, some in color.

For full annotation, see Part II-E.

MCGRAW-HILL ENCYCLOPEDIA OF WORLD DRAMA.

Contains numerous photographs and reproductions of stage designs originally created in various media.

For full annotation, see Part II-A.

Monro, Isabel Stevenson, and Cook, Dorothy E., eds. COSTUME INDEX; A SUBJECT INDEX TO PLATES AND TO ILLUSTRATED TEXTS. New York: H.W. Wilson, 1937. 388 p. Illustrated.

A specific subject index to plates and other illustrations of costume found in books. Includes historical costume of most countries. Excludes costume as actually worn onstage.

Monro, Isabel Stevenson, and Monro, Kate M., eds. SUPPLEMENT. New York: H.W. Wilson, 1957. 210 p. Illustrated.

Updates the COSTUME INDEX and has similar arrangement.

_____, eds. INDEX TO REPRODUCTIONS OF AMERICAN PAINTINGS; A GUIDE TO PICTURES OCCURRING IN MORE THAN EIGHT HUNDRED BOOKS. New York: H.W. Wilson, 1948. 731 p.

Includes references to reproductions in books and exhibition catalogs, entered by names of artists. Reference is also made to the locations of paintings in permanent collections.

_____, eds. SUPPLEMENT, 1ST. New York: H.W. Wilson, 1964. 480 p.

Adds references from 1948 to 1961.

_____, eds. INDEX TO REPRODUCTIONS OF EUROPEAN PAINTINGS; A GUIDE TO PICTURES IN MORE THAN THREE HUNDRED BOOKS. New York: H.W. Wilson, 1956. 668 p.

Entries are usually under artist, but some are under titles and their variants, while subject entries were also made selectively, e.g., "Circus" and "Musicians and Musical Instruments."

In addition to locating reproductions in books, this index shows locations of paintings in permanent collections.

MONUMENTA SCENICA.

See DENKMAELER DES THEATERS, above.

Mullin, Donald C. THE DEVELOPMENT OF THE PLAYHOUSE; A SURVEY OF THEATRE ARCHITECTURE FROM THE RENAISSANCE TO THE PRESENT. Berkeley: University of California Press, 1970.   xvi, 197 p.   Illustrated.

> Historical text plentifully illustrated with reproductions of architects'
> plans and models and with photographs and contemporary designs
> for scenery and theater buildings.

> Appendix I is a chronological record of theaters mentioned; Ap-
> pendix II, an alphabetical list of cities, with chronology of their
> theaters; Appendix III, an alphabetical list of architects; Appendix
> IV, "Observations on the Nineteenth Century Stage"; and Appendix
> V, illustrations for technical apparatus, sixteenth to nineteenth
> century.   Bibliography.

> See also Nicoll, Allardyce, below.

Nationalbibliothek.   Vienna.   KATALOGE DER THEATERSAMMLUNG.

> Reproduces some set designs by famous designers.   Also describes
> theatrical silhouettes and figurines in a special collection.

> For full annotation, see Part VI-A1.

> See also DENKMAELER DES THEATERS, above.

New York Public Library.   THE DEVELOPMENT OF SCENIC ART AND STAGE
MACHINERY.

> See Part VI-A4.

Nicoll, Allardyce.   THE DEVELOPMENT OF THE THEATRE; A STUDY OF
THEATRICAL ART FROM THE BEGINNINGS TO THE PRESENT DAY.   5th ed.,
rev.   New York: Harcourt, Brace, and World, 1967.   xix, 292 p.   Illustrated.

> The text, pp. 1-251, reviews developments in the theater, espe-
> cially in regard to techniques and design, from the ancient world
> to about 1950.   There is a good standard selection of reproductions.
> An appendix, "The Dialogues of Leone di Somi" (on stage affairs
> in the late sixteenth century) is here translated into English for the
> first time, pp. 252-78.   A selective classified bibliography, pp. 279-
> 83, has helpful evaluations.   General index.

OXFORD COMPANION TO THE THEATRE.

> Has a section devoted to illustrations of staging, theater buildings,
> etc., with notes.   Bibliography.

> For full annotation, see Part II-A.

Pegler, Martin.   THE DICTIONARY OF INTERIOR DESIGN.   New York:
Crown, 1966.   500 p.   Illustrated.

> Biographical notes on selected designers and architects are inter-
> filed in an alphabet consisting chiefly of English and foreign terms

used in interior design, e.g., "dos-a-dos," a seating device. Many drawings accompany the definitions throughout.

Picken, Mary. THE FASHION DICTIONARY; FABRIC, SEWING, AND AP-PAREL AS EXPRESSED IN THE LANGUAGE OF FASHION. Rev. ed. New York: Funk and Wagnalls, 1973. xii, 434 p. Illustrated.

First published in 1939 as THE LANGUAGE OF FASHION and revised in 1957 as THE FASHION DICTIONARY. The latest edition defines more than 10,000 words associated with the changing mode throughout history, e.g., the color "puce" or a "Gainsborough hat." For many items the pronunciation is given.

Very usefully illustrated with line drawings of costumes and details, e.g., "trunk-hose, 1600." Index of illustrations.

See also Wilcox, Ruth Turner, below.

Prisk, Berneice. STAGE COSTUME HANDBOOK. New York: Harper and Row, 1966. 198 p. Illustrated.

Discusses costumes of the world, with special reference to theatrical use. Part I, "Historical Costumes," is geographically arranged. (Note material on circus and commedia dell'arte.) Part II, "Construction of Costumes," has chapters on costuming the play, building a costume workshop, fabrics and patterns for stage use, dyeing and painting, mask and armor construction, etc. Illustrated with simple line drawings of costume and with patterns, pp. 124-55. Useful appendices: I, "Costume Crew Manual"; II, "Draping Historical Garments"; III, "Where Do I Get It?," a list of costume suppliers. Bibliography, pp. 189-94. Index.

See also Barton, Lucy, above, and Tompkins, Julia, below.

Racinet, Albert Charles Auguste. LE COSTUME HISTORIQUE. 6 vols. Paris: Firmin-Didot, 1888. Illustrated.

Surveys, pictorially and in French text, the costumes of the world from ancient times to the modern era in Europe, with some consideration of other areas.

Volume I, contents: Introduction, v-xxvii; analytical table for the plates and notes in Volumes II-VI; bibliography of costume, pp. 113-24; glossary, pp. 125-67; 22 plates of drawings for principal types of national costumes; comments on the drawings, pp. 193-96.

Volumes II-VI, plates, mainly in color, depicting costume, arms and armor, furniture, and modes of transportation. Geographical arrangement. Running text and notes.

Of the 500 fine plates throughout, 300 are in color, with silver, 200 in monochrome.

Rischbieter, Henning, comp. ART AND THE STAGE IN THE TWENTIETH CENTURY; PAINTERS AND SCULPTORS WORK FOR THE THEATER. New York: New York Graphic Society, 1968. 306 p. Illustrated.

Translation of BUEHNE UND BILDENDE KUNST IM XXTEN JAHR-HUNDERT (1968). Running text handsomely illustrated with photographs and with reproduced paintings, sketches, and models of stage settings, together with some costumes and a few programs. Ranges from Toulouse-Lautrec to "Op Art, Pop Art, Happening," in chronological sequence.

The compiler's introduction is followed by his comments throughout on designers and trends (e.g., "Futurism and the Theater"), accompanied by translations of artists' comments on stage productions. A "Catalog of Productions" is alphabetized by designers' names and includes mention of major collections, exhibitions, a list of all known drawings, and critical sources, (some with illustration) for each production of a designer. (Not limited to productions depicted in Rischbieter's work.)

"General Bibliography," pp. 300-301. List of theater exbibitions, p. 301. Source list for the translated remarks of designers, p. 302, and picture sources, p. 303. Name index includes artists, authors, composers, et al.

THEATRE ARCHITECTURE AND STAGE MACHINES. ENGRAVINGS FROM THE 'ENCYCLOPEDIE OU DICTIONNAIRE RAISONNE DES SCIENCES, DES ARTS, ET DES METIERS.' Edited by Denis Diderot and Jean le Rond d'Alembert. New ed. New York: B. Blom, 1969. 22 p. Illustrated.

Reproduces eighty-nine plates published in Paris between 1762 and 1772. These are of considerable historical interest. Text in French with introductory material in English.

Tilke, Max.

See Bruhn, Wolfgang, above.

TIME (magazine). ART IN 'TIME.'

See Havlice, Patricia Pate, above.

Tompkins, Julia. STAGE COSTUME AND HOW TO MAKE THEM. London: Pitman; Boston: Plays, Inc., 1969. xvi, 160 p. Illustrated.

Handy, practical text with many line drawings depicting costumes, accessories (e.g., a Mary Queen of Scots cap), and patterns. Restricted to England and arranged by periods. Index.

See also Barton, Lucy. PERIOD PATTERNS, and Prisk, Berneice, above.

Wasserman, Paul. MUSEUM MEDIA.

Has numerous references to exhibition catalogs available for purchase, some of which pertain to the work of theater designers,
e.g., "Inigo Jones and the Court Masques of James I," as shown
in 1968 at the Ringling Museum, Sarasota, Florida.

For full annotation, see Part VII-A, above.

Wilcox, Ruth Turner. DICTIONARY OF COSTUME. New York: Scribner's,
1969. 406 p. Illustrated.

This work is based on extensive research and is illustrated by line
drawings. Wilcox is also the author of more specialized books on
hats, headdress, and other details of costume.

See also Picken, Mary, above.

F. SONGS AND RECORDINGS (SOURCES AND REVIEWS)

THE AMERICAN RECORD GUIDE. Pelham, N.Y.: The American Record
Guide, 1935-   . Monthly. (Title varies.)

Supersedes MUSIC LOVERS' GUIDE. From 1944 to date it has
been THE AMERICAN RECORD GUIDE. It incorporates THE
AMERICAN TAPE GUIDE.

Has articles and illustrations but chiefly reviews of books and
recordings, ranging from opera to pop music. Spoken records are
also reviewed (See "Words Only"). The reviews are listed in
MUSIC INDEX; MULTI MEDIA REVIEWS INDEX; and in Maleady,
Antoinette O., below.

American Society of Composers, Authors, and Publishers. FORTY YEARS OF
SHOW TUNES; THE BIG BROADWAY HITS FROM 1917-1957. New York:
ASCAP, [1959]. 149 p.

Chronological list. Entries show title, composer, publisher, performing artists, and recording labels associated with each song.
Index of titles.

See also Lewine, Richard, and Simon, Alfred; and Burton, Jack,
in Part II-B.

ANNOTATED BIBLIOGRAPHY OF NEW PUBLICATIONS IN THE PERFORMING
ARTS.

Includes mention of drama recordings. For full annotation, see
Part VI-A1.

ANNUAL INDEX TO POPULAR MUSIC RECORD REVIEWS.

See Armitage, Andrew D., below.

Archive of American Folk Song.

> See U.S. Library of Congress. Music Division, both titles, below.

Archives of Recorded Music.

> See International Folk Music Council, below.

Armitage, Andrew D., with Tudor, Dean. ANNUAL INDEX TO POPULAR MUSIC RECORD REVIEWS. Metuchen, N.J.: Scarecrow Press, 1973. 467 p.

> Recordings are classified under twelve musical styles, each described in a brief essay. Ratings are given, based on the year's reviews.

> Also included are lists of books and articles; addresses of recording companies and record stores; record titles, including anthologies; and an artist index.

> See also MULTI MEDIA REVIEWS INDEX, below, and INTERNATIONAL INDEX TO MULTI-MEDIA INFORMATION in Part V.

Association for Recorded Sound Collections. A PRELIMINARY DIRECTORY OF SOUND RECORDINGS COLLECTIONS IN THE UNITED STATES AND CANADA. New York: New York Public Library, 1967. 157 p.

> Data obtained by questionnaire and arranged under state names (U.S.) and Canada. Information on materials in public and private collections, some of which are available for exchange. Some entries show there are catalogs for purchase or consultation on the spot. Entries describe kinds of materials (cylinders; discs, 78 rpm; specific brands of piano rolls; and tapes), as well as the scope of the collections, e.g., "New Orleans jazz." As some entries are not very informative, it may be necessary to correspond. Addresses are given.

Bate, John. HOW TO FIND OUT ABOUT SHAKESPEARE.

> Some notes on recordings.

> For full annotation, see Part VI-B.

Berkowitz, Freda Pastor. POPULAR TITLES AND SUBTITLES OF MUSICAL COMPOSITIONS. New York: Scarecrow Press, 1962. 182 p. New ed. in prep., 1973.

> Very useful for determining actual titles, opus numbers, and composers of serious musical compositions which are widely referred to by popular names, such as "Moonlight Sonata." Lists approximately 500 such names and explains their origin. Ranges from early seventeenth century to the present. Bibliography. List of composers. This work does not lead directly to recordings.

THE BEST PLAYS [AND THE YEAR BOOK OF THE DRAMA IN AMERICA].
Recent volumes have a discography, found under "Original Cast
Albums of New York Shows" or "Musical and Dramatic Recordings."

For full annotation, see Part II-A.

British Institute of Recorded Sound. Central Gramophone Library. CATA-
LOGUE 1965. London: 1965-   . 235 p.

The main section of this catalog lists composers in alphabetical
order, each with titles and label numbers for recorded works found
in this library. Mainly concert music, but a miscellaneous section
includes folksong and dramatic recordings.

Celletti, Rodolfo, ed. LE GRANDI VOCI.

Has an international discography for each opera star.

For full annotation, see Part II-B.

See also Kutsch, K.J.; and the VICTOR BOOK OF THE OPERA,
below.

Chicorel, Marietta. CHICOREL INDEX TO THE SPOKEN ARTS ON DISCS,
TAPES, AND CASSETTES. Chicorel Index Series, vol. 7. New York:
Chicorel Library Publishing Corp., 1973. 500 p.

Index to theatrical, literary, documentary, and speech recordings,
mainly from English-speaking nations. The index interfiles authors,
directors, performers, dramatic companies, readers, speakers, and
titles of works. Gives prices and names and addresses for distributors. No annotations or ratings.

See also Limbacher, James L., THEATRICAL EVENTS; Roach,
Helen Pauline; DIRECTORY OF SPOKEN-VOICE AUDIO-CASSETTES;
and Maleady, Antoinette O., below.

Chujoy, Anatole. THE DANCE ENCYCLOPEDIA.

Has a discography of theatrical dance music. See Part II-C.

Coover, James B., and Colvig, Richard. MEDIEVAL AND RENAISSANCE
MUSIC ON LONG-PLAYING RECORDS. Detroit Studies in Music Bibliography, no. 6. Detroit: Information Service, 1964. xii, 122 p.

Part I, Anthologies, has medieval and Renaissance sections. Part
II, arranged under composers, has individual discographies and indexes the anthologies also. Part III selectively lists choral groups,
other ensembles, and instrumental soloists, grouped under names of
instruments, e.g., viols and gambas. There are no evaluations,
but the complete listing of contents is helpful, e.g., the titles
of English folksongs in a Thomas Morley album.

A supplement covering through 1961 is on pp. 89-122 and has

similar arrangement.   For a second supplement, see below.

_____. SUPPLEMENT, 1962-1971.   Detroit Studies in Music Bibliography,
no. 26.   Detroit: Information Coordinators, 1973.   258 p.

> More than twice as long as the basic volume, for which it supplies
> addenda and corrigenda.   Not limited to currently available re-
> cordings.

Davies, J.H. MUSICALIA.

> Note Chapter 3, "The Theatre Conductor"; and 14, "The Gramo-
> phone Record Collector"; and pp. 122-23, "Film Music."

> For full annotation, see Part I-D.

De Charms, Desiree, and Breed, Paul Francis. SONGS IN COLLECTIONS;
AN INDEX. Detroit: Information Service, c. 1966.   xxxix, 588 p.

> Indexes solo songs with piano accompaniment, chiefly in the art
> song and operatic repertoire.   Collections indexed were those
> appearing between 1940 and 1957 and a few older collections
> not previously indexed--in all, 411 volumes containing 9,493
> songs.   In addition to songs shown under composers, there is a
> geographically arranged section which indexes representative collec-
> tions of folksongs.   Other sections list carols and sea songs.   Using
> De Charms's index, it is easy to find texts of "Silent Night" in
> many languages or to locate the words for numerous spirituals.
> In addition to a title and first-line index, there is an author in-
> dex.   The work does not include recordings.

> See also Leigh, Robert; and Sears, Minnie Earl, below.

DIRECTORY OF SPOKEN-VOICE AUDIO-CASSETTES.   Los Angeles: Cassette
Information Services, 1972-   . Annual. 82 p.

> Available cassettes are listed, chiefly those suitable for college
> programs.   Broad subject classification.   See "Drama," pp. 26-28,
> for a title list of recorded plays; but note also, under "Contempo-
> rary Issues," such items as "Walter Kerr's Guide to the Theatre,"
> "Lorraine Hansberry on her Art and the Black Experience," etc.
> See also "Old Time Radio" entries.

> Each item briefly described, with price and source noted.   Several
> indexes of cassette companies, pp. 72-82.

> See also Chicorel, Marietta, above.

Duckles, Vincent. MUSIC REFERENCE AND RESEARCH MATERIALS.

> Note especially "Discographies."

> For full annotation, see Part I-D.

Greenfield, Edward, et al. THE SECOND PENGUIN GUIDE TO BARGAIN
RECORDS. Edited by Ivan March. Harmondsworth: Penguin, 1971. xxiii,
584 p.

> In-print recordings of all types of serious music are evaluated,
> e.g., Britten, Benjamin. THE PRINCE OF THE PAGODA (complete
> ballet). There are interesting notes on the origin of a composition,
> its influence, etc.

> See also evaluations of humor recordings, pp. 583-84, and of
> "The Spoken Word," pp. 478-81.

Greenfield, Edward.

> See STEREO RECORD GUIDE, below.

GUIDE TO THE PERFORMING ARTS.

> See such headings as "Audio-Visual Library Services," "Film
> Libraries," and "Phonograph Records." Under the last heading
> there are general references to sources where reviews of record-
> ings are regularly carried. This list is less complete than that in
> MUSIC INDEX, see below.

> For full annotation, see Part IV-A.

Harris, Kenn. OPERA RECORDINGS; A CRITICAL GUIDE. New York: Drake
Publishers, 1973. 328 p.

> Discusses and compares in-print recordings, mainly those available
> in the United Kingdom and the United States. Some are reissues.
> Operas commented on are in the standard repertoire. Index of
> persons and institutions.

> See also Greenfield, Edward, above.

Haywood, Charles. A BIBLIOGRAPHY OF NORTH AMERICAN FOLKLORE
AND FOLKSONG.

> See Part VI-A3.

HIGH FIDELITY. RECORDS IN REVIEW. Great Barrington, Mass.: Wyeth
Press, 1955-   . Annual. (Title and publisher vary.)

> Lists recordings under composers and annotates fully. There are
> also comments on "Recitals and Miscellany," but no spoken records
> are evaluated. Index of performers.

> See also STEREO RECORD GUIDE, below.

Huerta, Jorge A. A BIBLIOGRAPHY OF CHICANO AND MEXICAN DANCE,
DRAMA, AND MUSIC.

> See Part VI-A2.

"Index of Record Reviews." Compiled by Kurtz Myers et al.

> See Music Library Association. NOTES, below.

AN INDEX TO 'FILMS IN REVIEW, 1950-1959.'

> See pp. 18-20 for a short bibliography of film music and a list of films discussed in the column "Sound Track."

> For full annotation, see Part V.

International Folk Music Council. INTERNATIONAL CATALOGUE OF RE-CORDED FOLK MUSIC. Archives of Recorded Music, series C., vol. 4. Edited by Norman Fraser. Preface by R. Vaughan Williams. Introduction by Maud Karpeles. London: Published for UNESCO by Oxford University Press, 1954. 210 p.

> (Not examined.)

> Ethnographic in emphasis, this catalog lists both commercially available recordings, Part 1, and those held by institutions, Part 2.

> See also U.S. Library of Congress. Music Division. FOLK MUSIC; A CATALOG, below.

Junge, Ewald. "World Drama on Records." THEATRE RESEARCH 1, no. 1 (1964): 16-49.

> A list mainly of "complete plays recorded in their original languages," with the addition of some authors' readings (with stage directions). The "complete" plays are often acting versions.

> The list is alphabetized under authors' names. Each entry gives names of cast and director, as well as recording label number, speed, diameter, and other information such as inclusion of a brochure. Index of record labels and their publishers, with addresses.

Kutsch, K.J. A CONCISE DICTIONARY OF SINGERS FROM THE BEGIN-NING OF RECORDED SOUND TO THE PRESENT [1969].

> For each singer, companies are named which have made recordings, reissues, or re-recordings.

> For full annotation, see Part II-B.

> See also Celletti, Rodolfo, above, and the VICTOR BOOK OF THE OPERA, below.

Lawless, Ray McKinley. FOLKSINGERS AND FOLKSONGS IN AMERICA.

> See Part VI-A3.

Leigh, Robert. INDEX TO SONG BOOKS. Stockton, Calif.: The Author,

1964.   237 p.

> Intended to continue some aspects of Minnie Earl Sears's SONG-
> INDEX. (See below.) Leigh lists by title approximately 6,800
> songs in song books published in the United States between 1933
> and 1962, all containing both words and music. Books indexed
> were those most often found in libraries. There are cross-references
> from alternate titles and "memorable lines." No author or com-
> poser index. Does not list recordings.

> See also De Charms, Desiree, and Breed, Paul Francis; above,
> and Sears, Minnie Earl, below.

Lewine, Richard, and Simon, Alfred. SONGS OF THE AMERICAN THEATER.

> For some productions, recording labels are mentioned.

> For full annotation, see Part II-B.

Limbacher, James L. FILM MUSIC: FROM VIOLIN TO VIDEO.

> Has an extensive discography.

> For full annotation, see Part VI-A3.

_____. THEATRICAL EVENTS; A SELECTED LIST OF MUSICAL AND DRA-
MATIC PERFORMANCES ON LONG-PLAYING RECORDS. 5th ed. Dearborn,
Mich.: Dearborn Public Library, 1968. 95 p.

> Selected titles are arranged alphabetically under the headings
> "Musical Events," "Film Musicals," and "Television Musicals,"
> followed by a name index for authors, composers, lyricists, and
> performers. Gives dates of original performances and of New
> York revivals as well as information on recordings.

> See also Chicorel, Marietta; and DIRECTORY OF SPOKEN-VOICE
> AUDIO-CASSETTES, above, and Maleady, Antoinette O.; and
> Roach, Helen Pauline, below.

Maleady, Antoinette O. RECORD AND TAPE REVIEWS INDEX, 1971.
Metuchen, N.J.: Scarecrow Press, 1972. 234 p.

> Chiefly composer entries leading to reviews of serious music in
> sixteen periodicals. Section II, "Music in Collections," shows
> records or tapes with several composers on one disc or tape, e.g.,
> "The Voice of the Computer," "Music by Black Composers," etc.
> Section III, pp. 227-34, leads to reviews of spoken recordings
> in such periodicals as AMERICAN RECORD GUIDE, LIBRARY
> JOURNAL, and SATURDAY REVIEW. These are listed under
> literary author.

> See also Music Library Association, below.

MULTI MEDIA REVIEWS INDEX. Edited by C. Edward Wall and B. Penny

Northern. Ann Arbor, Mich.: Pierian Press, 1970- . Annual.

> Cites reviews in more than 70 periodicals and services such as AMERICAN RECORD GUIDE, BOOKLIST, EFLA EVALUATIONS, HIGH FIDELITY, LANDERS FILM REVIEWS, LIBRARY JOURNAL, STEREO REVIEW, and VARIETY. Assigns qualitative ratings based on reviews.

> Reviews cited cover nonclassical records and tapes, films, filmstrips, slides, transparencies, and other illustrative materials, especially those needed by educators.

> Supplemented in the issues of AUDIOVISUAL INSTRUCTION.

> See also INTERNATIONAL INDEX TO MULTI-MEDIA INFORMATION in Part V, and Armitage, Andrew D.; and Maleady, Antoinette O., above.

MUSIC INDEX. 1949- .

> Indexes recordings listed in many sources, primarily music periodicals in the United States and abroad. See references under names of composers and performers.

> See the heading "Recordings" for a list of sources which regularly review recordings. (See also GUIDE TO THE PERFORMING ARTS.)

> For full annotation, see Part V.

Music Library Association. NOTES. "Index of Record Reviews." Compiled by Kurtz Myers et al. In NOTES, 2d series, vol. 5, no. 2- . March 1948- . Quarterly.

> Reviews are noted in American and British periodicals, with reviewers' ratings shown. Predominantly, serious music is considered; no spoken recordings.

THE MUSICIAN'S GUIDE.

> Has brief selected lists of classical, jazz, and rock recordings (Section 4). In Section 7 are names and addresses of music publishers, instrument manufacturers, and recording companies.

> For full annotation, see Part III.

New York Public Library. CATALOG OF THE THEATRE AND DRAMA COLLECTIONS.

> The "Author List" includes dramatic phonodiscs. For full annotation, see Part IV-A.

_____. DICTIONARY CATALOG OF THE DANCE COLLECTION.

Will include taped interviews.

For full annotation, see Part VI-A1.

RECORD AND TAPE REVIEWS INDEX.

See Maleady, Antoinette O., above.

Roach, Helen Pauline. SPOKEN RECORDS. 3d ed. Metuchen, N.J.: Scarecrow Press, 1970. 288 p.

Discursive bibliographic essay, pp. 9-157, followed by a list of recordings discussed, pp. 157-61; a "Selected Discography of Shakespeare's Plays" by Arthur J. Weiss, pp. 162-77; Appendix A: essays by various writers on oral history, the uses of recordings, etc.; Appendix B: a list of recording companies. Index of performers, authors, and titles.

See also Chicorel, Marietta; Junge, Ewald; and Limbacher, James L. THEATRICAL EVENTS; DIRECTORY OF SPOKEN-VOICE AUDIO-CASSETTES; and Maleady, Antoinette O., above.

Rust, Brian, and Debus, Allen G. THE COMPLETE ENTERTAINMENT DISCOGRAPHY FROM THE MID-1890s to 1942. New Rochelle, N.Y.: Arlington House, 1973. 677 p.

Biographies and discographies for 500 popular entertainers. Despite the title, some exclusions were made, e.g., jazz, blues, and commercial dance bands. There is material (in many cases complete lists of recordings) on artists, both major and minor, notable in the entertainment field, including radio, film, and vaudeville.

SCHWANN RECORD AND TAPE GUIDE. Boston: W.W. Schwann, 1949- . Monthly. (Title varies.)

Formerly SCHWANN'S LONG-PLAYING CATALOG. The main section of the guide is devoted to classical and contemporary serious music listed under composer. Conductors and performers are named for various recordings of each composition, along with label numbers. Price information is found at the end of each issue. A group of new listings for the month precedes the main list.

Note special location of "Musical Shows," listed by title, under "Collections," both in main and new listings.

A SUPPLEMENTARY RECORD GUIDE has been issued since 1968 and is now semiannual. This shows spoken records (including plays listed by title), motion picture and musical comedy records, as well as some special categories such as religious and pop records not in heavy demand.

Back issues of Schwann and its former, irregularly issued ARTIST ISSUE CATALOG (with records listed under performers and conductors) are still of use, although recordings may now be collector's items.

Sears, Minnie Earl. SONG INDEX; AN INDEX TO MORE THAN 12,000 SONGS IN 177 SONG COLLECTIONS COMPRISING 262 VOLUMES, AND SUPPLEMENT, 1934. New York: H.W. Wilson, 1926. Reprint. 2 vols. in 1. Hamden, Conn.: Shoe String Press, 1966.

"This volume is a facsimile reproduction of both the SONG INDEX and SONG INDEX SUPPLEMENT." (Publisher's note.)

The basic volume was published in 1926. The main alphabet interfiles first lines, titles, and composers' and authors' names. Classified list of collections indexed, Volume 2, pp. xxi–xxxvii.

As Constance M. Winchell has noted in GUIDE TO REFERENCE BOOKS, this index is also a locator for poems, if they have been set to music, and it serves to complement GRANGER'S INDEX TO POETRY (Edith Granger, 6th ed. New York: Columbia University Press, 1973. 2,223 p.). Neither the index nor its supplements will lead to recordings.

The supplement indexes more than 7,000 songs in 104 collections comprising 124 volumes.

See also De Charms, Desiree, and Breed, Paul Francis; and Leigh, Robert, above.

Shapiro, Nat. POPULAR MUSIC; AN ANNOTATED INDEX OF AMERICAN POPULAR SONGS. 6 vols. New York: Adrian Press, 1964-   .

Volumes published so far have covered the years 1920–69. Song titles are listed chronologically under copyright year, then alphabetically. Composer, lyricist, publisher, and first recording are noted. Both Broadway and film productions are named, as well as singers associated with each song, e.g., "Introduced by Ethel Merman in...." Each volume has an index of song titles and a list of publishers with addresses and performing rights affiliations.

The preface notes that the series is intended as a "selective... list of the significant popular songs of our time." Volume coverage is as follows: Volume 1: 1950–59; Volume 2: 1940–49; Volume 3: 1960–64; Volume 4: 1930–39; Volume 5: 1920–29; Volume 6: 1965–69.

SONG INDEX.

See Sears, Minnie Earl, above.

SONGS.

In addition to sources listed here, see Part VI–A3.

Sonneck, Oscar George Theodore. CATALOGUE OF OPERA LIBRETTOS PRINTED BEFORE 1800.

> Note the aria index in Volume II.

> For full annotation, see Part IV-A.

Steane, J.B. THE GRAND TRADITION; SEVENTY YEARS OF SINGING ON RECORD (1900-1970). London: Duckworth; New York: Vienna House, 1974. 628 p. Illustrated.

> Comparative discussion of singers' styles and techniques, with reference to recordings.

STEREO RECORD GUIDE. London: Long Playing Record Library; New York: Taplinger, 1960-   . Annual.

> Volumes covering 1900-68 prepared by Edward Greenfield et al. Planned as a survey of wide range. Mainly musical recordings (and a few albums of spoken humor) are rated.

Thiel, Joern. INTERNATIONAL ANTHOLOGY OF RECORDED MUSIC. Vienna and Munich: Jugend und Volk, 1971. 208 p.

> Edited under the patronage of the International Music Centre, Vienna.

> Classified guide with critical evaluations of musical recordings. Of two volumes planned one has appeared. Considers non-European music (biwa, Peking opera, etc.) but emphasizes European musical history. The notes on historical albums and series are very informative. Various indexes, including one entitled "Spotlights on Instruments." List of firms in Europe and the United States.

U.S. Library of Congress. LIBRARY OF CONGRESS CATALOG. MUSIC AND PHONORECORDS.

> See Part VI-A3.

U.S. Library of Congress. General Reference and Bibliography Division. LITERARY RECORDINGS: A CHECKLIST OF THE ARCHIVE OF RECORDED POETRY AND LITERATURE IN THE LIBRARY OF CONGRESS. Washington, D.C.: Library of Congress, 1966. 190 p.

> Reports on the inventory of literary recordings in the archive through June 1965. These are recordings made at the library, others made by poets for the archive, and some acquired as gifts. Copies of many tapes and recordings (78 and 33 1/3 rpm) may be purchased. (See p. iv.)

> Arrangement is alphabetical by names of persons or events recorded. There are some entries for drama, e.g., "American National The-

atre and Academy...Matinee Theatre Series," as well as
recitals by actors, e.g., MacLiammoir, Michael. THE IMPOR-
TANCE OF BEING OSCAR, and some interviews, with Maurice
Evans and others. (See especially "Turning Point Interviews.")
Name index.

U.S. Library of Congress. Music Division. CHECK-LIST OF RECORDED
SONGS IN THE ENGLISH LANGUAGE IN THE ARCHIVE OF AMERICAN
FOLK-SONG TO JULY 1940. ALPHABETICAL LIST WITH GEOGRAPHICAL
INDEX. 3 vols. Washington, D.C.: Library of Congress, 1942.

The first two volumes comprise an alphabetical list of titles, indicating singer, recording date, etc. Volume III arranges titles
under state and county.

Copies of the recordings can be purchased on application. See
Preface.

_____. FOLK MUSIC; A CATALOG OF FOLK SONGS, BALLADS, DANCES,
AND INSTRUMENTAL PIECES, AND FOLK TALES OF UNITED STATES AND
LATIN AMERICA ON PHONOGRAPH RECORDS. Washington, D.C.: U.S.
Government Printing Office, 1964. 110 p.

The 166 discs listed contain 1,240 titles selected from the Archive
of American Folk Song. The recordings are sold by the Library
of Congress.

See also International Folk Music Council, above.

VICTOR BOOK OF THE OPERA. 13th ed. (1968).

Contains a discography of operas from several recording companies.

For full annotation, see Part II-B.

See also Celletti, Rodolfo; and Harris, Kenn, above.

Young, William C. AMERICAN THEATRICAL ARTS.

"Oral History" entries lead to some collections of theatrical history
recordings.

See Part III.

G. FILMS FOR THE STUDY OF THE PERFORMING ARTS

Batcheller, David R. SIXTEEN MILLIMETER FILMS FOR USE IN TEACHING
DRAMA AND THEATRE. AETA AUDIO-VISUAL AIDS PROJECT. Washington,
D.C.: American Educational Theatre Association, 1967. 77 p.

Lists rental sources for training films in the field of theater and
for filmed plays.

See also BRITISH NATIONAL FILM CATALOGUE; National Information Center for Educational Media; and United Nations Educational, Scientific, and Cultural Organization, below.

BRITISH NATIONAL FILM CATALOGUE. 1963- .

Includes films on ballet, drama, opera, puppets, and the stage.

For full annotation, see Part VI-A5.

Bukalski, Peter J. FILM RESEARCH.

See Part VI-A5.

EDUCATORS' GUIDE TO FREE FILMS. Compiled by M.F. Horkheimer and J.C. Diffor. Randolph, Wis.: Educators' Progress Service, 1941- . Annual.

This guide is directed toward the educator at various levels, through college. Broad subject classification. There are films on architecture, dance, movie making, music, Shakespeare, etc. Title and subject indexes. List of sources in Canada and the United States.

EDUCATORS' GUIDE TO FREE FILMSTRIPS. Edited by M.F. Horkheimer and J.C. Diffor. Randolph, Wis.: Educators' Progress Service, 1949- . Annual. (Title varies.)

First through tenth editions were issued as EDUCATORS' GUIDE TO FREE SLIDE-FILMS. Has broad subject classification. Subject index has entries for architecture, artists, arts and crafts. List of U.S. and Canadian sources.

See also National Information Center for Educational Media. INDEX TO 35mm EDUCATIONAL FILMSTRIPS, below.

FEATURE FILMS ON 8mm AND 16mm.

See Part VI-A5.

FILMS, GENERAL.

For films other than instructional, see Part VI-A5.

FILMS ON ART.

See Humphrys, Alfred W., below.

Gottesman, Ronald. GUIDEBOOK TO FILM.

See Part I-A.

Humphrys, Alfred W., comp. FILMS ON ART. National Art Education Association. Uses of the Newer Media Project Publication no. 1. Introduction by Vincent Lanier. Washington, D.C.: NAEA, 1965. 60 p.

> Title list of films concerned with a broad range of arts. Entries include "Ballet Mecanique," "Design," "Directing a Play," The Film and Reality," "Marcel Marceau," "Images Medievales," "Mask," "Marionettes," etc.

> Each entry has information on grade level, dimension, color, sound, duration, producer or distributor, and cost, with a brief descriptive phrase. List of producers and distributors, pp. 53-60.

> See also International Institute of Films on Art, below.

INTERNATIONAL FILM GUIDE.

> Lists films for loan.

> For full annotation, see Part V.

International Folk Music Council. FILMS ON TRADITIONAL MUSIC AND DANCE, A FIRST INTERNATIONAL CATALOGUE. Edited by Peter Kennedy. Paris: UNESCO, 1970. 261 p.

> Mainly of anthropological interest. Some of the films are by German specialists connected with the Institut fuer den Wissenschaftlichen Film at Goettingen (Federal Republic of Germany) where many of the films are kept. Entries, along with a brief description, show availability for rental, purchase, or exchange. Arrangement is geographical. There are indexes of titles and subjects.

INTERNATIONAL INDEX TO MULTI-MEDIA INFORMATION.

> Has a good subject approach to films and other media, inclusive of many documentary films usable for instruction.

> For full annotation, see Part V.

International Institute of Films on Art. LE FILM SUR L'ART; REPERTOIRE GENERAL INTERNATIONAL DU FILM SUR L'ART, 1953-1960. Raccolta Pisana di Saggi e Studi, no. 12. Par les soins de Pasquale Rocchetti et Cesare Molinari de l'Institut International du Film sur l'Art. Venice: Pozza, 1963. 524 p.

> Continues a catalog of the same title issued by the predecessor of the institute, the International Committee for the Cinema and the Figurative Arts (Rome, 1953). In the 1963 catalog films are grouped under country of origin, alphabetized by title. Most concern art, architecture, and the decorative arts; a few deal with filmmaking, e.g., (United States) "Origins of the Motion Picture" (1955).

As there is no subject index, the catalog is difficult to use.
There are indexes of artists, of titles, of art works and places,
e.g., Vicenza (Palladian architecture). The indexes cover both
the 1953 and 1963 volumes.

Entries give name and address of producer, film credits, duration,
and dimension, with a brief summary.

See also Humphrys, Alfred W., above.

International Music Centre, Vienna. FILMS FOR MUSIC EDUCATION AND
OPERA FILMS; AN INTERNATIONAL SELECTIVE CATALOGUE. General intro-
duction by Egon Kraus; Introduction to Opera Films by Jack Bornoff. Paris:
UNESCO, 1962. 114 p.

Separate lists, the first of which is directed toward music educators.
Included are a few films of interest for theater studies, e.g.,
"Richard Wagner," and several films on the court dance and music
of Japan. Ballet is not treated. "Opera Films," pp. 91-114,
has short descriptions of available films, each with cast, technical
details, and distributor's name and address.

See also BRITISH NATIONAL FILM CATALOGUE, above.

_____. TEN YEARS OF FILMS ON BALLET AND CLASSICAL DANCE, 1956-
1965. Paris: UNESCO, 1968. 105 p.

(Not examined.)

Entries, arranged under countries of origin, include synopses, production credits, names of distributors. Indexes of composers and of
choreographers.

See also BRITISH NATIONAL FILM CATALOGUE, above.

Kone, Grace Ann. 8mm FILM DIRECTORY, 1969-70. New York: Educational
Film Library Association; Produced and distributed by Comprehensive Service
Corp., New York, 1969. xiv, 532 p. Illustrated. (To be supplemented.)

Films on all subjects, distributed in the United States, are classified under broad subjects, each with technical and ordering information and some with a short description. See "Performing Arts,"
which includes items on circus, dance, motion pictures, music
(e.g., theater organists, etc.), television, and theater (only two
entries, one for makeup, one for set design). Materials in loop
and reel form for various projectors are listed. Grade levels are
shown, and they include college. A few films are advanced or
technical.

List of producers and distributors, pp. xii-xiv. Illustrated guide to
8mm equipment, pp. 403-16. Index of film titles and subjects.

Manchel, Frank. FILM STUDY.

See Part VI-A5.

244

Mirwis, Allan. A DIRECTORY OF 16mm FILM COLLECTIONS IN COLLEGES AND UNIVERSITIES IN THE UNITED STATES.

> Some institutions permit rental or exchange and issue catalogs.

> For full annotation, see Part III.

MULTI MEDIA REVIEWS INDEX.

> See Part VII-F, above.

National Art Education Association. Uses of the Newer Media Project. FILMS ON ART.

> See Humphrys, Alfred W., above.

National Information Center for Educational Media. INDEX TO 16mm EDUCA-TIONAL FILMS. NICEM Media Indexes Series. 2d ed. New York: R.R. Bowker, 1969. 1,111 p.

> Alphabetical title list. See entries in "Subject Guide" under "Fine Arts" (Dance, Motion Pictures, Music, and Theater). Entries show color, duration, date, grade level (through adult), producer, and distributor. List of producers and distributors, with addresses.

> See also Batcheller, David R., above.

_____. INDEX TO 35mm EDUCATIONAL FILMSTRIPS. NICEM Media Indexes Series. 2d ed. New York: R.R. Bowker, 1970. 872 p.

> Similar in format to the same organization's INDEX TO 16mm EDUCATIONAL FILMS. (See above.)

> Entries for "Drama" are under "Literature" and those for "Architecture" and "Theater" are under "Fine Arts" in a subject guide, which leads to the main list, alphabetized by title of filmstrip. Reference code letters refer to a "Producer-Distributor Credit" section arranged by code letters and another arranged by names of producers and distributors. Addresses are given in the coded list.

> See also EDUCATORS' GUIDE TO FREE FILMSTRIPS, above.

New York Public Library. FILMS; A CATALOG OF THE FILM COLLECTION IN THE NEW YORK PUBLIC LIBRARY. Rev. ed. New York: New York Public Library, 1966. 80 p.

> Lists 16mm films under subject and also alphabetically by title, with short descriptions. A few entries for circus, dance, music, and theater. All films are available for rental in New York City.

Rocchetti, Pasquale. LE FILM SUR L'ART.

See International Institute of Films on Art, above.

United Nations Educational, Scientific, and Cultural Organization. CATA-
LOGUE DES FILMS SUR LE THEATRE ET L'ART DU MIME. Paris: 1965.
283 p.

Text and catalog are in French. Contents: Prefatory note by
Jun Watanabe on the importance of film as a medium for the international study of theater, pp. 11-12; Andre Veinstein's remarks
on the preparation of this catalog by an international committee,
with a description of the film categories included, pp. 13-20.

In the catalog 395 films are entered alphabetically by title, under
country of origin. Films not available for distribution were omitted,
e.g., a large number owned by the British Broadcasting Corp.

Films on musical theater were excluded because they had been
included in another UNESCO publication. Mime films account
for 70 percent of the entries. Second largest group consists of
films involving biography or the history of a theater or organization. Two other groups are represented: (1) those depicting some
aspect or genre of theater; (2) those relating to the staging of a
production.

Each entry gives date of film, producing company, dimension,
duration, color, language, general content, audience suitability,
and a short criticism.

Indexes of titles, authors (for mimodramas), persons, organizations,
and general subjects.

See also Batcheller, David R.; BRITISH NATIONAL FILM CATA-
LOGUE; and Humphrys, Alfred W., above.

U.S. Library of Congress. LIBRARY OF CONGRESS CATALOG. MOTION
PICTURES AND FILMSTRIPS, 1953- .

See Part VI-A5.

Note also U.S. Library of Congress. NATIONAL UNION CATA-
LOG: FILMS AND OTHER MATERIALS FOR PROJECTION, below.

_____. NATIONAL UNION CATALOG: FILMS AND OTHER MATERIALS
FOR PROJECTION, 1973- .

Intended to include all materials of educational value in all film
media (except microfilm). There is a subject index, which leads
to items such as "Theatrical Costume" (Filmstrip).

For full annotation, see Part VI-A5.

H. AUDIOVISUAL EQUIPMENT, SERVICES, INFORMATION

AUDIO-VISUAL EQUIPMENT DIRECTORY. Edited by Laurie Shirey and Kathleen A. Ryan. Evanston, Ill.: National Audio-Visual Association, 1953– . Annual. Illustrated.

> The editors do not claim comprehensiveness, nor do they endorse the products described, such as projectors, recorders, playback equipment, and storage units. These are illustrated with photographs. Technical information and prices are noted. There are charts of screen sizes, lamp nomenclature, etc., and a list of trade names.

AUDIO VISUAL MARKET PLACE.

> Details concerning rental services, manufacturers, etc.
>
> For full annotation, see Part III.

BACK STAGE--TV FILM/TAPE AND SYNDICATION DIRECTORY. New York: Back Stage Publications, 1963– . Title and frequency have varied.

> Lists manufacturers, suppliers, and services, mainly in New York, Chicago, and Hollywood. Classified arrangement.

Bukalski, Peter J. FILM RESEARCH.

> See Part VI-A5.

Chisholm, Margaret E. MEDIA INDEXES AND REVIEW SOURCES. College Park: University of Maryland School of Library and Information Services, 1972. 84 p.

> Directed toward public and academic librarians and educators, this guide evaluates periodicals, indexes, and bibliographies, both those which lead to audiovisual materials and those listing criticism of them.
>
> Part I is a survey of the field. Part II is a title list, with short critical evaluations. Part III includes a general guide to subjects and an index of titles grouped under types of media.
>
> See also Rufsvold, Margaret Irene, and Guss, Carolyn, below.

DIRECTORY OF FILM LIBRARIES IN THE U.S.A.

> Also leads to some media other than films. See Part III.

DIRECTORY OF SPOKEN-VOICE AUDIO-CASSETTES.

> See Part VII-F, above.

INTERNATIONAL FILM GUIDE.

> Lists films for loan, equipment suppliers, etc.
>
> For full annotation, see Part V.

INTERNATIONAL MOTION PICTURE ALMANAC. New York: Quigley, 1956–   . Annual. Illustrated. (Title varies.)

> In 1956 superseded, in part, MOTION PICTURE AND TELEVISION ALMANAC, which had been published since 1929.
>
> See names and addresses in "Equipment and Supplies," "Services," "Guilds and Unions," and also in a separate list of 16mm feature film distributors.
>
> For full annotation, see Part III.

INTERNATIONAL TELEVISION ALMANAC. New York: Quigley, 1965–   . Annual. (Title varies.)

> Supersedes, in part, MOTION PICTURE AND TELEVISION ALMA-NAC.
>
> Similar to INTERNATIONAL MOTION PICTURE ALMANAC, above.

Kone, Grace Ann. 8mm FILM DIRECTORY.

> Has a list of distributors and a guide to 8mm equipment.
>
> See Part VII-G, above.

Limbacher, James L. A REFERENCE GUIDE TO AUDIO-VISUAL INFORMATION.

> See Part I-A.

THE MUSICIAN'S GUIDE.

> Has addresses of instrument manufacturers and recording companies.
>
> For full annotation, see Part III.

National Information Center for Educational Media. INDEX TO PRODUCERS AND DISTRIBUTORS. 2d ed. Los Angeles: 1973. 134 p.

> Lists names and addresses only. No subject approach.

Rufsvold, Margaret Irene, and Guss, Carolyn. GUIDES TO EDUCATIONAL MEDIA; FILMS, FILMSTRIPS, KINESCOPES, PHONODISCS, PHONOTAPES, PROGRAMMED INSTRUCTION MATERIALS, SLIDES, TRANSPARENCIES, VIDEO-TAPES. 3d ed. Chicago: American Library Association, 1971. 116 p.

> The first edition was published in 1961 under the title GUIDES TO

NEWER EDUCATIONAL MEDIA.   The second edition appeared in 1967.

Critically annotated list of audio visual catalogs, services, and specialized periodicals providing information on nonprint educational media, pp. 1-89.   Supplementary list of items no longer available in 1971, pp. 90-94.   Selected periodicals, pp. 81-89. Index of titles, names, and subjects.

See also Chisholm, Margaret E., above.

SIMON'S DIRECTORY OF THEATRICAL MATERIALS, SERVICES, AND INFOR-MATION.

See especially the headings "Sound Equipment," "Sound Effects," "Recording Studios," "Multi-Media," and "Audio-Visual."

For full annotation, see Part III.

Wasserman, Paul.   MUSEUM MEDIA.

See Part VII-A, above.

INDEX

The index provides author, subject, and title access, in one alphabet. Titles are shown entirely in capital letters. Alphabetization is letter by letter.

In addition to authors there are entries for coauthors, compilers, editors, and translators, when known. Organizations may appear either as corporate authors or as added entries.

Library of Congress headings are used, with the exception of a few adaptations for the sake of economy of space (e.g., Rhetoric and speech), a few direct entries where they seem practical (e.g., Medieval drama, not Drama, medieval), and a few new terms to reflect current theatrical developments (e.g., Theater collectives). See references are from terms not used (such as synonyms) to those chosen for use; see also references are to related subject matter.

References are to page numbers, as follows: A single number means an item can be found on that page; two numbers, e.g., 65-66, indicate that the item continues from one page to the next; three or more numbers in sequence mean that items can be found on each page; three or more, followed by passim, will indicate references on at least every other page of that sequence.

A

A.L.A. PORTRAIT INDEX 210
Abbey Theatre 173, 180
Abstracts. See Bibliographies, indexes, and abstracts
ABSTRACTS OF ENGLISH STUDIES 169
Academy Award winners (music) 152
Academy of Motion Picture Arts and Sciences 21
Acoustics 46, 155, 157-58. See also Design for the Theater; Stage settings, scenery, lighting, etc.

Actors. See Biographical sources
Adams, William Davenport 21
Adaptations. See Play indexes and finding lists
Adelman, Irving 105
Adkins, Cecil 184-85
Advertisements. See Posters, playbills, programs, advertisements, etc.
African Bibliographic Center 133
AFRICAN THEATRE 136
Agencies and agents: directories 3, 57, 61-67 passim, 162
Alembert, Jean le Rond d' 229
Allevy, Marie-Antoinette 133

Index

Index

Index

Holzknecht, Karl J.   30
Horkheimer, M.F.   242
Horn-Monval, Madeleine   99
Houle, Peter J.   175
Howard, Diana   60, 208, 216
Howard, Patsy C.   188
Howard-Hill, Trevor Howard   12, 175, 208
Hoyo, Arturo del   30
Huenefeld, Irene Pennington   60
Huerlimann, Martin   30, 224
Huerta, Jorge A.   137
Hume, Samuel J.   222
Humphrys, Alfred W.   243
Hunter, Frederick James   3-4
Huntington [Henry E.] Library.   Larpent Plays   84

I

Iberian theater.   See Catalan theater; Portuguese-language theater; Spanish-language theater
ILLUSTRATION INDEX   200
Illustrative sources   195-230
    architectural illustration   215-18
    art and design illustration   218-30
    bibliographies   196
    dictionaries   45-47
    directories   203, 205, 221
    general illustration   195-205
    guides   4, 5-7
    performing arts illustration   195-205
    portrait catalogs and indexes   210-14
    posters, playbills, programs, advertisements   205-10
    See also Audiovisual sources; Design for the theater; Films for the study of the performing arts
Indexes.   See Bibliographies, indexes, and abstracts
"Index of Record Reviews"   237
INDEX TO AMERICAN DOCTORAL DISSERTATIONS   187, 188
INDEX TO AMERICAN LITTLE MAGAZINES   175-76

INDEX TO ART PERIODICALS   156
INDEX TO BOOK REVIEWS IN THE HUMANITIES   121
INDEX TO CHILDREN'S PLAYS IN COLLECTIONS   82
INDEX TO COMMONWEALTH LITTLE MAGAZINES   110-11
INDEX TO 'FILMS IN REVIEW,' AN   111, 201, 235
INDEX TO FULL-LENGTH PLAYS   81-82, 93
INDEX TO ILLUSTRATIONS   199
INDEX TO LITTLE MAGAZINES   17, 175-76
INDEX TO MONOLOGS AND DIALOGS, AN   82
INDEX TO ONE-ACT PLAYS, AN   83-84
INDEX TO PLAYS   77
INDEX TO PLAYS, WITH SUGGESTIONS FOR TEACHING   84
INDEX TO PLAYS IN COLLECTIONS   87
INDEX TO PLAYS IN PERIODICALS   82, 88
INDEX TO SKITS AND STUNTS, AN   82
INDEX TRANSLATIONUM; INTERNATIONAL BIBLIOGRAPHY OF TRANSLATIONS   74, 81
INDUSTRIAL ARTS INDEX   155
Interior design   46, 225, 227.   See also Art and design illustration; Design for the theater
International Centre of Arts and Costumes   60
INTERNATIONAL DIRECTORY OF LITTLE MAGAZINES AND SMALL PRESSES   17
INTERNATIONALE BIBLIOGRAPHIE DER REZENSIONEN   121
INTERNATIONAL ENCYCLOPEDIA OF FILM   30
INTERNATIONALE FILMBIBLIOGRAPHIE, 1952-1962   164
International Federation of Film Archives   164
International Federation of Library Associations   61, 201, 208
INTERNATIONAL FILM GUIDE   111, 243, 248

Index

Index

Index

Index

Index

Index